ANURAG MATHUR

GWALIOR
· HERITAGE CITY OF FORT & MUSEUMS ·

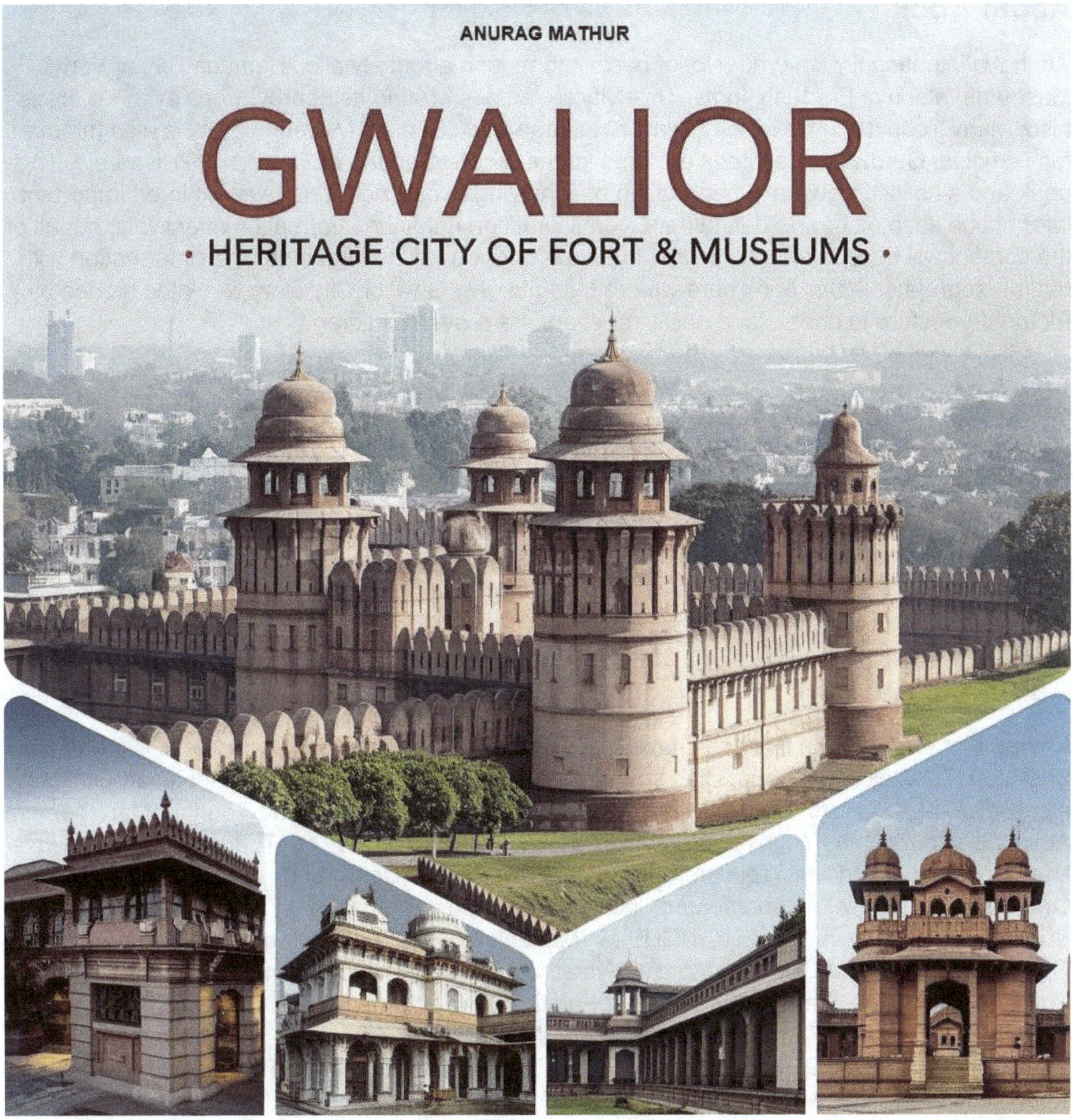

GWALIOR- HERITAGE CITY OF FORT & MUSEUMS

About Book

We have intentionally covered a lot of basic information about Gwalior-Heritage City of Fort & Museums, Madhya Pradesh, India. This City so famous around its nearby areas even far areas also. Many Tourists come to see Gwalior-Heritage City of Fort & Museums. City is also famous for Temples, Gurdwara, devotees are present them here Garland of Flowers & Prasad etc. This book and a holistic view have been taken of achieving excellence. We have explored important information such as how to define the Overall direction enhance information effectively, not all of the content will have been new to you, but hopefully you will have gained fresh information with real photographs. In this book here we are trying to give Gwalior City story & related stories by Picture by Picture to understand easily for everyone & even Children.

ISBN: 9798302947352

ANURAG MATHUR

About the Author

Anurag Mathur Author of this book have 32 years vast experience of 5 Star Hotels, like Mughal Sheraton ITC Welcome Group, Clarks Shiraj, Park Plaza Agra, Sahara Shahar Resort Lucknow etc. (B.Sc., M.A. - History, Ph.D. Level Research, P.G. Dip. in Hotel and Tourism Management Advance Course in Tourism from IITTM – Indian Institute of Tourism & Travel Management-Ministry of Tourism Govt. of India, New Delhi and WTO (World Tourism Organization-Geneva). Represented India on Tourism Promotion in "International Tourism Summit" at New Delhi in 1990. PGDBIM (MBA-Delhi). Ex. Lecturer of History, Hotel & Tourism Management Deptt. At Agra University. Agra and also Numismatist (Coins Collector), Philatelist, Antiques, Rare Photographs & Paintings Collector etc, Lucknow. U.P. India. Winner of State level Prizes. (Father of Author Anurag Mathur, Late. Shri. O.N. Mathur, Archaeological Survey of India (ASI), Govt. of India -Posted at Taj Mahal & other Historical Monuments at Agra-Year 1975 - 89. Author Anurag Mathur's forefather was posted at Royal Imperial Court of Emperor Shah Jahan as Finance Minister (Treasury Incharge –*Shaahi Khazana)* as per Author's Family Tree Records & generations Chronology & rest all ancestors were educated from Kayastha family and served in Royal Mughal Court after one by one.

Acknowledgements

This book would not have been possible without the blessings of Radhasoami Dayal & Karni Mata. My Guru & friends contribution is also great. My guru guardian Late. Proff. Agam Prasad Mathur Head of Radhasoami Faith Agra was great. He was twice Ex. Vice Chancellor of Agra University & Head of Department History of Agra College. He wrote so many History & Radhasoami Books in his life time. His contribution in History, Travel & Tourism was great & very informative for readers, students, Historians, Travellers to increase Travel, Tourism & Indian Culture. I am also grateful to my both children Jitesh Mathur & Shreshtha Mathur in contribution of writing this book. I generally use to travel extensively whenever I got the time from my profession of Hotel Industry to write books, being as Hotelier having vast experience of 35 years of Hotel Industry. I also got valuable inputs from the staff of Hotel Mughal Sheraton, Hotel Clark Shiraz and Hotel Howard Park Plaza American Chain Hotel Agra & Sahara Shahar Resort of Sahara Group of Hotels Lucknow where I worked.

Disclaimer

It may be possible that text, few Paintings & Photographs looks like someone work, here in this book we are using all replicas, Copies & material generally available all over India in all form of hard, soft copies at public social media, Internet, Libraries etc. It does not concern with any one, Particular person, any Religion, any Faith, any Temple, Society, Trust, Club & Cult. Here through this book the aim of giving general information for general awareness for general people to build stronger bonds of Indian Cultural values & ethics between all of us, Indians are living beyond boundaries of their mother land & for new upcoming generations for many years of the whole world due to regular changing of social & living ethics of families, decentralization & broken families Social & Cultural values & ethics in present scenario to improve future. We do not want to hurt anyone sentiment through this. Today is Internet World so it may be possible that some Information like Text/Photographs/Paintings may be viral through electronic social media via email & others. As writer I am trying to give my best Historic facts& figures in this modern present scenario of Internet World with various website links for easy access of more information by readers like Social websites Face book, what's app etc. Myself and its Service Providers shall under no circumstance be liable to you, and/or any third party for any lost profits or lost opportunity, indirect, special, consequential, incidental, or punitive damages whatsoever, even it has been advised of the possibility of such damages like social media viral images, videos etc. I am using my own smart mobile camera for various images with many angles for new coming generations' awareness those are internet savvy and want to see everything on internet & do not want to visit many Historical Heritage Buildings personally. This disclaimer is made on behalf of me, its affiliates and its third party information with any of these entities officers, employees, directors, or agents. All information contained herein is obtained by me from sources believed by in travel to be accurate and reliable and every effort is taken to verify, correct and update the information provided in this site at the time of uploading. Because of the possibility of human and mechanical error as well as other factors or omissions, we cannot accept responsibility for any authenticity of the data provided, travel information, rules and conditions that are incorrectly represented within this system. I make any warranty regarding the correctness or reliability of the information and all information is provided "as is". The authenticity of the data provided is to be verified by one who is planning to use the information, as they are bound to change. I and its information Providers make no representations and subject to below, disclaim all express, implied, and statutory warranties of any kind to user and/or any third party including warranties as to accuracy, timeliness, completeness, merchantability, or fitness for any particular purpose.

Introduction

Gwalior, a historic city in the Indian state of Madhya Pradesh, is renowned for its rich cultural heritage, architectural grandeur, and significant role in India's history. This city is a tapestry of diverse dynastic influences, offering a glimpse into India's storied past.

Historical Significance

Gwalior's history stretches back to the 8th century, with the city flourishing under the rule of various dynasties such as the Tomars, Mughals, Marathas, and Scindias. Each dynasty contributed to the city's cultural and architectural evolution:

- The **Tomar dynasty**, particularly under Raja Man Singh Tomar, laid the foundation of Gwalior's grandeur by constructing the iconic **Gwalior Fort** in the 8th century.
- Successive rulers, including the **Mughals**, **Marathas**, and **Scindias**, left their indelible marks, enriching Gwalior's historical landscape with unique artistic and cultural imprints.

Gwalior Fort: A Monument of Splendour

The **Gwalior Fort**, a UNESCO World Heritage Site, stands as a testament to the city's historical and architectural prowess. Often referred to as "The Pearl of Fortresses," it boasts a remarkable blend of **Hindu** and **Islamic architectural styles**, reflected in its palaces, temples, and water reservoirs.

Key attractions within the fort include:

- **Man Mandir Palace** – A dazzling example of medieval Indian architecture.
- **Gujari Mahal Museum** – Showcasing artifacts that highlight the region's rich history.

Other Iconic Attractions

- **Jai Vilas Palace:** Constructed in the 19th century by the Scindia dynasty, this palace is an exquisite amalgamation of **European** and **Indian architectural styles**, renowned for its opulent interiors and the world's largest chandelier.
- **Sas-Bahu Temples:** Dating back to the 11th century, these intricately designed temples dedicated to **Lord Vishnu** showcase the artistic brilliance of ancient Indian craftsmanship.
- **Tansen Samaroh:** An annual music festival in honor of **Mian Tansen**, one of the nine jewels of Emperor Akbar's court, celebrating Gwalior's rich legacy in Hindustani classical music.

Cultural Essence of Gwalior

Gwalior is a vibrant cultural hub where tradition meets modernity. The city is particularly famous for:

- **Classical Music:** As the birthplace of the Gwalior gharana, a prominent school of Hindustani classical music.
- **Handicrafts:** Renowned for **Chanderi sarees** and **Gwalior cotton**, which reflect the region's textile artistry.
- **Folk Art and Dance:** Traditional dance forms and festivals that bring the city's culture to life.

Gwalior's timeless charm, architectural marvels, and cultural vibrancy make it a treasure trove for historians, travelers, and art enthusiasts alike.

Economy of Gwalior

Gwalior's economy has seen consistent growth, driven by key sectors such as **textiles**, **manufacturing**, and **tourism**. The city's rich historical and cultural heritage makes it an attractive destination for travelers, further boosting its economic prospects.

History of Gwalior Heritage City

The name **Gwalior** is rooted in a legend about the sage **Gwalipa**, who is said to have cured the local ruler, **Suraj Sen**, of leprosy. As a token of gratitude, Suraj Sen founded the city and named it after the sage. The fort on **Gopachal Hill**, which later became synonymous with Gwalior, played a pivotal role in shaping its legacy.

The precise date of Gwalior Fort's construction remains uncertain. According to local legend, it was established around 600 CE by a regional king named Suraj Sen. The story goes that the king, suffering from leprosy, was cured after a sage named Gwalipa provided him with water from a sacred pond within the fort's premises. In gratitude, Suraj Sen built the fort and named it after the sage. The sage conferred upon him the title "Pala" (protector) and prophesied that the fort would remain under his family's control as long as they upheld the title. This lineage persisted for 16 generations before the 17th ruler, Tej Karan, lost the fort.

Archaeological evidence and inscriptions suggest the fort existed as early as the 6th century. For instance, an inscription references a sun temple built during the reign of the Huna emperor Mihirakula in the same era. Later, the Teli ka Mandir, a masterpiece of Gurjara-Pratihara architecture, was constructed in the 9th century. The fort is definitively recorded in history by the 10th century, under the rule of the Kachchhapaghatas, likely as vassals of the Chandelas.

From the 11th century onward, Gwalior Fort witnessed numerous invasions by Muslim dynasties. In 1022 CE, Mahmud of Ghazni besieged it for four days, lifting the siege after receiving 35 elephants as tribute. In 1196, the Ghurid general Bahauddin Tourghil captured it after a prolonged siege. Iltutmish of the Delhi Sultanate later regained control in 1232 CE. By 1398, the Tomar dynasty seized the fort, ushering in a golden era under the rule of Raja Man Singh Tomar, who commissioned several iconic structures within its walls.

Despite its strength, the fort faced multiple sieges. Sikander Lodi unsuccessfully attempted to capture it in 1505, but his son Ibrahim Lodi succeeded in 1516 after a year-long siege, resulting in Man Singh's death. Soon after, the fort passed to the Mughal Emperor Babur, who made it a symbol of Mughal dominance. During Akbar's reign, it served as a political prison, with notable prisoners such as Abu'l-Kasim, Akbar's cousin, who was executed there.

Gwalior Fort also bears significance in Sikh history. Guru Hargobind, the sixth Sikh Guru, was imprisoned here by Emperor Jahangir in 1609 for non-payment of fines levied on his father, Guru Arjan. According to Sikh tradition, the Guru's release on Diwali is commemorated as Bandi Chhor Divas.

In subsequent years, the fort was embroiled in power struggles among the Mughals, Marathas, and British. The Marathas captured it in the mid-18th century, only to lose it to the British East India Company in 1780. Control shifted between these powers until the Scindia dynasty secured it as a British protectorate in 1844. During the 1857 rebellion, the fort became a focal point, with many sepoys rebelling against British rule. However, after the uprising was suppressed, the fort was handed back to the Scindias, who maintained it until Indian independence in 1947.

The modern-day Gwalior Fort comprises two primary palaces: **Man Mandir**, a 15th-century citadel, and **Gujari Mahal**, built by Man Singh Tomar for his queen, Mrignayani. It also houses numerous Jain temples and inscriptions, including one of the world's oldest records of the numeral zero. The **Teli ka Mandir**, an architectural marvel blending northern and southern Indian styles, further enriches its heritage.

The fort's intricate carvings, rock-cut Jain sculptures, and sprawling courtyards continue to attract historians and tourists alike. Spanning 3 square kilometers, it is accessible via two grand gates—**Hathi Pul (Elephant Gate)** and **Badalgarh Gate**. Its massive reservoirs once provided water for a garrison of 15,000, underscoring its strategic importance.

Even today, Gwalior Fort stands as a testament to India's rich history, blending legends, military conquests, and architectural grandeur.

Gwalior Fort: A Marvel of Architecture and History

The **Gwalior Fort**, perched on an outcrop of Vindhyan sandstone on **Gopachal Hill**, boasts a rich history intertwined with legends and dynastic battles. Its ochre sandstone, basalt-covered geology, and massive structure make it a breathtaking sight, with its **342-foot elevation** offering strategic defensive advantages.

Origin and Early Construction

The exact period of the fort's construction is debated. Local legend attributes its origins to **Suraj Sen**, who, in gratitude to sage Gwalipa, built the fort in 600 CE. Inscriptions and historical records suggest the fort's existence as early as the **6th century**, during the reign of **Huna Emperor Mihirakula**, who built a sun temple within its premises.

Medieval and Mughal Periods

The fort changed hands among various rulers:

- **Kachchhapaghatas** ruled the fort as feudatories of the Chandelas

Economy of Gwalior

Gwalior's economy is steadily growing, supported by industries such as **textiles**, **manufacturing**, and **tourism**. The city's rich historical and architectural heritage, combined with its vibrant cultural scene, attracts both domestic and international visitors, making tourism a key contributor to economic development.

Gwalior Fort: - Heritage beautiful Architectural Fort

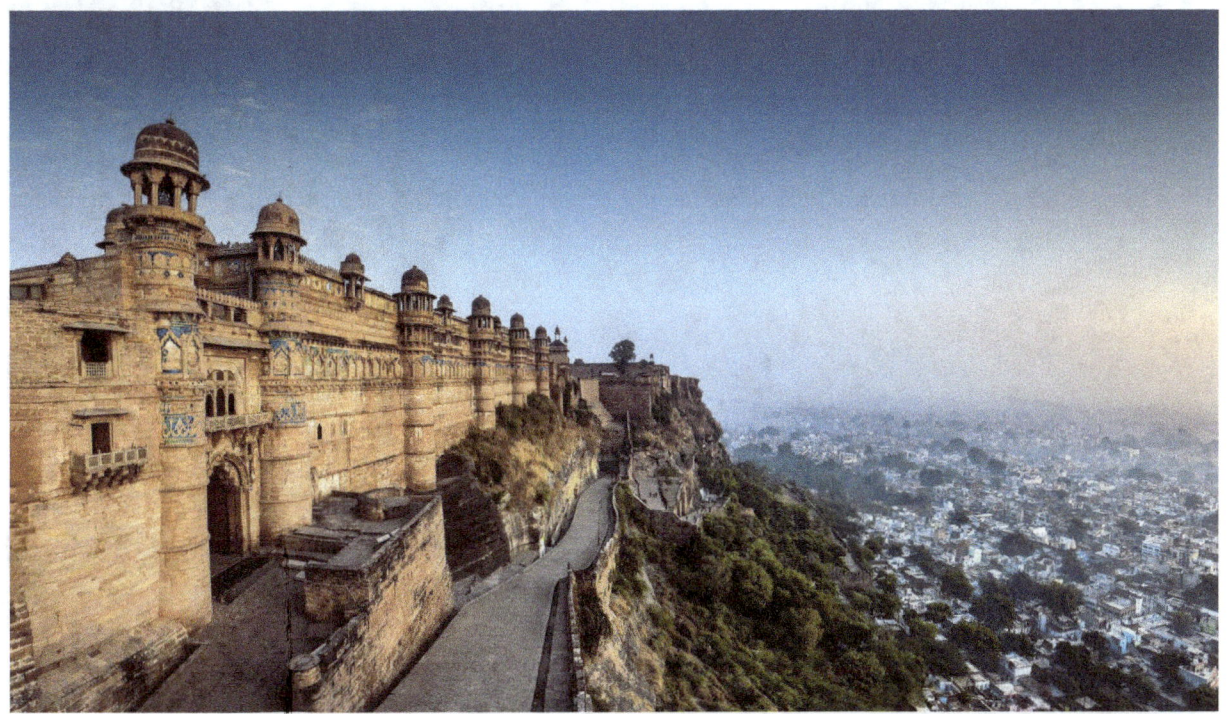

Gwalior City view from Hill top of Gwalior Fort

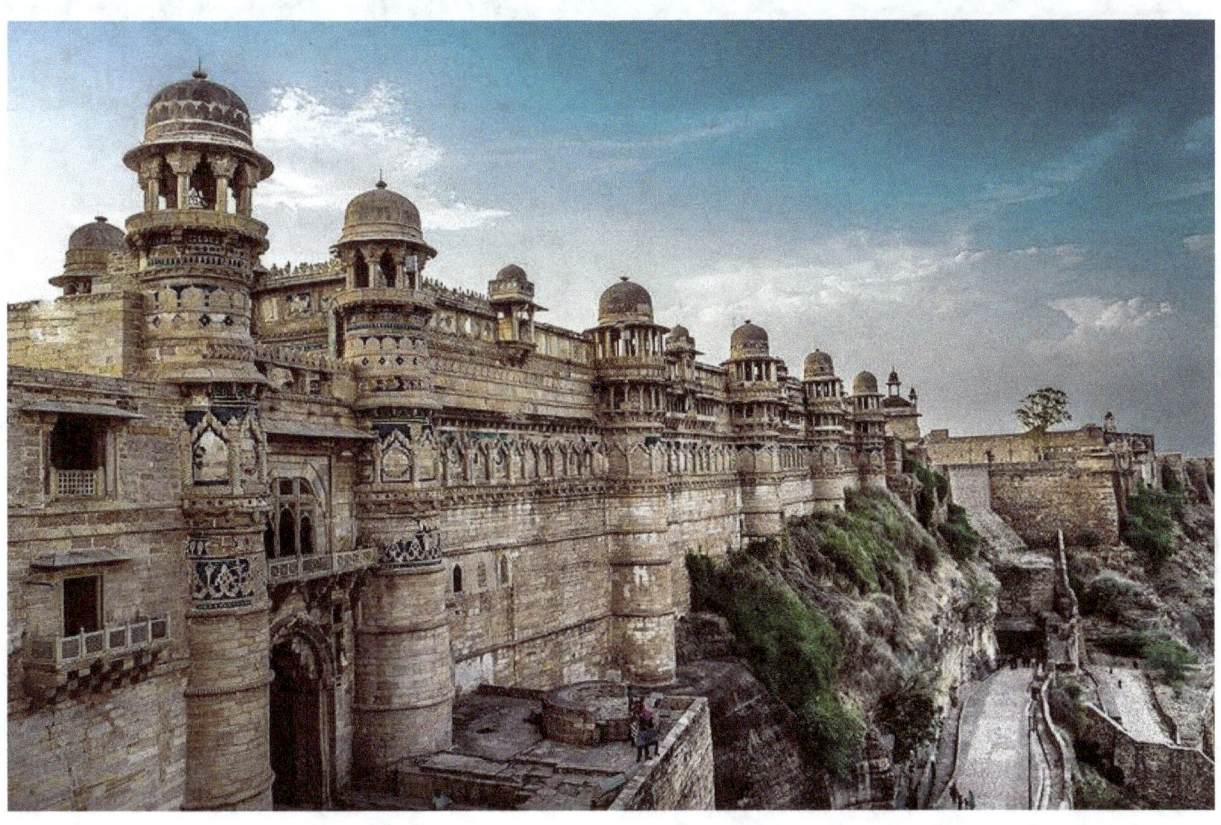

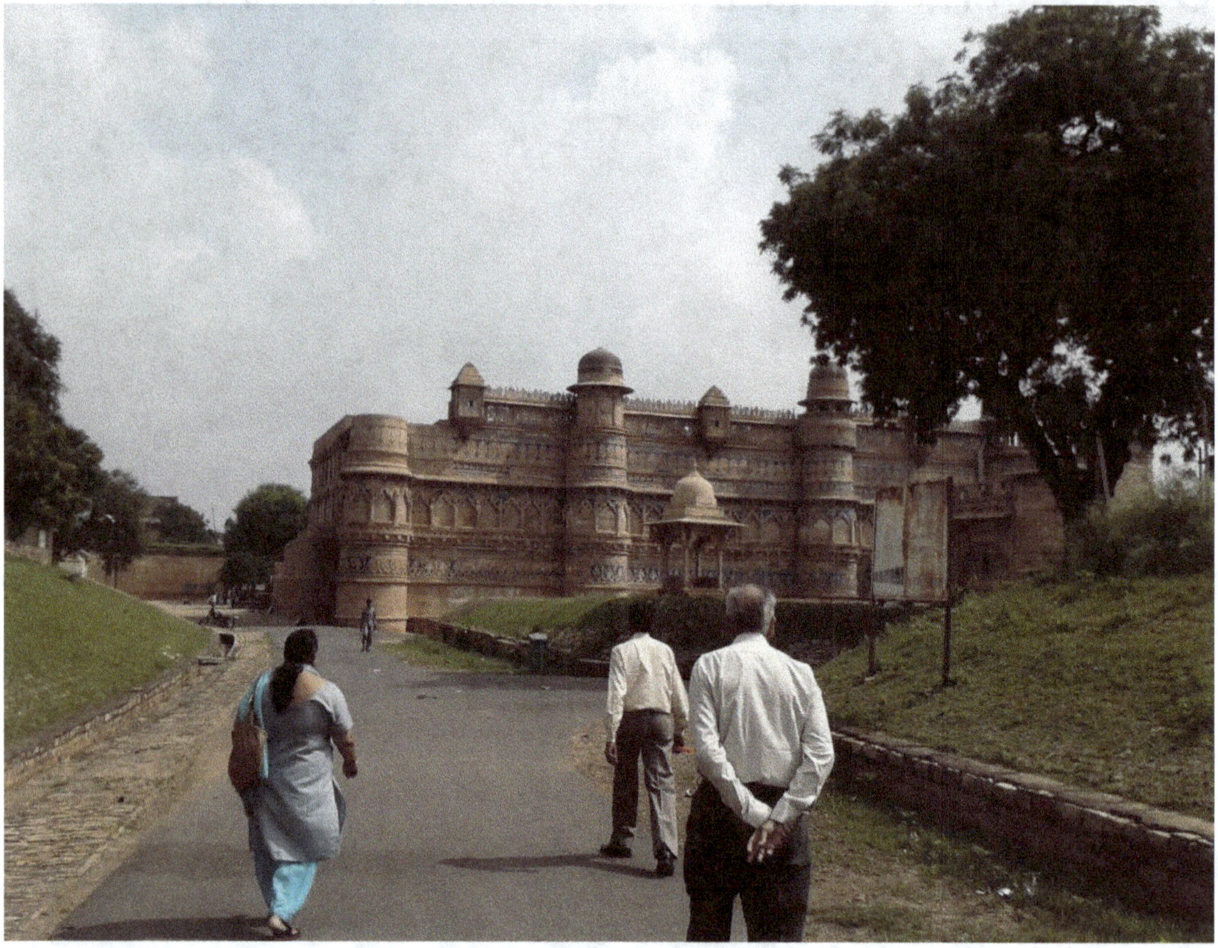

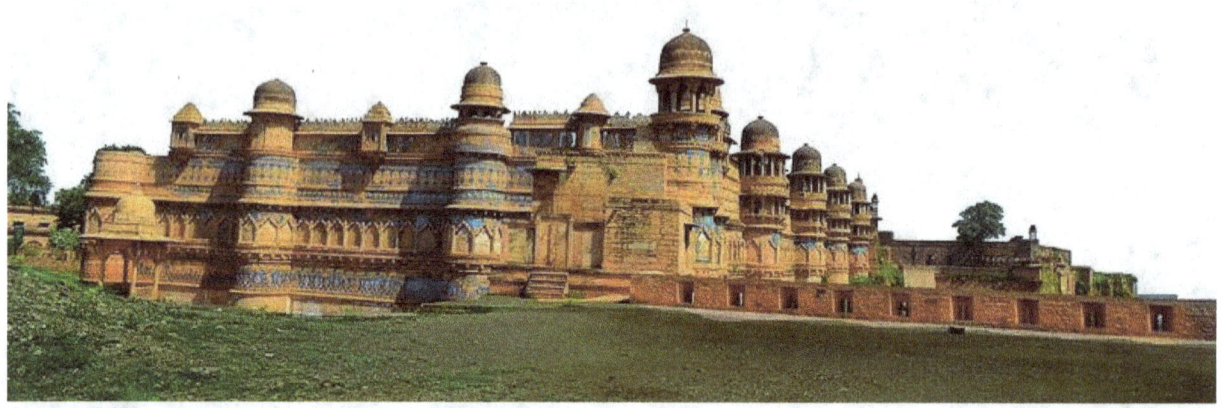

Gwalior Fort inside view

Gwalior Fort: A Symbol of Strength and Culture

The **Gwalior Fort**, situated atop Gopachal Hill, is a monumental fortress renowned for its architecture and historical significance. Built with Vindhyan sandstone, the fort's geology features a unique ochre-colored sandstone and basalt foundation. Its elevated position, rising **342 feet**, offered strategic advantages, making it a coveted stronghold.

Founding and Early History

While the exact origins of the fort are debated, local legends suggest it was built by **Suraj Sen** in the **6th century CE** after sage Gwalipa directed him to a sacred pond whose water healed his illness. The fort's early records include a **6th-century inscription** referencing a sun temple built during the reign of the Huna emperor **Mihirakula**. By the **9th century**, the **Gurjara-Pratiharas** had added structures like the **Teli ka Mandir**, blending northern and southern architectural styles.

Medieval Era and Dynastic Struggles

From the **10th century** onward, Gwalior Fort became a contested site:

- The **Kachchhapaghatas** ruled the fort, likely under the **Chandelas**, adding their architectural contributions.
- In **1022 CE**, the fort withstood a siege by **Mahmud of Ghazni**, who eventually retreated after receiving tribute.
- In 1196 CE, **Bahauddin Tourghil**, a commander of **Muhammad of Ghor**, captured the fort. It later fell to the **Delhi Sultanate**, with **Iltutmish** retaking it in **1232 CE**.

The Tomar Dynasty

The **Tomar dynasty**, beginning in the **14th century**, ushered in a golden age for Gwalior. **Man Singh Tomar**, its most celebrated ruler, constructed the **Man Mandir Palace** and fortified the fort's defenses. The Tomars' reign ended after repeated sieges by the Delhi Sultanate, culminating in the fort's surrender to **Ibrahim Lodi** in **1516**.

Mughal and Post-Mughal Era

The **Mughals** captured Gwalior Fort under Emperor **Babur** and later used it as a political prison. Notable figures imprisoned here included Guru **Hargobind Sahib**, the sixth Sikh Guru, and various Mughal royals such as **Aurangzeb's brother Murad Baksh** and son **Muhammad Sultan**. The fort also witnessed the **Bandi Chhor Divas**, marking Guru Hargobind's release.

The **Marathas** took control in the 18th century under **Mahadaji Shinde (Scindia)**, who lost the fort briefly to the British during the **Second Anglo-Maratha War** but regained it as part of Gwalior State under British suzerainty.

Architectural Highlights

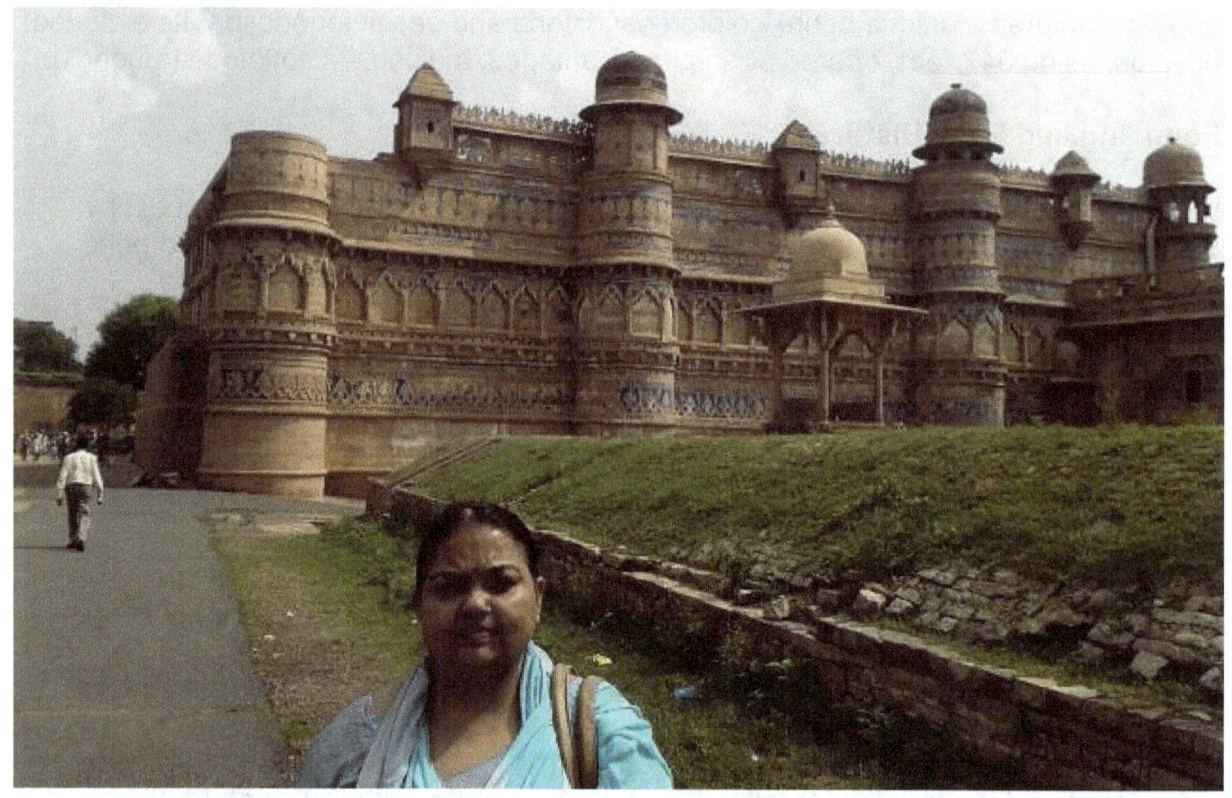

Gwalior Fort inside view

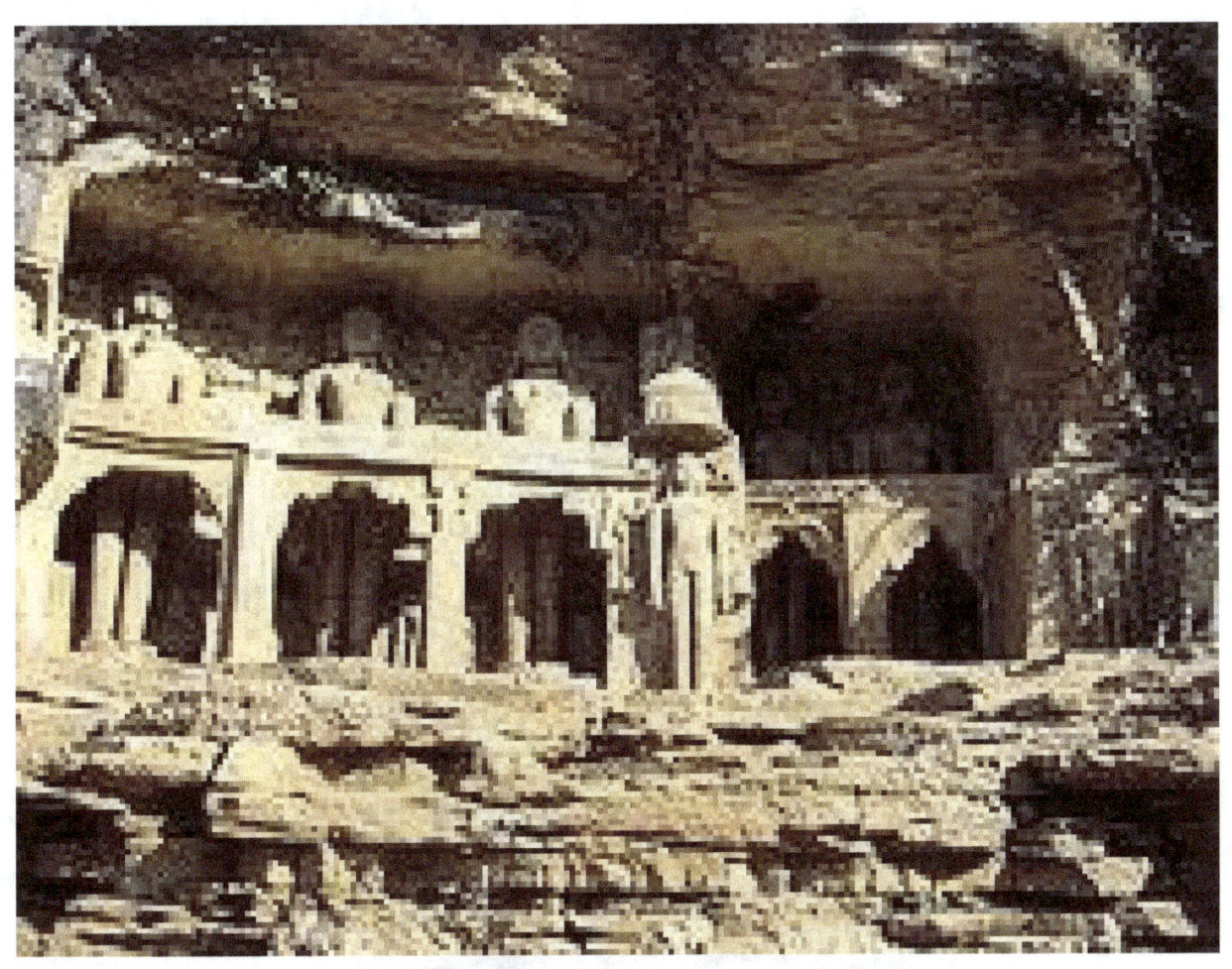

Rock cut images of the Tirthankaras

Main Temple Urvahi: -

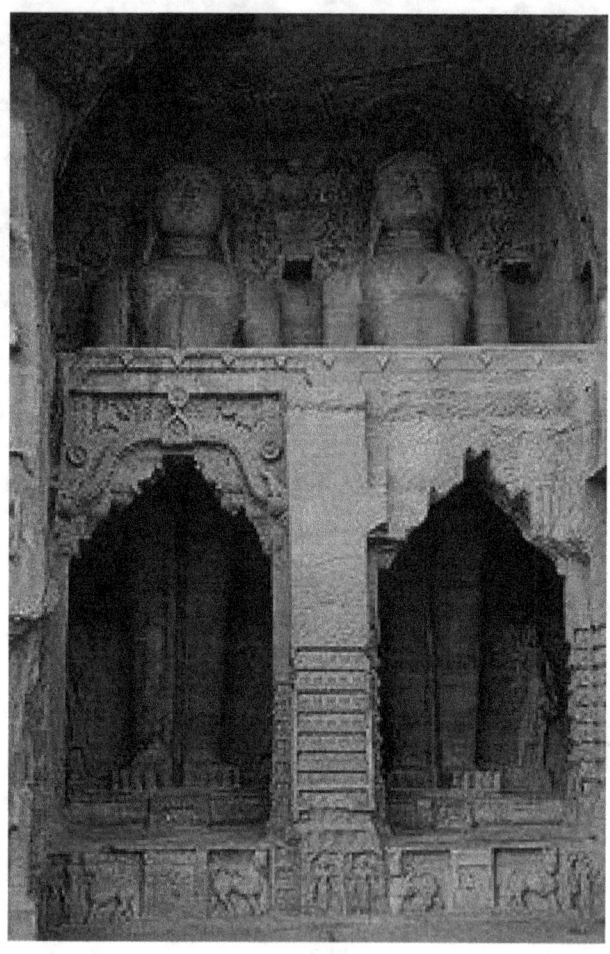

Jain statues carved out of rock in the Gwalior Fort near the Urwai Gate

The expansive Gwalior Fort complex is divided into five distinct areas: **Urvahi**, **Northwest**, **Northeast**, **Southwest**, and **Southeast**. Among these, the **Urvahi area** is renowned for its extraordinary collection of Jain sculptures, making it a significant site of religious and historical importance.

In the Urvahi region alone, there are **24 idols of Tirthankaras** seated in the **Padmasana posture**, **40 in the Kayotsarga posture**, and approximately **840 intricately carved figures** adorning the walls and pillars. These carvings represent the unparalleled artistic dedication of the craftsmen and serve as a testimony to the fort's Jain heritage.

One of the most iconic sculptures in this area is the colossal **58 feet 4-inch statue of Adinatha**, the first Tirthankara, standing tall outside the Urvahi gate. This awe-inspiring figure is considered one of the largest Jain idols in the world, symbolizing serenity and spiritual enlightenment. Another notable idol is the **35-foot statue of Suparshvanatha**, also in the Padmasana posture, located in the **Paththar-ki Bavadi** (Stone Tank) area.

These monumental carvings reflect the religious fervor and artistic ingenuity of the Tomar period, showcasing a harmonious blend of spirituality and craftsmanship. Despite centuries of invasions and attempts at destruction, these sculptures have endured, preserving their magnificence and continuing to inspire admiration among visitors and devotees.

Gopachal:-

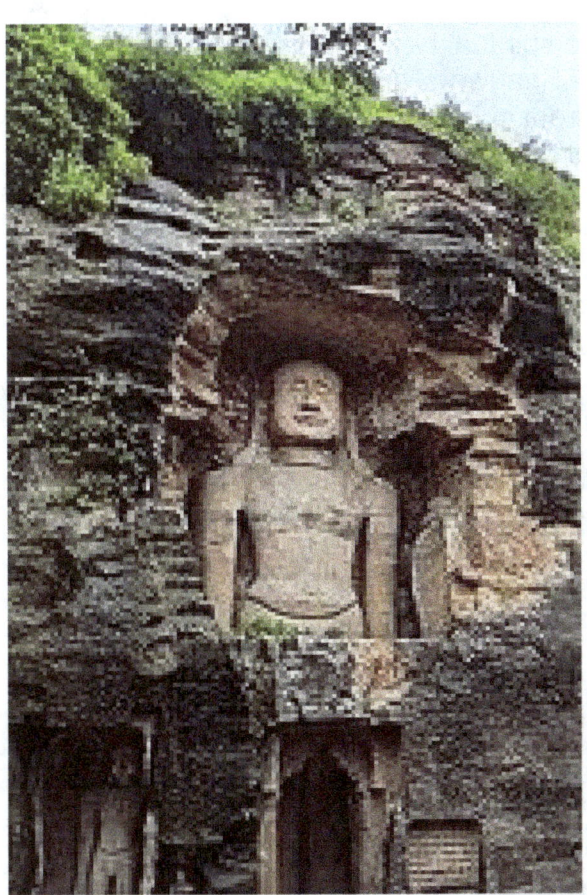

58.4 feet (17.8 m) high idol of Bhagwan Adinatha.

The **Gopachal Hill**, situated within the Gwalior Fort complex, is another significant site, known for its remarkable array of Jain sculptures. It houses approximately **1,500 idols**, ranging in size from small 6-inch carvings to towering figures as tall as **57 feet**. These idols, intricately carved from the natural rock of the hill, are a testament to the artistic excellence of the craftsmen of the Tomar dynasty. Most of these masterpieces were created during the reigns of **King Dungar Singh** and **Keerti Singh** between **1341 and 1479 CE**.

One of the most awe-inspiring statues is the colossus of **Bhagwan Parsvanath**, depicted in the **Padmasana posture**, standing at **42 feet in height** and **30 feet in width**. This magnificent idol is revered not only for its artistic grandeur but also for the miraculous legend associated with it. According to local lore, when Mughal Emperor Babur captured the fort in 1527, he ordered his soldiers to destroy these idols. As one soldier struck the thumb of the Parsvanath statue, a miraculous event is said to have occurred, causing fear among the invaders and forcing them to retreat. Despite these attacks, the idols endured significant damage, and fragments of the destroyed sculptures remain scattered throughout the fort complex, serving as silent witnesses to the turmoil of history.

The main colossus of Parsvanath stands as the spiritual heart of this site. It is complemented by the **place of precept**, where Bhagwan Parsvanath is believed to have delivered teachings. This hill also holds great significance in Jain tradition, as it is where **Shri 1008 Supratishtha Kevali** attained **nirvana**, marking it as a sacred site.

Gopachal Hill is further adorned with **26 additional Jain temples**, each showcasing intricate carvings and spiritual symbolism. Together, these temples and sculptures form one of the most comprehensive collections of Jain art and architecture, illustrating the cultural and religious importance of the site during the Tomar dynasty.

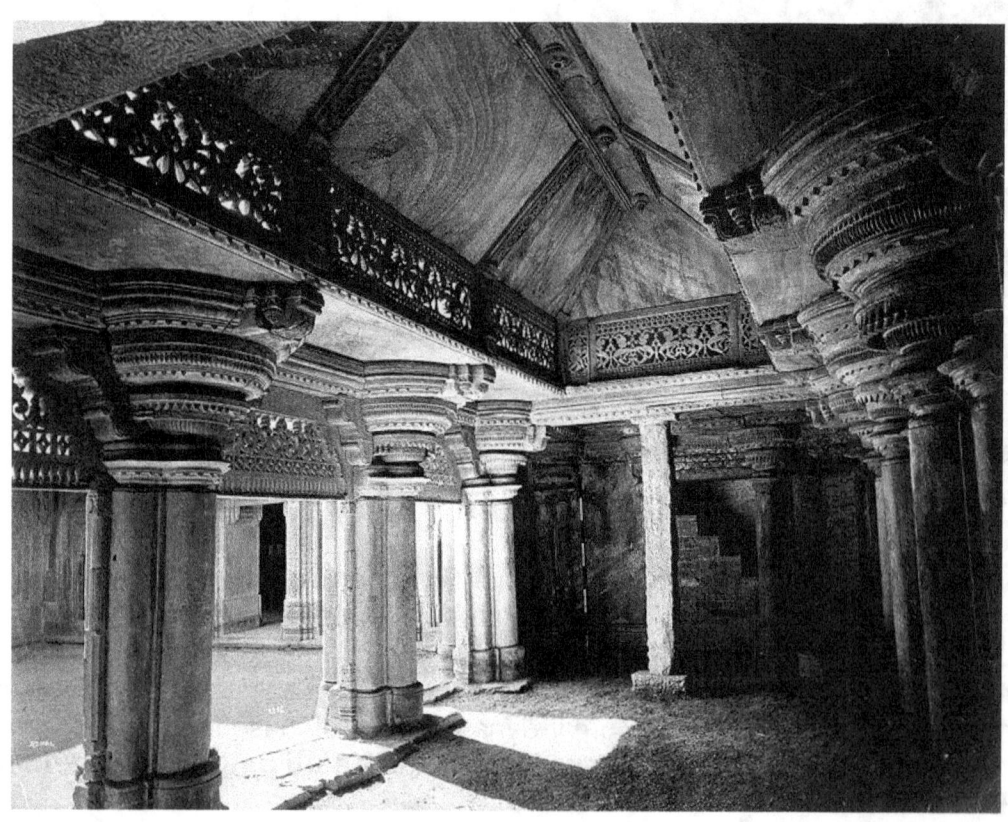

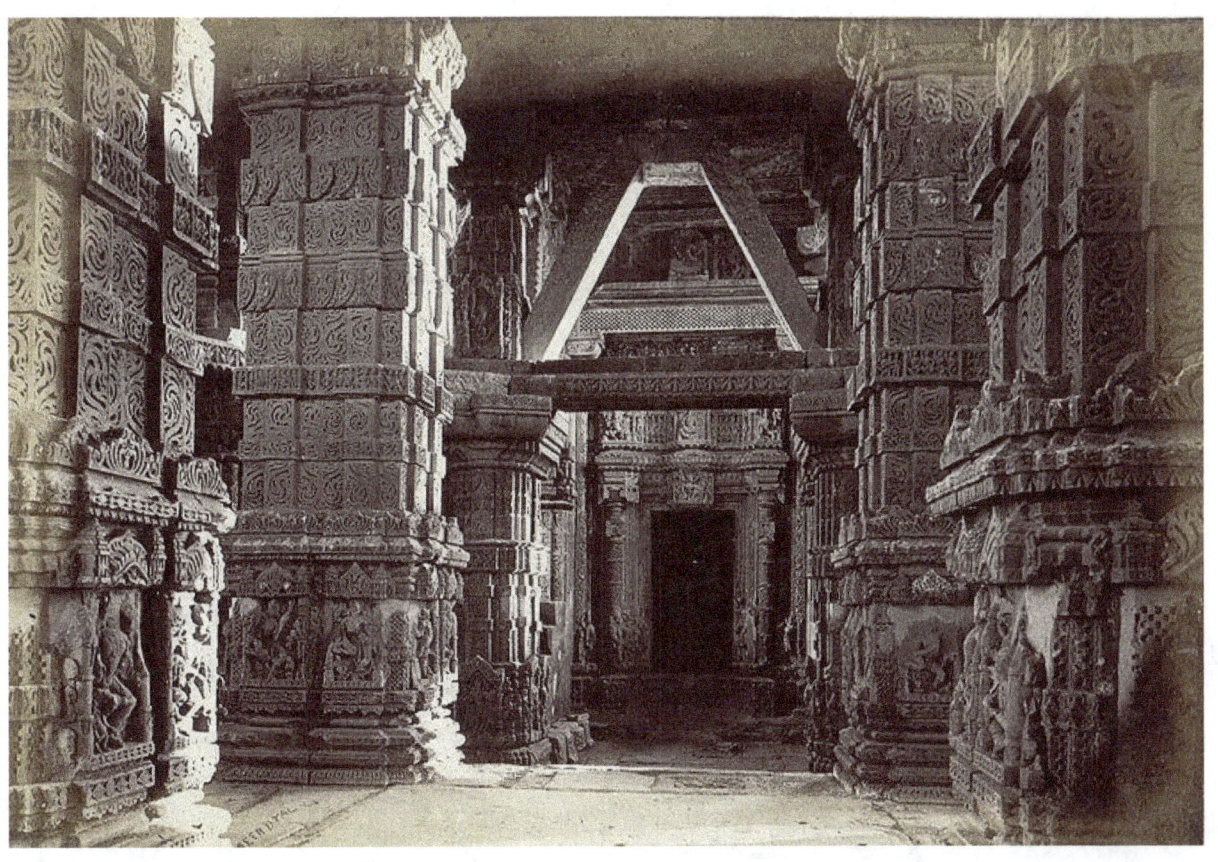

Interior of Jain Temple Gwalior Fort

Teli ka Mandir: -

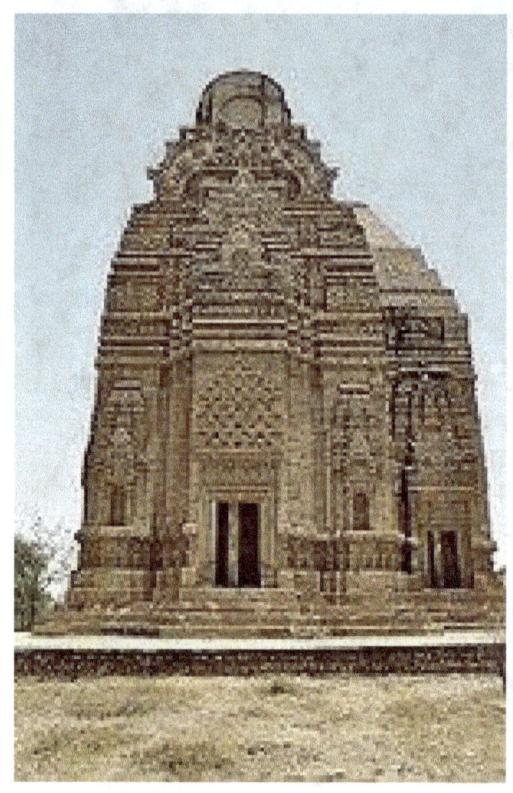

Teli ka Mandir was built by the Pratihara emperor Mihira Bhoja.

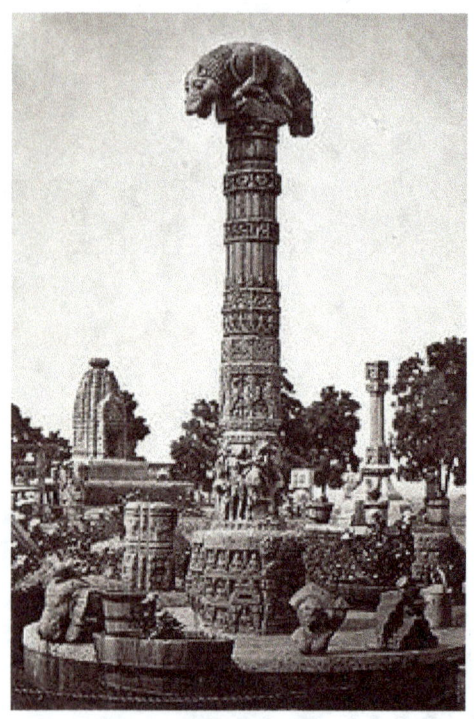

Sculptures near Teli ka Mandir, Gwalior Fort.

The Name "Teli ka Mandir":

The name "Teli ka Mandir" is derived from the Hindi word **"Teli"**, meaning **oil**. Historical accounts suggest this nomenclature may have originated because the temple's upkeep or construction was possibly funded by an oil merchant community. However, there is no definitive evidence linking the temple to oil traders, and the name might also refer to local folklore or linguistic evolution.

An exquisite temple built by the **Pratihara Emperor Mihira Bhoja**, it combines northern Nagara and southern Dravidian architectural styles. Originally dedicated to **Vishnu**, it later housed a **Shiva Linga**.

The **Teli ka Mandir**, located within the Gwalior Fort, is a remarkable Hindu temple attributed to the **Pratihara emperor Mihira Bhoja**. It is the oldest surviving structure in the fort complex and exemplifies a unique blend of **South Indian and North Indian architectural styles**.

The temple's design is distinctive and innovative. It features a **rectangular layout** with a shrine that lacks the typical **pillared pavilions (mandapa)** found in many Hindu temples. The structure is crowned with a **South Indian barrel-vaulted roof**, while its **masonry tower**, standing at an impressive height of **25 meters (82 feet)**, embodies the **Nagara architectural style** of North India. This fusion of styles makes the Teli ka Mandir architecturally unique and a landmark of early temple construction.

Key Architectural Features:

1. **Exterior Niches and Chandrashalas**:
   - The temple's outer walls once housed intricately carved statues, which have now been replaced by **Chandrashalas** (horseshoe-shaped ventilator openings), a hallmark of traditional North Indian design. These Chandrashalas, resembling trefoil or honeycomb patterns, are composed of **receding pointed arches within an arch**, adding an ornamental charm to the structure.
2. **Entrance Doorway**:
   - The temple's grand **torana (archway)** is adorned with elaborate sculptures, including images of **river goddesses**, **romantic couples**, intricate **foliage patterns**, and a **Garuda**, the vehicle of Lord Vishnu.
   - The vertical bands flanking the doorway feature simpler decorative motifs, though many of these carvings have been weathered over time.
3. **Dama Laka**:
   - Above the main entrance is a grouping of small discs, symbolizing the **dama laka (finial)** of a traditional **shikhara** (temple tower), which adds to the structure's spiritual and architectural significance.

History and Restoration:

Originally dedicated to **Lord Vishnu**, the Teli ka Mandir faced significant damage during repeated invasions and **Muslim raids**, leading to the destruction of many of its original features. During its restoration, the temple was rededicated as a **Shaivite shrine** by installing a **Shiva linga**, while retaining its Vaishnava symbols, including the **Garuda**.

The temple underwent further restoration between **1881 and 1883** under the patronage of the British, ensuring its preservation for future generations. Despite the changes in its use and architectural elements, the Teli ka Mandir stands as a monumental testament to India's rich cultural and religious heritage.

Sahastrabahu (Sas-Bahu) Temple: -

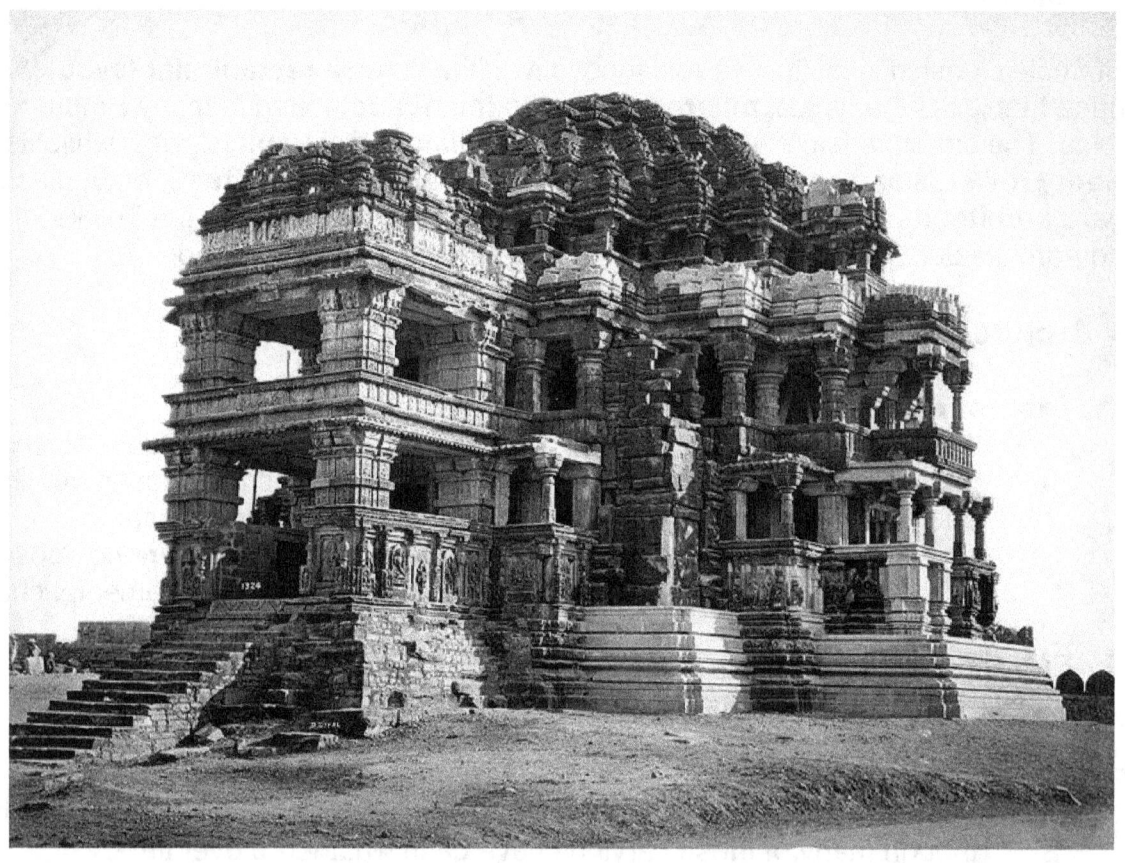

Sahastrabahu (Sas-Bahu) Temple inside Gwalior fort

The **Sas-Bahu Temple**, located within the Gwalior Fort complex, is an extraordinary example of **medieval Indian temple architecture**, constructed during the reign of the **Kachchhapaghata dynasty** in **1092–93 CE**. The temple derives its name not from familial relations but from a combination of the words **"Sahasrabahu,"** an epithet of Lord Vishnu, to whom the temple is dedicated. Over time, the name evolved into the colloquial "Sas-Bahu."

Sahastrabahu (Sas-Bahu) Temple

The **Sas-Bahu Temple**, constructed in **1092–93 CE** by the **Kachchhapaghata dynasty**, is an exquisite example of temple architecture. Dedicated to **Lord Vishnu**, the temple is distinguished by its **pyramidal shape**, built using red sandstone. Its structure is adorned with intricate carvings, featuring multiple stories of beams and pillars, but notably no arches. The name "Sas-Bahu" (mother-in-law and daughter-in-law) is derived from local lore, as the temple housed smaller shrines symbolizing familial harmony.

Architectural Highlights:

1. **Pyramidal Structure**:
    - The temple is designed in a **pyramidal shape**, showcasing the architectural ingenuity of the era. Its rising tiers create a visual harmony that is both grand and balanced, emphasizing the verticality often seen in North Indian temple styles.
2. **Material**:
    - Constructed from **red sandstone**, the temple has withstood the passage of time and numerous invasions, showcasing the durability and craftsmanship of the period.
3. **Beams and Pillars**:
    - The structure is characterized by **multiple stories of intricately carved beams and columns**, which form the temple's primary support system. Notably, **arches** are absent, indicating the temple's reliance on traditional post-and-lintel construction methods prevalent during its era.
4. **Intricate Carvings**:
    - The temple walls and columns are adorned with exquisite carvings, depicting **mythological stories, floral patterns**, and **geometrical motifs**. These carvings reflect the artistic expertise of the Kachchhapaghata artisans and their devotion to Lord Vishnu.

Historical and Cultural Significance:

The Sas-Bahu Temple stands as a testimony to the **religious and cultural prosperity** under the Kachchhapaghata dynasty. Although originally dedicated to **Vishnu**, the temple's name and legends surrounding it have added layers of historical and cultural richness to its identity.

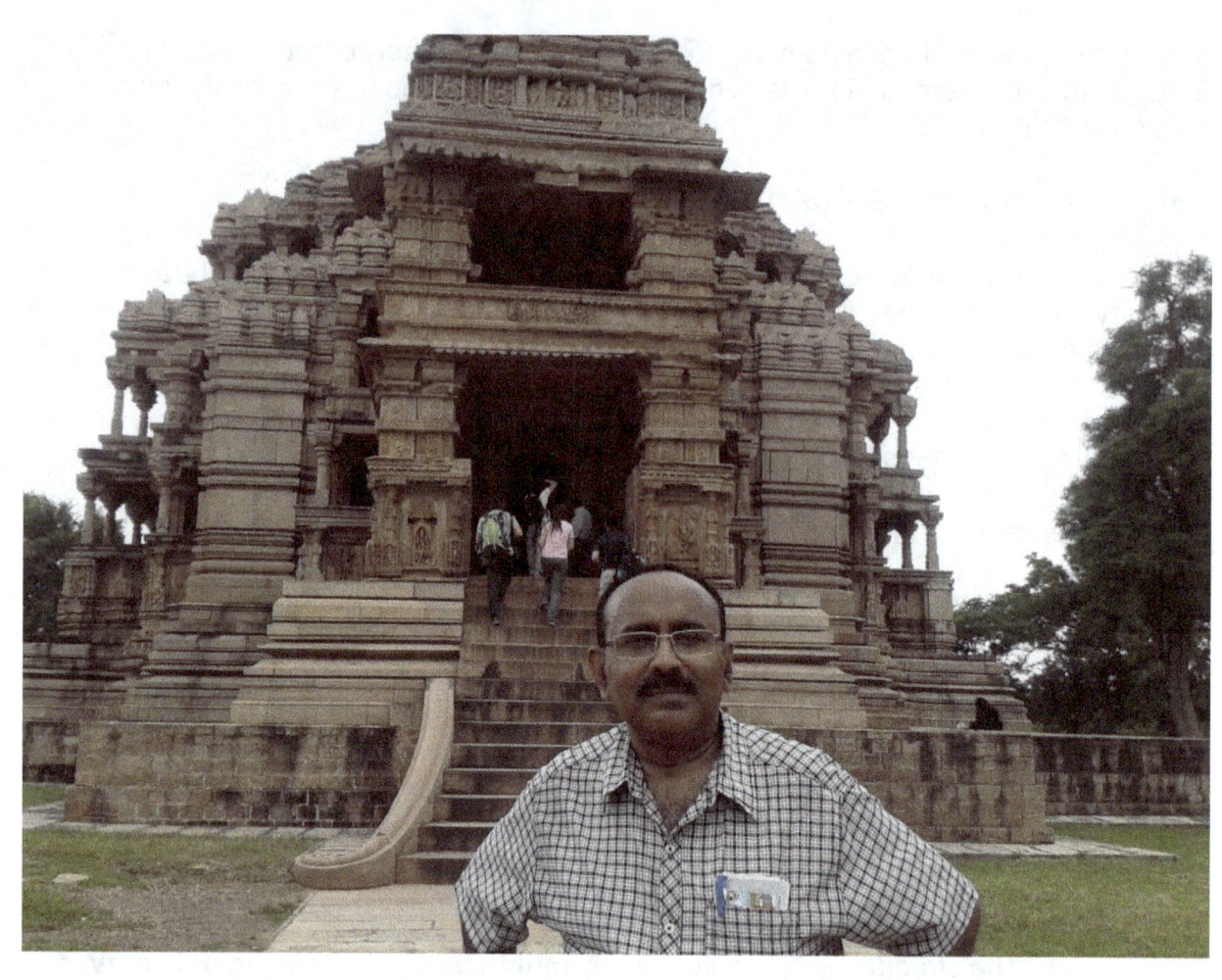

Sahastrabahu (Sas-Bahu) Temple inside Gwalior Fort

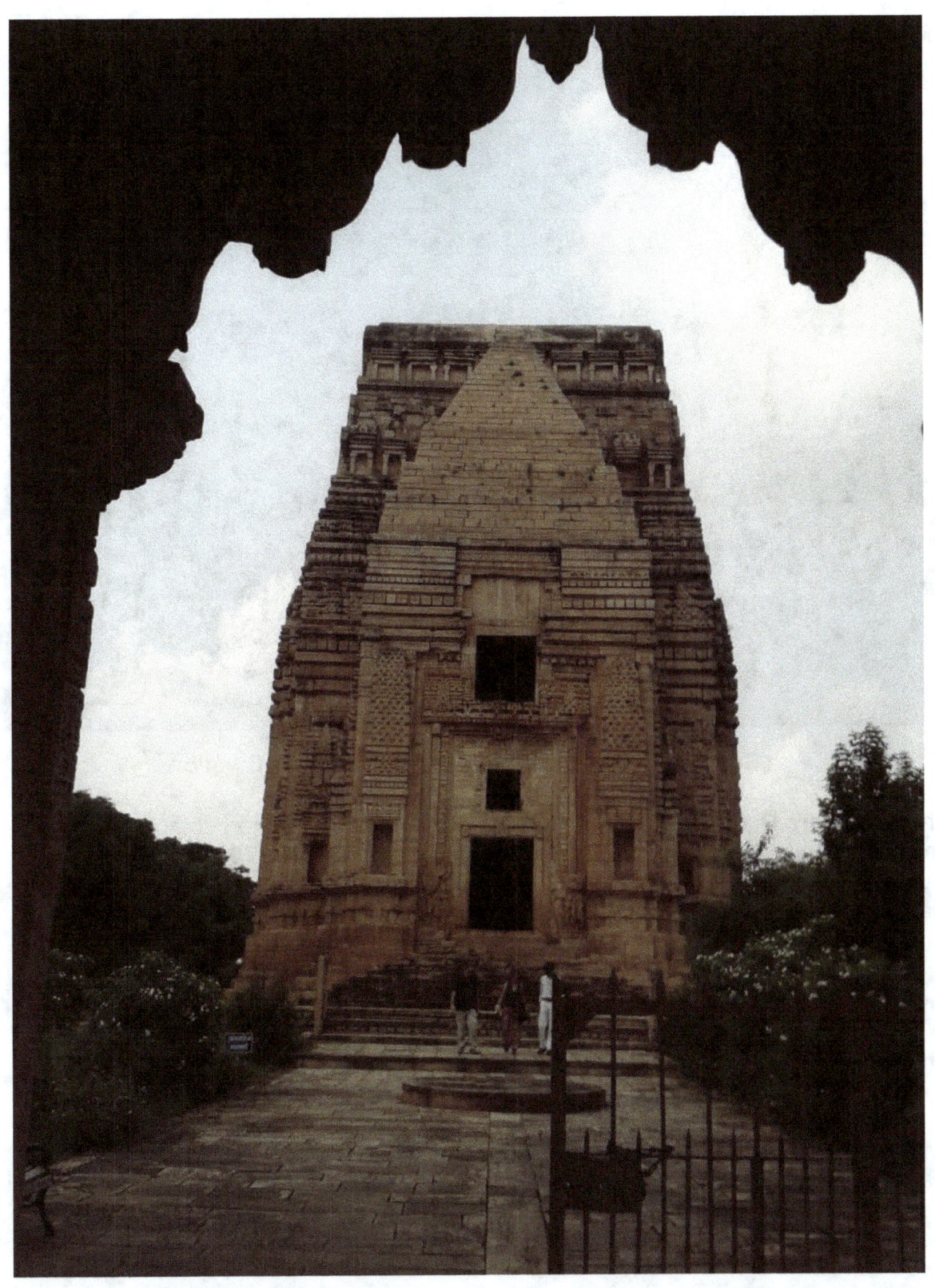

Sahastrabahu (Sas-Bahu) Temple inside Gwalior Fort

Gurdwara Data Bandi Chhor Shahib-

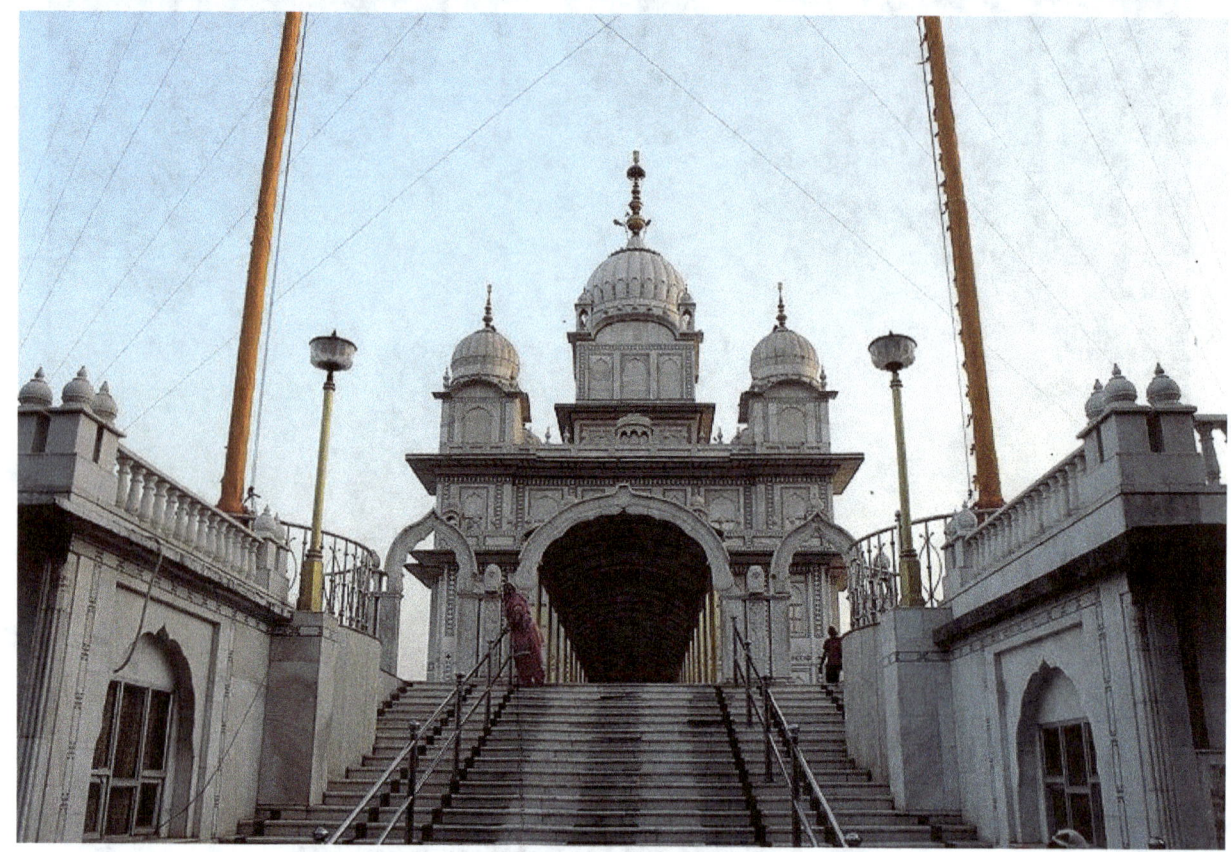

Gurudwara Shri Data Bandi Chhor Shahib Gwalior

The **Gurdwara Data Bandi Chhor**, located within the Gwalior Fort complex, holds profound significance in Sikh history. Constructed during the **1970s and 1980s**, the Gurdwara commemorates the historic episode where the **6th Sikh Guru, Guru Hargobind Sahib**, was imprisoned and subsequently released under extraordinary circumstances.

Gurdwara Data Bandi Chhor

The **Gurdwara Data Bandi Chhor**, constructed during the **1970s and 1980s**, commemorates the imprisonment of **Guru Hargobind Sahib**, the sixth Sikh Guru, at **Gwalior Fort** in 1609 by Mughal Emperor **Jahangir**. Guru Hargobind was detained over unpaid fines attributed to his father, **Guru Arjan Dev Ji**. According to Sikh history, Guru Hargobind secured the release of **52 Hindu Rajas** imprisoned as hostages by Jahangir. He wore a special cloak with **52 hems**, allowing each king to hold on and be freed alongside him. The event is celebrated annually as **Bandi Chhor Divas**.

Historical Background: -

1. **Imprisonment of Guru Hargobind Sahib**:
    - In **1609 CE**, Guru Hargobind, then only **14 years old**, was imprisoned by **Mughal Emperor Jahangir** in the fort. This act was purportedly due to the Sikhs' inability to pay a fine imposed on his father, **Guru Arjan Dev Ji**, who had been martyred under Jahangir's orders.
2. **The Plight of the 52 Hindu Rajas**:
    - At the time, **52 Hindu Rajas** were also held captive in the fort, reportedly as hostages for **"millions of rupees"** and for opposing the Mughal Empire. These rulers regarded Guru Hargobind as a spiritual mentor, and his imprisonment disheartened them.
3. **Guru's Compassionate Appeal**:
    - Upon his release, Guru Hargobind Sahib requested that the captive Rajas be freed as well. Jahangir agreed to the condition that only those who could hold onto the Guru while leaving could be released.
4. **The Cloak with 52 Hems**:
    - To ensure the freedom of all 52 Rajas, Guru Hargobind had a special **cloak stitched with 52 hems**. As he left the fort, each of the captive kings held onto a hem, symbolizing unity and liberation. This act not only secured their freedom but also immortalized Guru Hargobind's legacy as a **spiritual and temporal leader**.

Modern-Day Gurdwara:

The **Gurdwara Data Bandi Chhor** was established to honor this event, symbolizing **compassion, justice, and selflessness**. Its serene architecture and spiritual atmosphere attract pilgrims and visitors from around the world. The gurdwara also serves as a reminder of the **Bandi Chhor Divas**—a Sikh festival coinciding with **Diwali**, celebrating the Guru's return and the liberation of the Rajas.

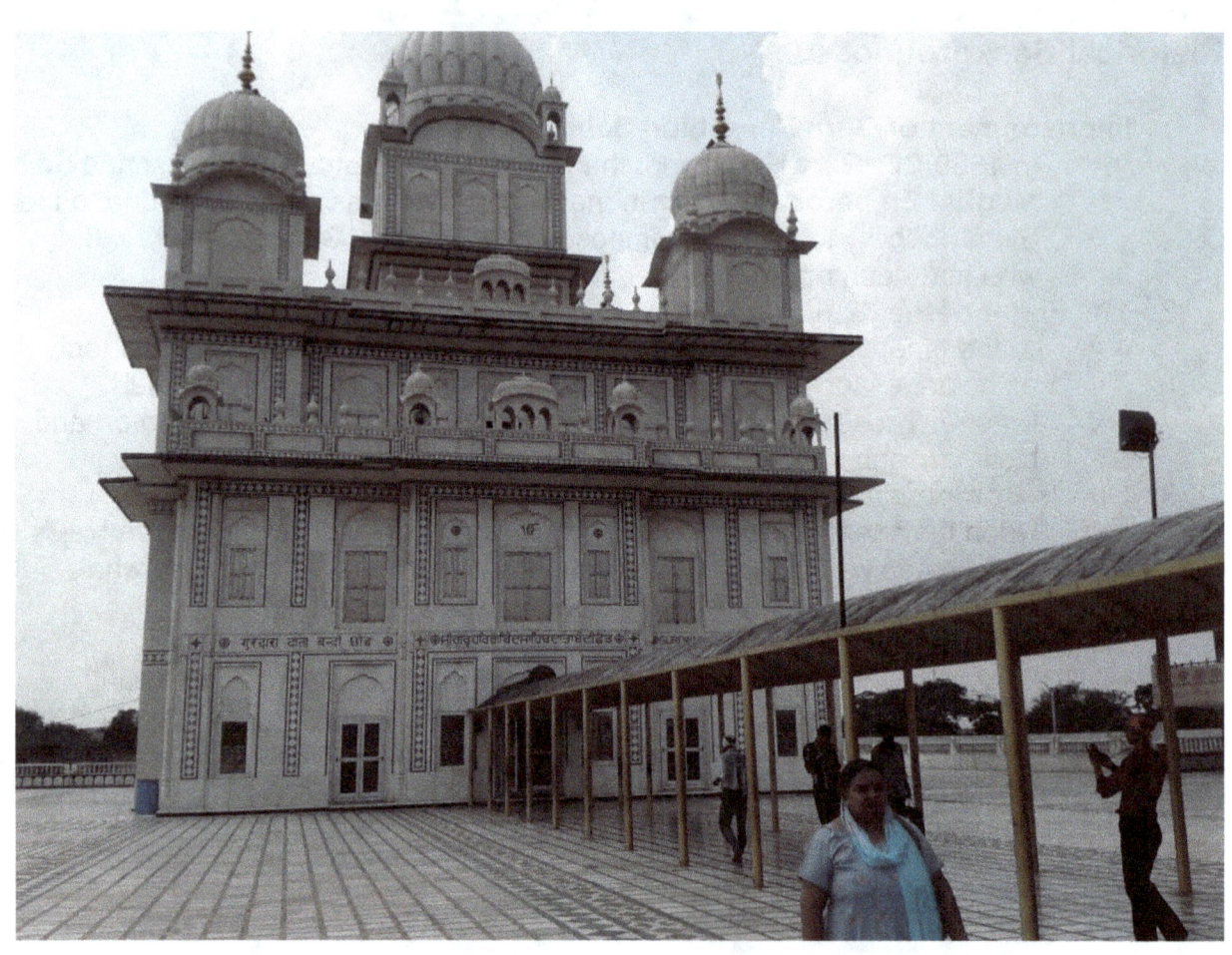

Gurudwara Shri Data Bandi Chhor Shahib Gwalior

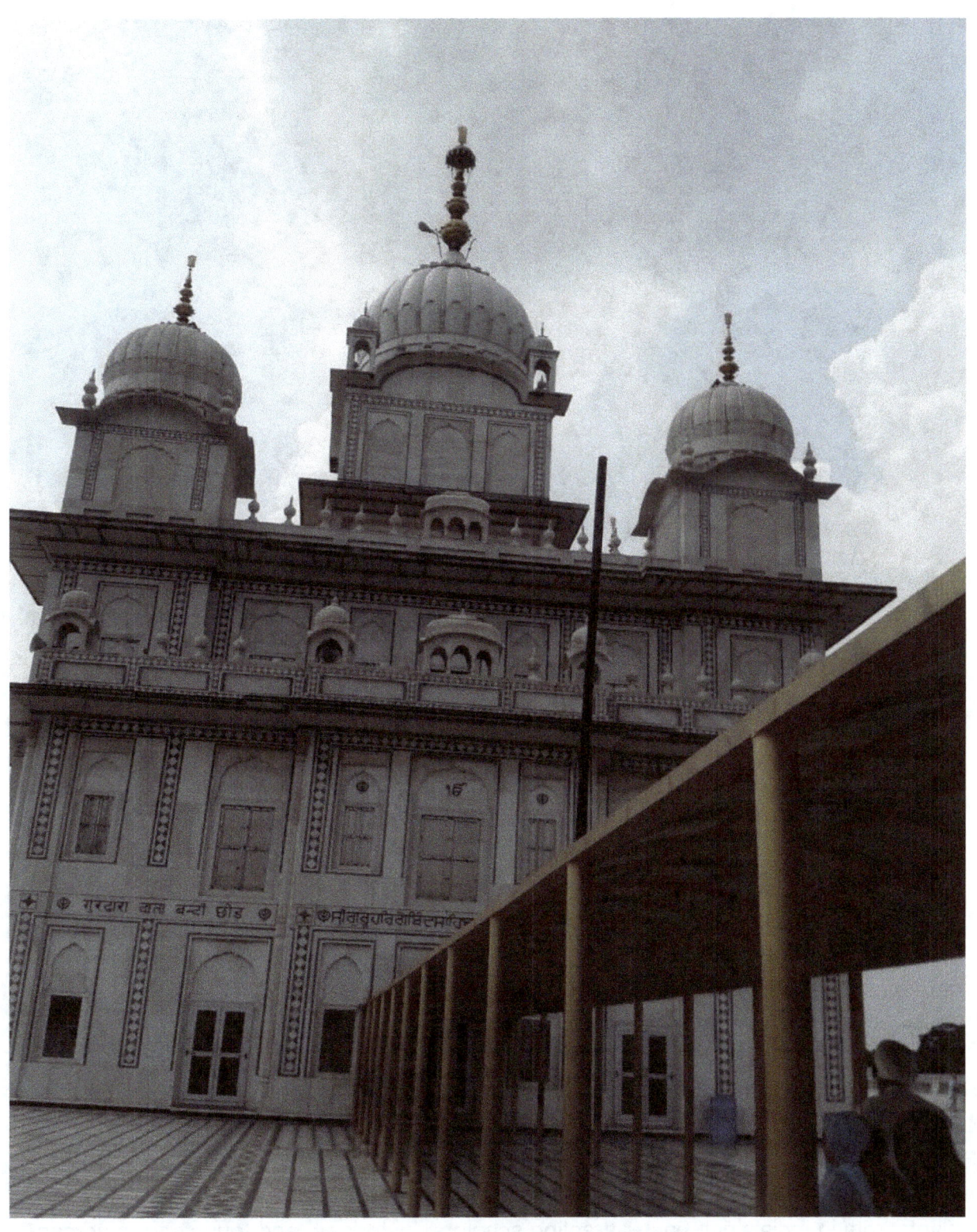
Gurudwara Shri Data Bandi Chhor Shahib Gwalior

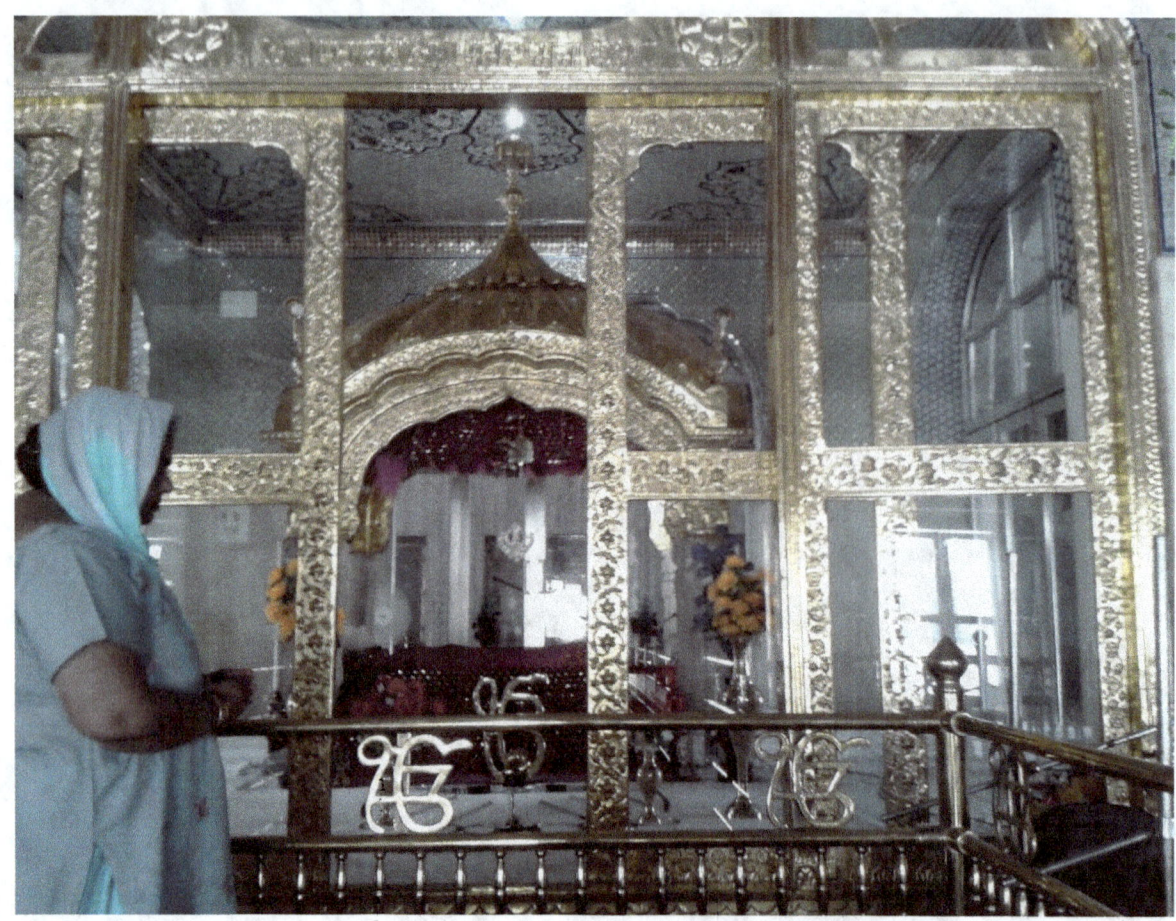

Gurudwara Shri Data Bandi Chhor Shahib Gwalior

Siddhachal Jain Temple Caves

Dating from the **7th to 15th centuries**, these rock-cut Jain temples feature intricately carved Tirthankara statues. The largest idol, a **58-foot figure of Rishabhanatha**, stands as a testament to Gwalior's artistic heritage.

Cultural Significance

The Gwalior Fort serves as a treasure trove of history, blending influences from various dynasties and cultures. Today, it stands as a symbol of the city's resilience and its pivotal role in India's rich past, attracting scholars, historians, and tourists from across the globe.

Vikram Mahal

The **Vikram Mahal**, also known as **Vikram Mandir**, was built by **Vikramaditya Singh**, the elder son of Maharaja Man Singh Tomar. A temple dedicated to **Lord Shiva** originally stood within its premises but was destroyed during the Mughal period. The temple has since been re-established in the palace's courtyard.

Chhatri of Bhim Singh Rana

This **chhatri** (memorial pavilion) was erected by **Chhatra Singh**, as a tribute to **Bhim Singh Rana** (1707–1756), a ruler of **Gohad state**. Bhim Singh occupied the fort in **1740 CE** and constructed a lake, **Bhimtal**, as a monument. The chhatri, built near Bhimtal, is an enduring symbol of his legacy.

Gujari Mahal Archaeological Museum

The **Gujari Mahal**, a palace built by **Raja Man Singh Tomar** for his wife, **Mrignayani**, is now an archaeological museum. The palace, known for its innovative aqueduct system sourcing water from the Rai River, houses artifacts including **1st- and 2nd-century BCE sculptures**, terracotta items, and replicas of frescoes from the **Bagh Caves**.

Garuda

Near the **Teli ka Mandir**, within the **Gwalior Fort**, stands the **Garuda Monument**, a striking structure dedicated to **Lord Vishnu**. This monument is notable for its height, making it the tallest within the fort premises, and serves as an enduring symbol of devotion to Vishnu.

Architectural Features:

1. **Fusion of Styles**:
   The Garuda monument reflects a **blend of Indian and Muslim architectural influences**, showcasing intricate design elements from both traditions. This fusion is emblematic of the cultural exchanges that shaped much of India's medieval architecture.

2. **Height and Prominence**:
   As the highest monument in the fort, it offers a commanding presence and is visible from various points within the fort, enhancing its spiritual and visual appeal.

Man Mandir Palace

This 15th-century palace is known for its ornate carvings, colourful tiles, and artistic stone latticework. It remains one of the fort's architectural jewels.

The **Man Mandir Palace**, constructed in the **15th century** by **Maharaja Man Singh** of the **Tomar Dynasty**, is one of the most remarkable structures within **Gwalior Fort**. It is frequently referred to as the **"Painted Palace"** due to its distinctive **decorative tiles**, which give the palace its vibrant appearance.

Architectural Highlights:

1. **Tile Decoration**:
   - The palace is renowned for its **turquoise, green, and yellow tiles**, which are arranged in **geometric patterns** throughout the structure. These colorful tiles were used extensively, creating an eye-catching, painted effect that defines the palace's aesthetic.
   - The intricate tilework is an example of the advanced **art and craftsmanship** of the Tomar dynasty and reflects the architectural trends of the period.
2. **Structure and Design**:
   - The **Man Mandir Palace** is a **multi-story** building with several courtyards and rooms that once served as royal quarters, featuring fine stone carvings and an intricate layout.
   - The palace also includes **decorative motifs** such as **arches, intricate carvings**, and **jharokhas** (overhanging enclosed balcony), which are characteristic of the **Rajput style**.

Significance:

- The palace was not only a royal residence but also served as a symbol of the **wealth and power** of the Tomar dynasty.
- Today, it is one of the most visited attractions in **Gwalior Fort**, admired for its aesthetic beauty and historical importance.

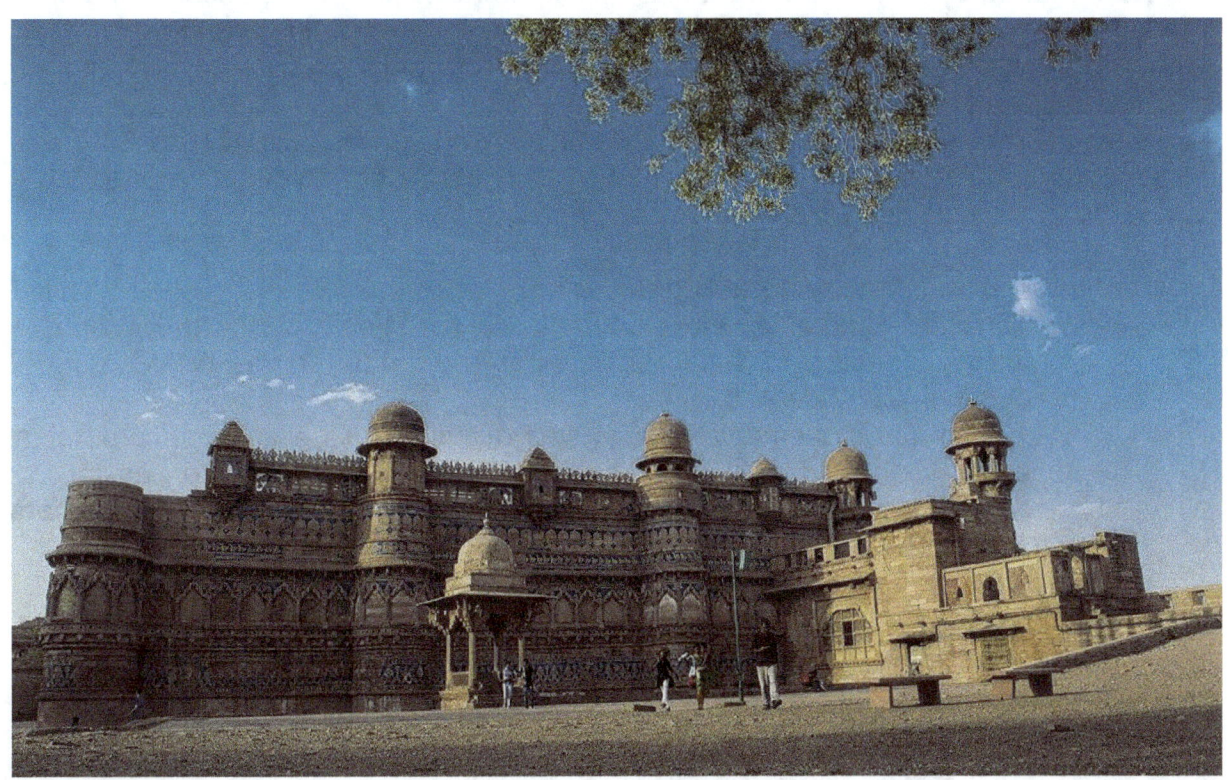

Hathi Pol

Hathi Pol Gate

The **Hathi Pol Gate** (also known as **Hathiya Paur**) is one of the most significant and visually striking gates at **Gwalior Fort**. Located on the **southeastern side**, it serves as the gateway leading to the **Man Mandir Palace**. The gate is the **last of the seven gates** of the fort, making it a crucial entry point.

- **Architectural Features**:
    - The gate is **built in stone** and features **cylindrical towers** topped with **cupola domes**. These domes add a distinctive aesthetic to the structure.
    - The **carved parapets** connecting the domes provide both structural support and ornamental beauty.
    - The gate was originally **adorned with a life-sized statue of an elephant (hathi)**, which is why it was named **Hathi Pol**. Although the statue is no longer present, the gate's historical and architectural significance remains evident.

Karan Mahal

The **Karn Mahal**, built by **Kirti Singh**, also known as **Karn Singh**, the second king of the Tomar dynasty, is another significant structure within the fort. It exemplifies the dynasty's architectural prowess and their devotion to fortifying Gwalior.

The **Karan Mahal** is another key monument within **Gwalior Fort**, built by **Kirti Singh**, the second ruler of the **Tomar Dynasty**. Known as **Karn Singh**, he commissioned the palace, which reflects the wealth and artistic heritage of his reign.

- **Historical and Architectural Significance**:
    - The **Karan Mahal** is renowned for its **Rajput style architecture**, which includes features such as **intricate carvings**, **pillared verandas**, and decorative arches.
    - The palace is often admired for its **layout and design**, which incorporates elements that were typical of the Tomar dynasty's royal residences.
    - **Karan Mahal** is a testament to the grandeur of the Tomar rulers and offers a glimpse into the fort's royal past.

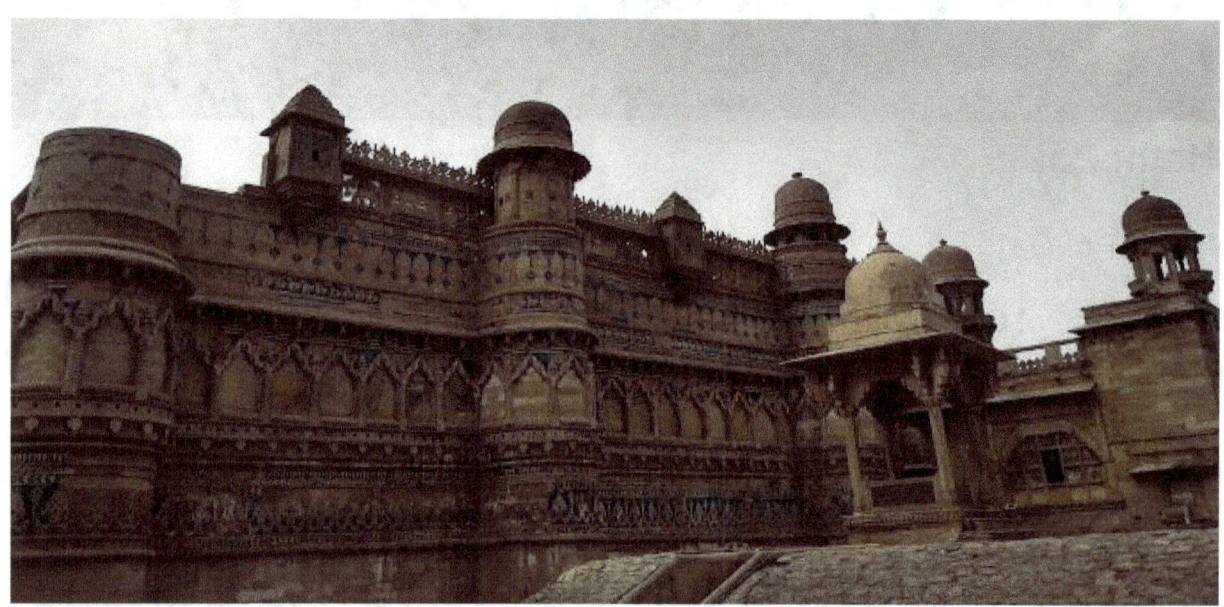

Vikram Mahal

The **Vikram Mahal** (also known as **Vikram Mandir**) was built by **Vikramaditya Singh**, the elder son of **Maharaja Man Singh**. A devoted follower of **Shiva**, Vikramaditya Singh initially constructed a **Shiva temple** within the palace. The temple was later destroyed during the **Mughal period**, but efforts have been made to **re-establish the temple** in the front open space of the **Vikram Mahal**.

- **Historical Context**:
    - Vikramaditya Singh, who was a devout Hindu, dedicated the original structure to **Lord Shiva**.
    - Despite its destruction during the Mughal era, the **Vikram Mahal** still holds a deep spiritual and architectural significance.
    - Today, the re-established Shiva temple continues to attract visitors who admire its historical and religious heritage.

Chhatri of Bhim Singh Rana

The **Chhatri of Bhim Singh Rana** is a commemorative monument built to honor **Bhim Singh Rana**, a ruler of **Gohad state** from 1707 to 1756. The chhatri is a domed pavilion, symbolizing both the region's architectural style and the respect paid to a significant ruler.

- **Historical Background**:
    - **Bhim Singh Rana** played a key role in the **Gwalior Fort's history**, notably by occupying the fort in **1740**, when the Mughal Satrap **Ali Khan** surrendered.
    - In **1754**, he created the **Bhimtal**, a lake within the fort, as a lasting monument to his rule.
    - After his death, his successor, **Chhatra Singh**, constructed the **Chhatri** near the **Bhimtal** to honor Bhim Singh's legacy.
- **Architectural Features**:
    - The **Chhatri** stands as a symbol of **Rajput memorial architecture**, with a **dome** that signifies the respect given to rulers and heroes of the time.
    - It is located near the **Bhimtal**, the lake that Bhim Singh Rana constructed, adding an element of tranquility and beauty to the memorial.

These two monuments, **Vikram Mahal** and the **Chhatri of Bhim Singh Rana**, reflect the fort's blend of **religious** and **political history**, showcasing both **devotion** and **military significance**

Museum

Gujari Mahal Archaeological Museum

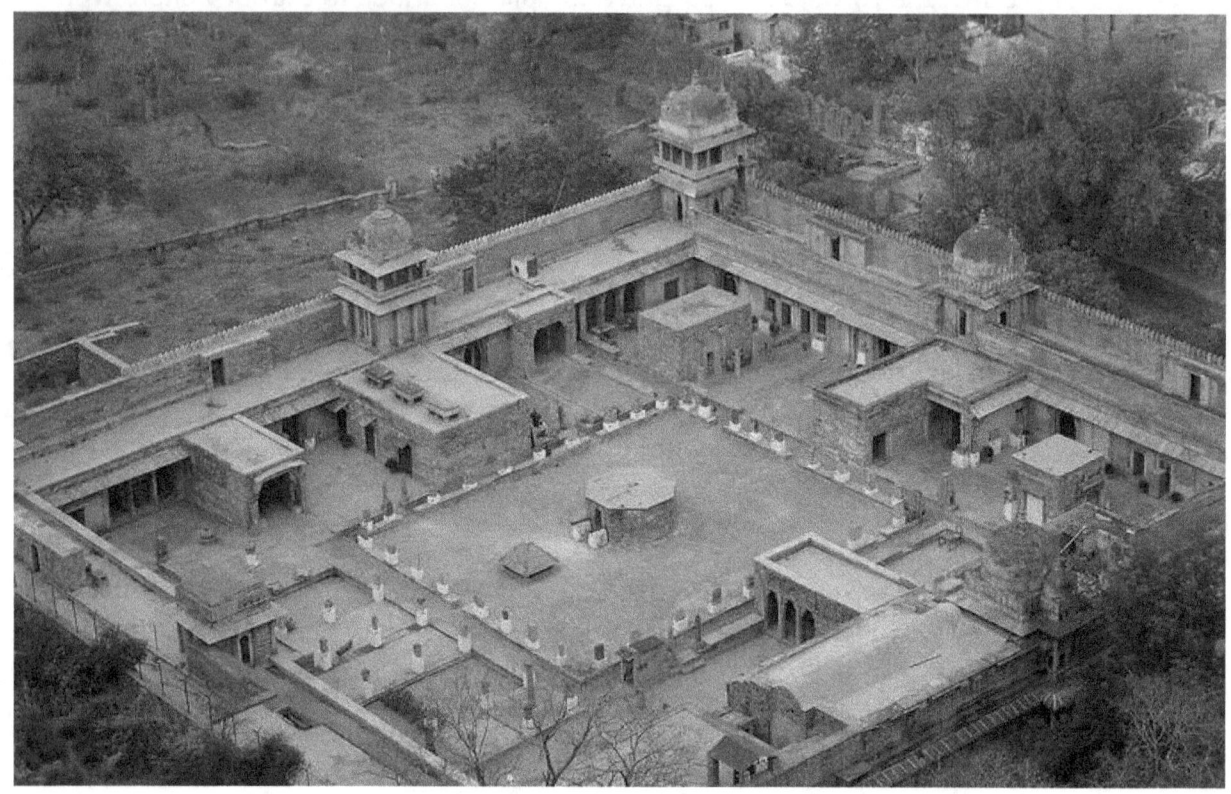

Gujari Mahal inside the fort

Gujari Mahal

The **Gujari Mahal**, now an **archaeological museum**, was built by **Raja Man Singh Tomar** in the **15th century** for his beloved wife, **Mrignayani**, a **Gujar princess**. The palace's unique design and construction were influenced by Mrignayani's request for a **separate living space** that would provide her with comfort and convenience. One of her significant demands was a **regular water supply**, which was achieved through an **aqueduct** bringing water from the nearby **Rai River**.

- **Historical Significance**:
    - The **Gujari Mahal** is named after Mrignayani, reflecting its connection to the **Gujar** community, which Mrignayani hailed from. It stands as a testament to the **love** and **dedication** of Raja Man Singh to his queen.
    - The palace was designed to offer luxury and practicality, catering to the specific needs of the royal couple.
- **Museum Features**:

- The **Gujari Mahal** has been transformed into an **archaeological museum** that showcases a **rich collection of artefacts** from various periods of Indian history.
- Rare exhibits at the museum include:
  - **Hindu and Jain sculptures**, dating back to the **1st and 2nd centuries BC**.
  - A **miniature statue of Salabhanjika**, which is an iconic image of an apsara or divine woman.
  - **Terracotta items** that highlight the artistic craftsmanship of ancient India.
  - **Replicas of frescoes** from the **Bagh Caves**, which are renowned for their exquisite ancient wall paintings.
- **Architectural Features**:
  - The **Gujari Mahal** is known for its **unique blend of Mughal and Rajput architectural styles**, featuring **elegant arches, intricate carvings**, and a **water management system** that is quite ahead of its time.

The **museum** not only preserves the architectural grandeur of the **Gujari Mahal** but also serves as an important repository of ancient art and culture.

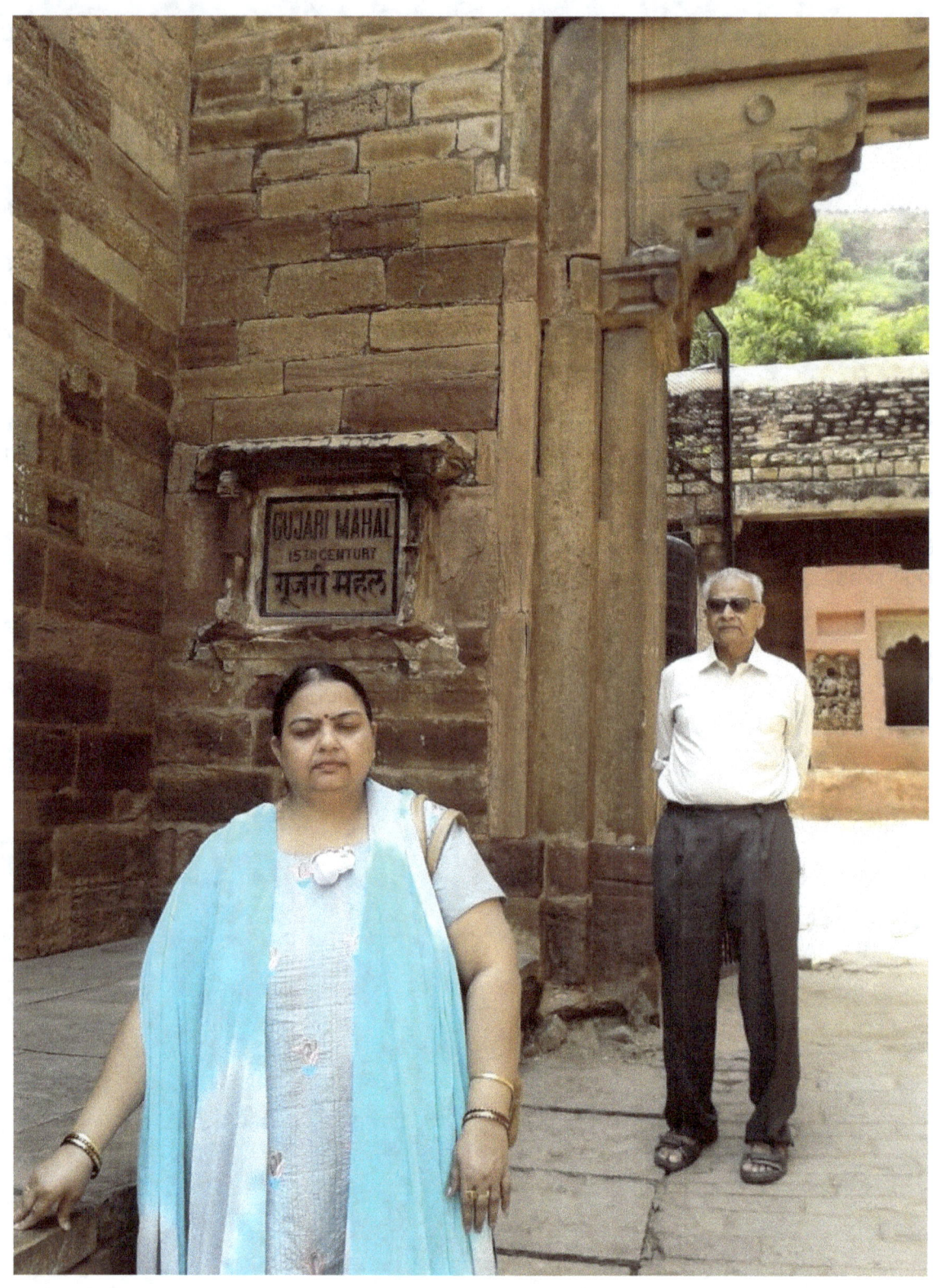

Gujari Mahal Entrance Gate of Gwalior Fort

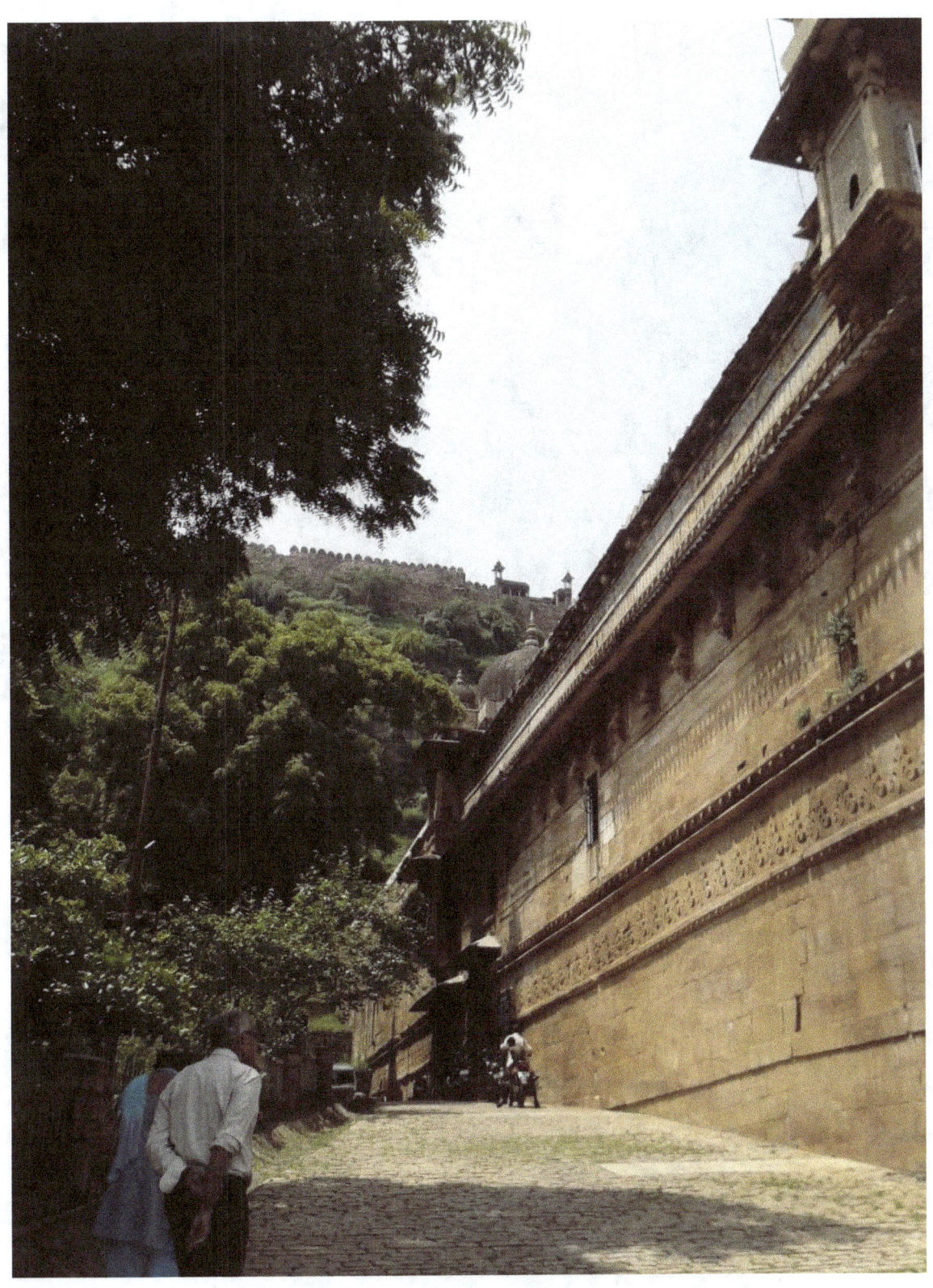

Towards Fort Entrance Gate of Gwalior Fort

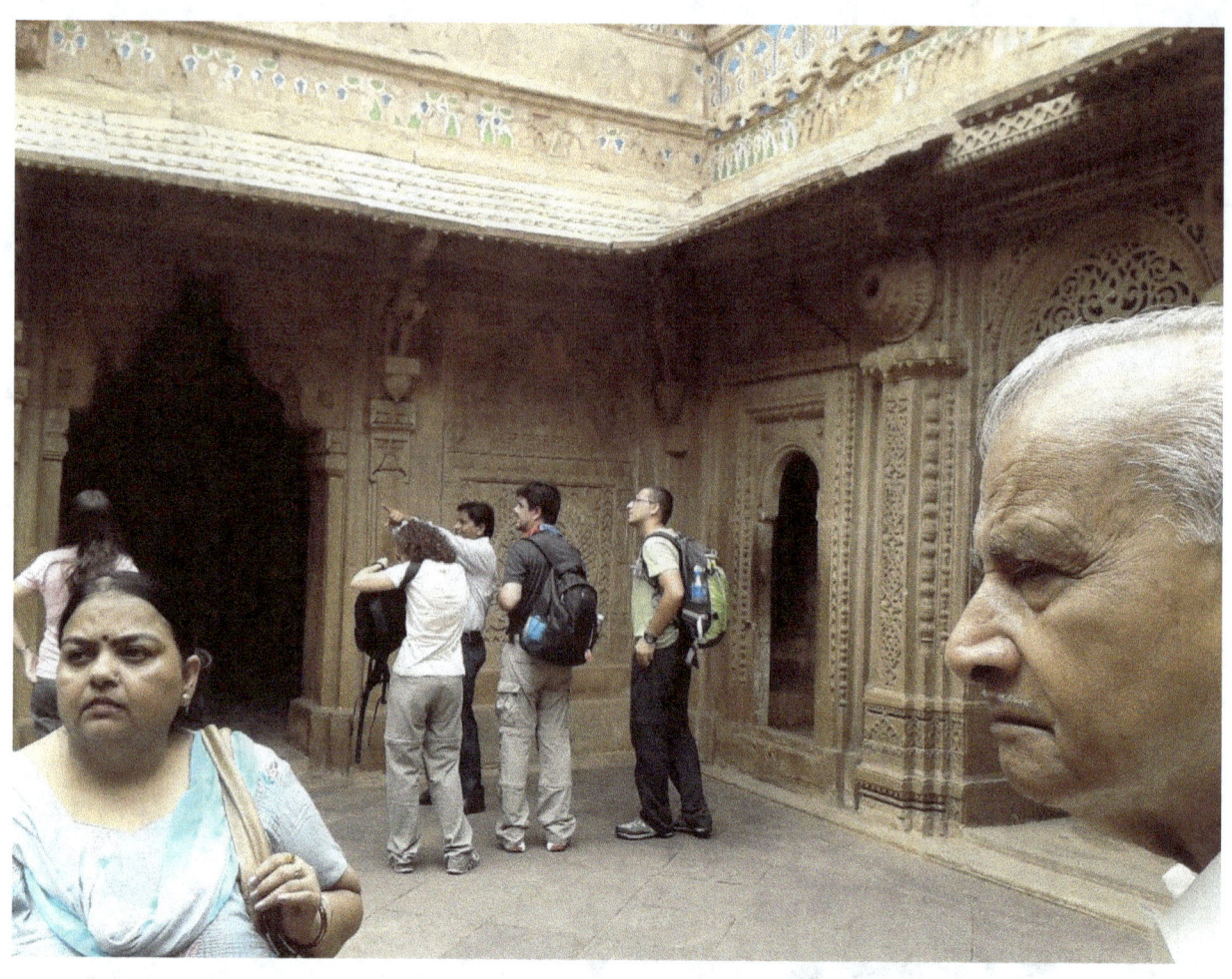

Visitors inside the Gwalior Fort

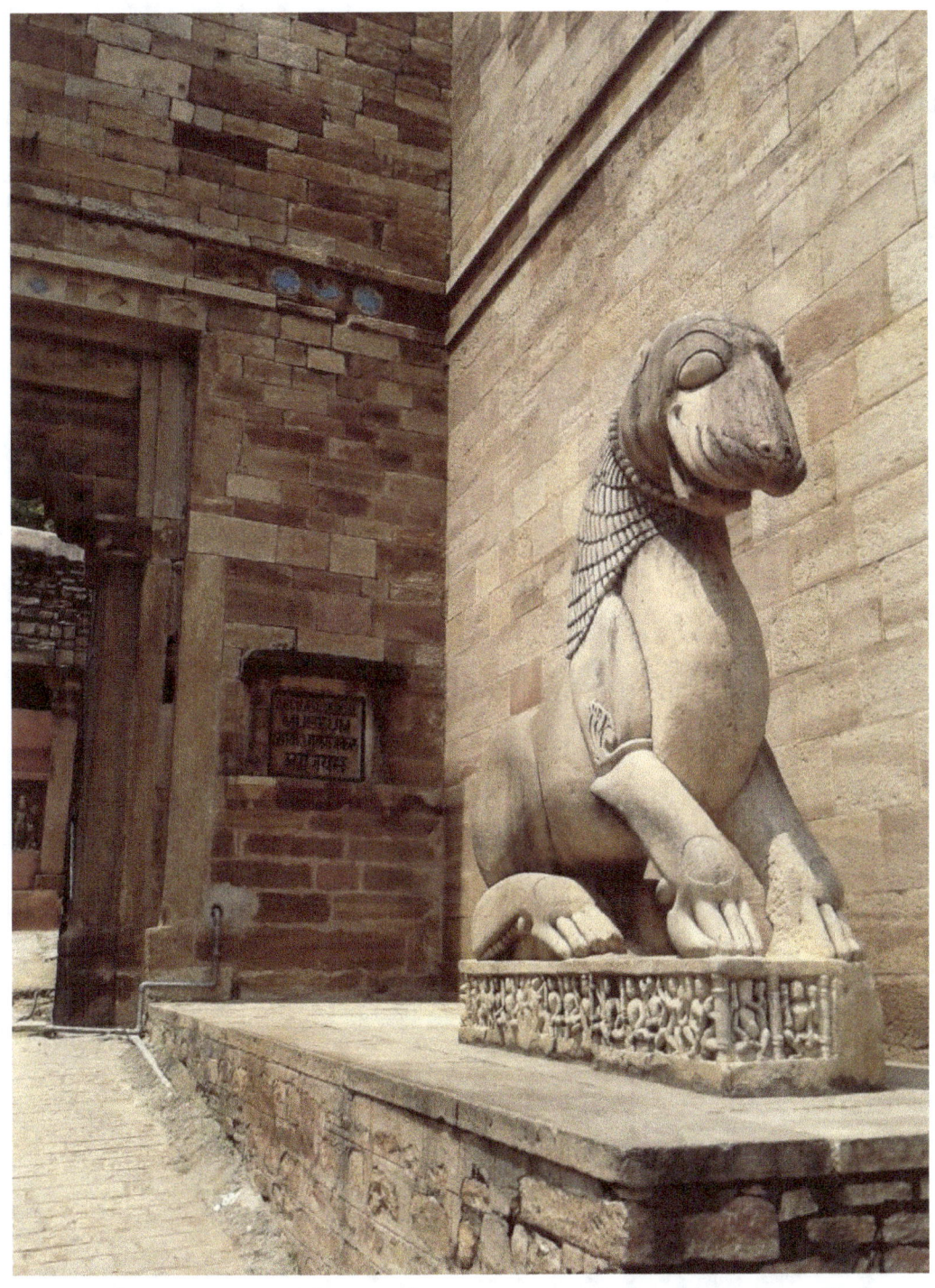

Archaeological Museum Entrance Gate inside Gwalior Fort

Other Monuments

There are several other monuments built inside the fort area. These include the Scindia School (Originally an exclusive school for the sons of Indian princes and nobles) that was founded by Madho Rao Scindia in 1897.

Scindhiya Museum Gwalior: -

About Jai Vilas Palace Museum: -

This 19th-century European-style palace features glass furniture & a model train in the dining room.

Address:

Jai Vilas Palace, Lashkar, Gwalior, Madhya Pradesh 474009

Phone: 1800 233 7777

Opening Hours:

Open Tue-Sun (10AM-6PM). Closed Monday

Entry Ticket: -

Indian Nationals: ₹300
Foreign Nationals: ₹850

Jai Vilas Palace History & Amazing Architecture: -
Picture Gallery: -

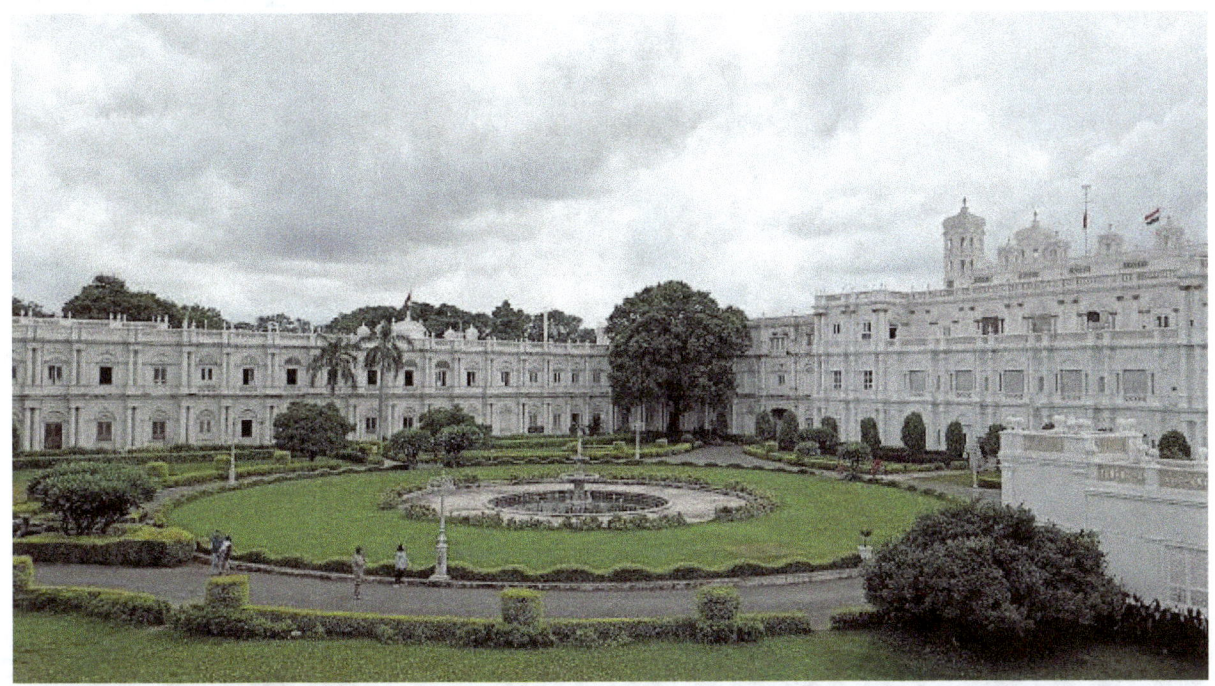

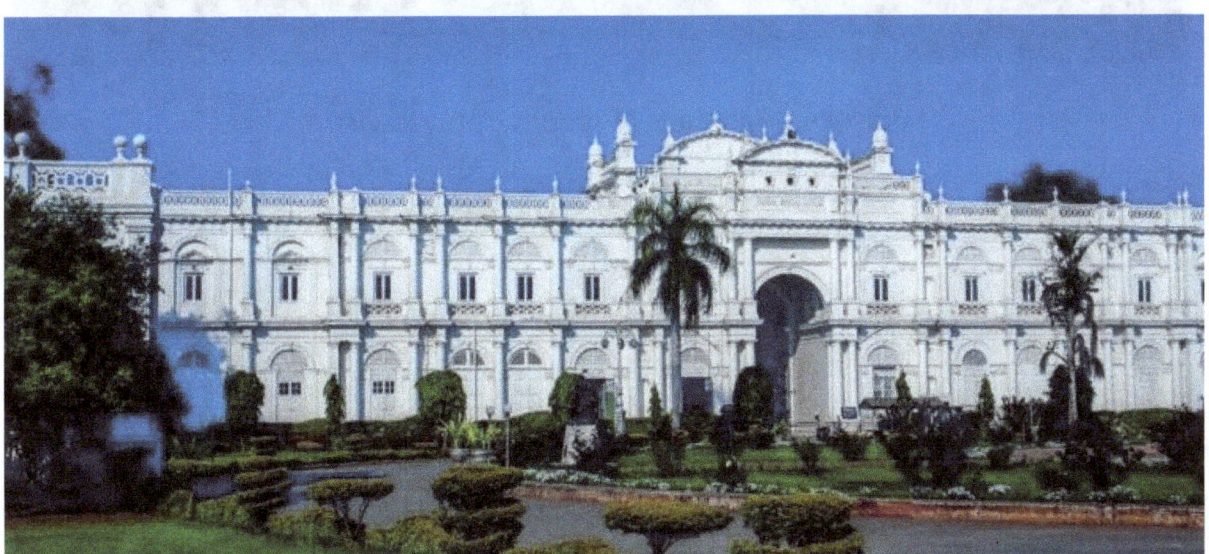

Gwalior Jai Vilas Palace & Museum outside view

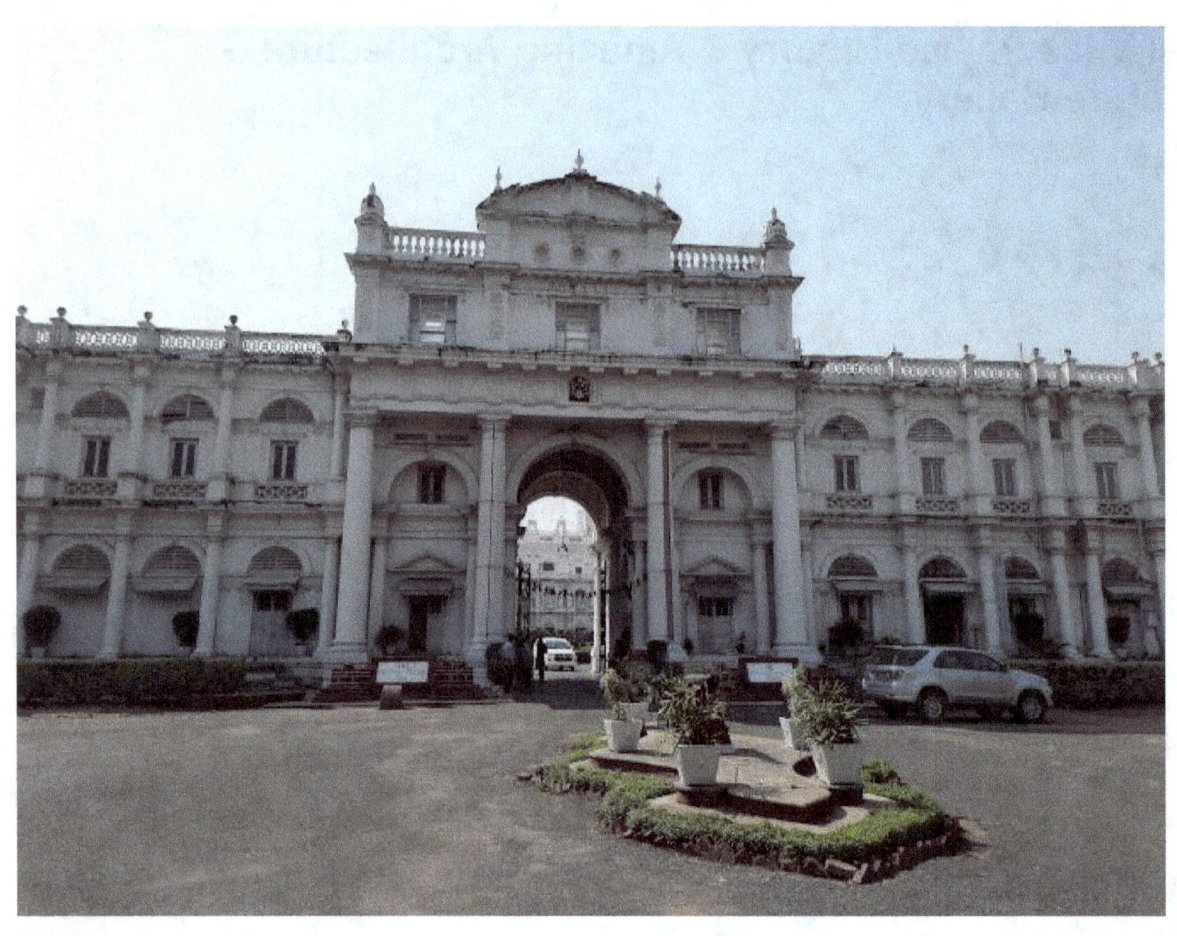

Jai Vilas Palace & Museum outside view

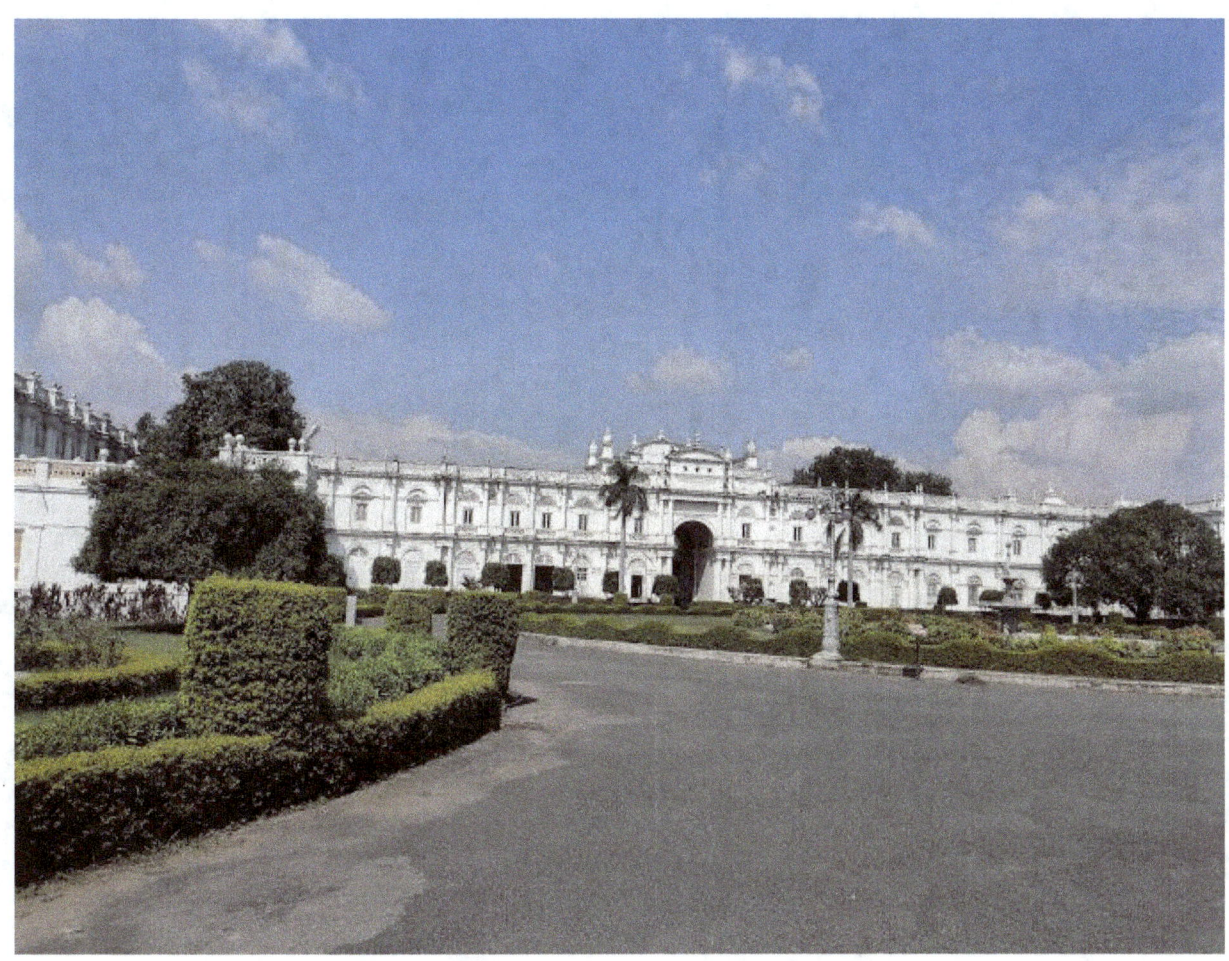

Jai Vilas Palace and Museum

Constructed in **1874** by **Maharaja Jayajirao Scindia**, the **Jai Vilas Palace** is a grand residence blending **Tuscan, Italian Doric, and Corinthian architectural styles**. Renowned for its **Durbar Hall**, which features **gold furnishings** and the world's largest pair of chandeliers, the palace is a masterpiece of European-inspired design.

In **1964**, portions of the palace were converted into the **Jiwajirao Scindia Museum**, showcasing **Maratha heritage** and artifacts like royal carriages, silver dining sets, and arms. Highlights include a **silver train** used to serve after-dinner drinks and the intricate steps of wrapping a **Maratha-style turban**.

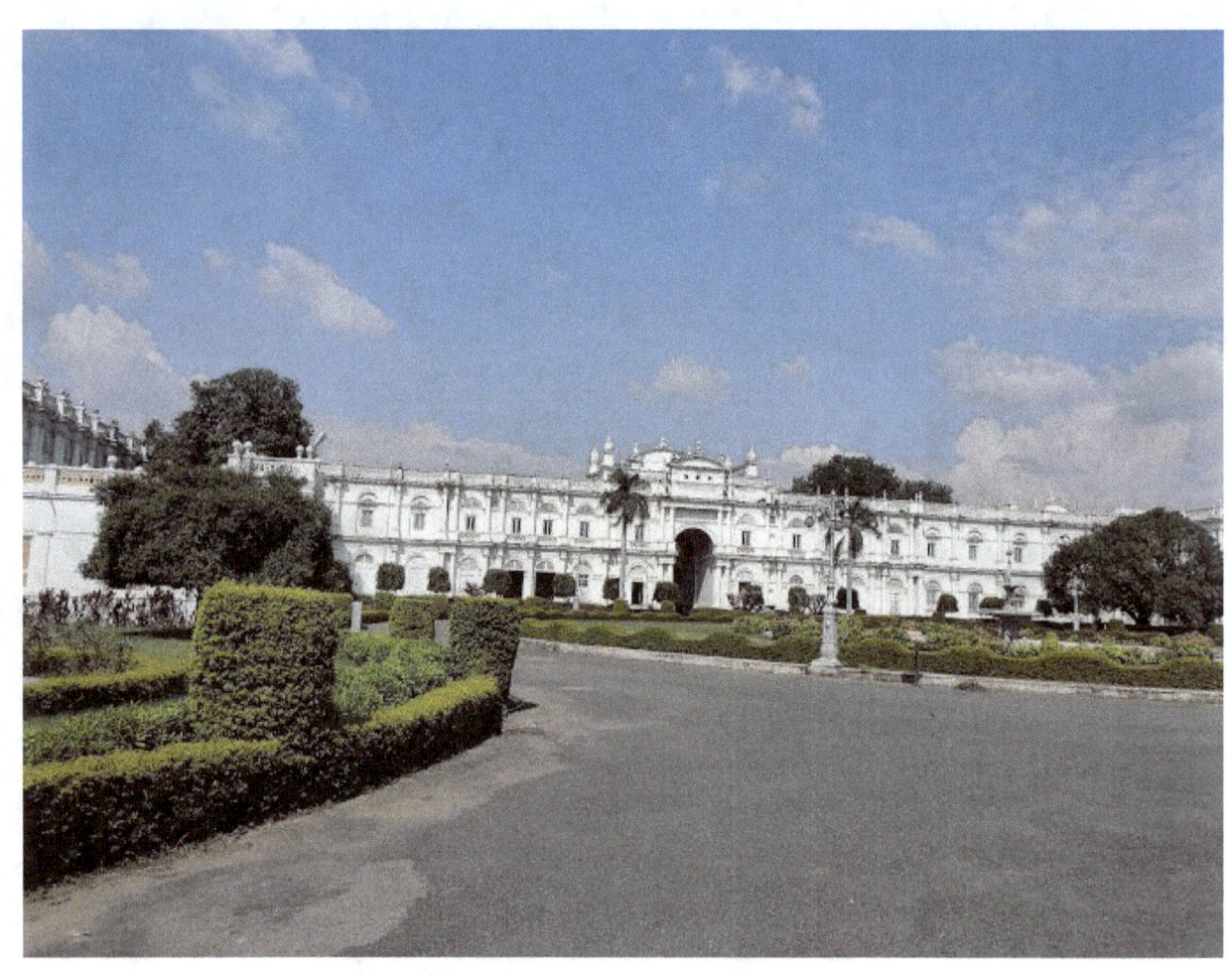

Jai Vilas Palace & Museum outside view

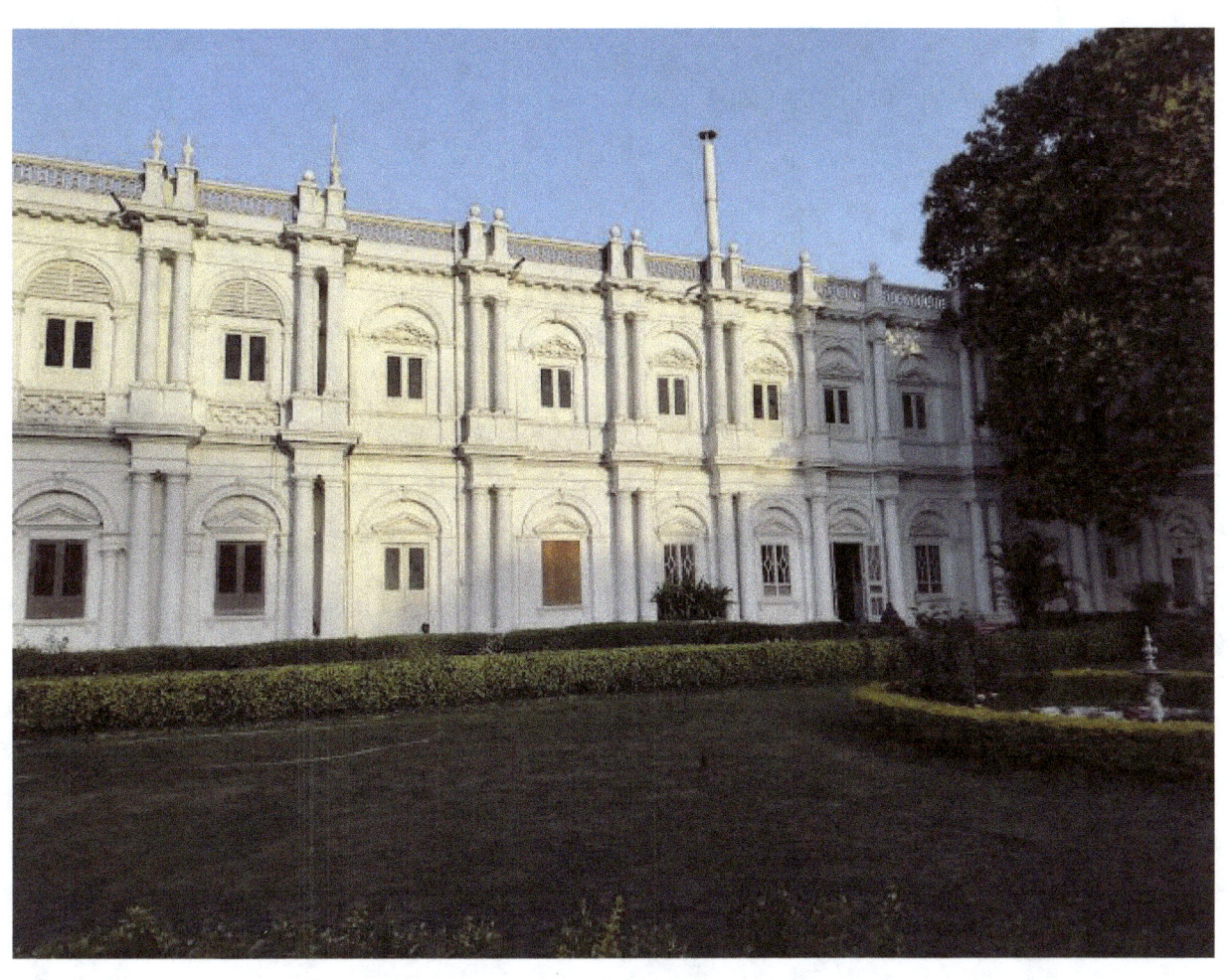

Jai Vilas Palace & Museum outside view

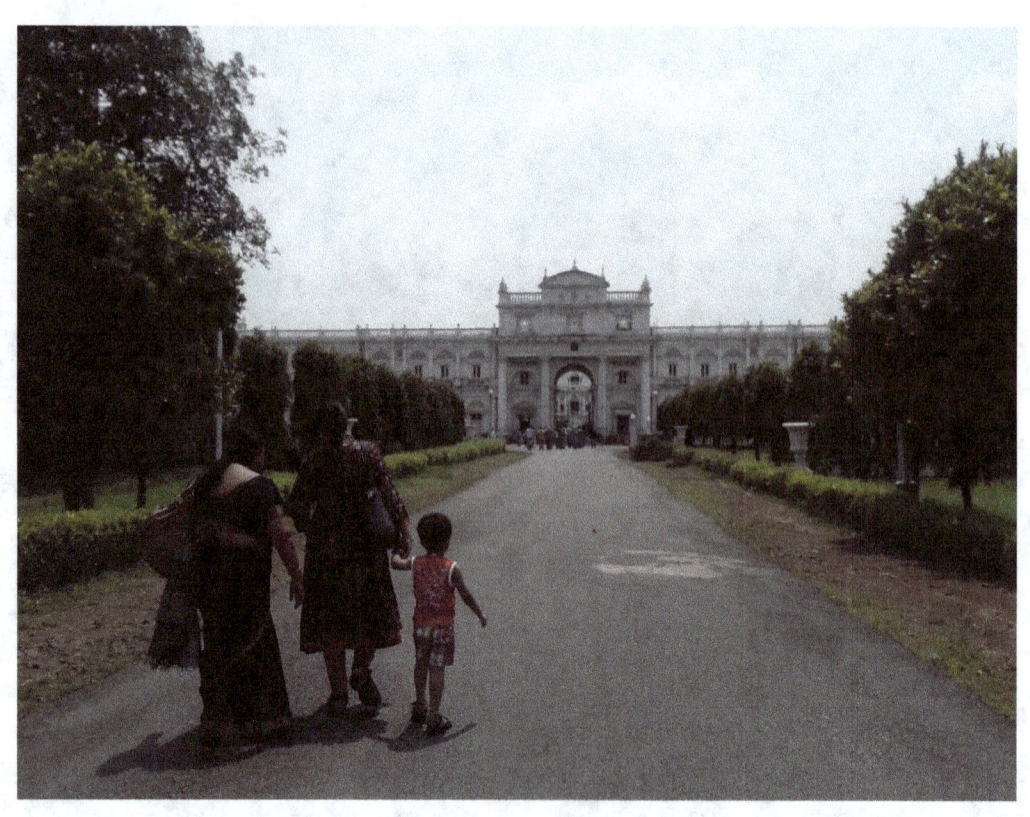
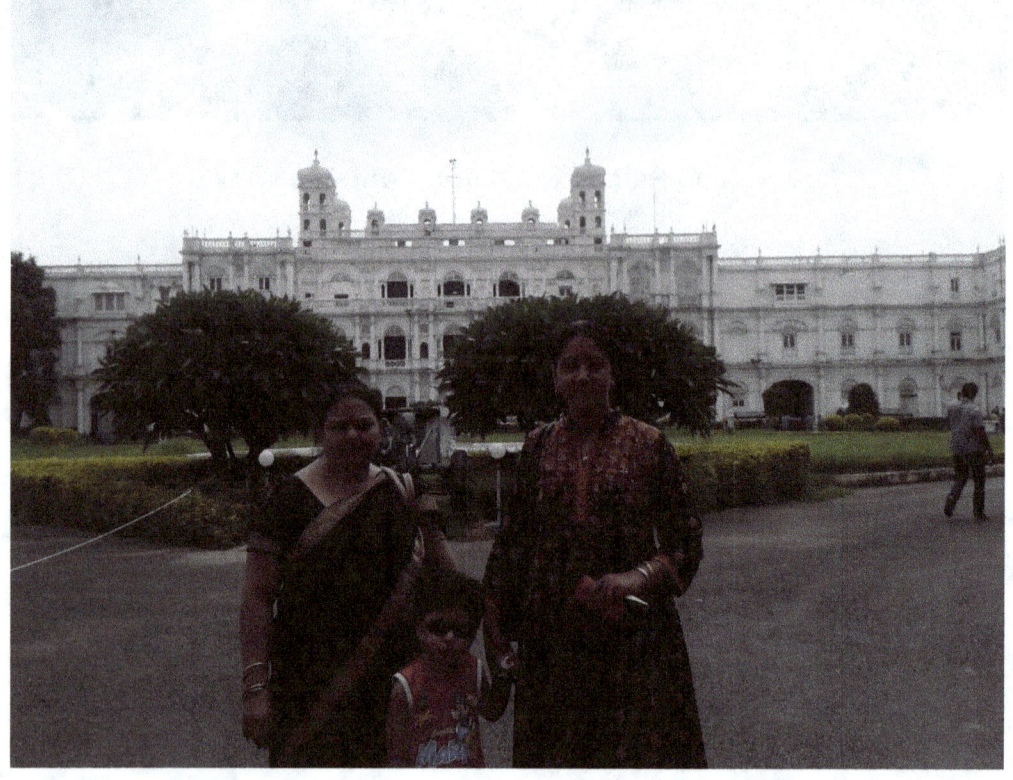

Jai Vilas Palace & Museum outside view

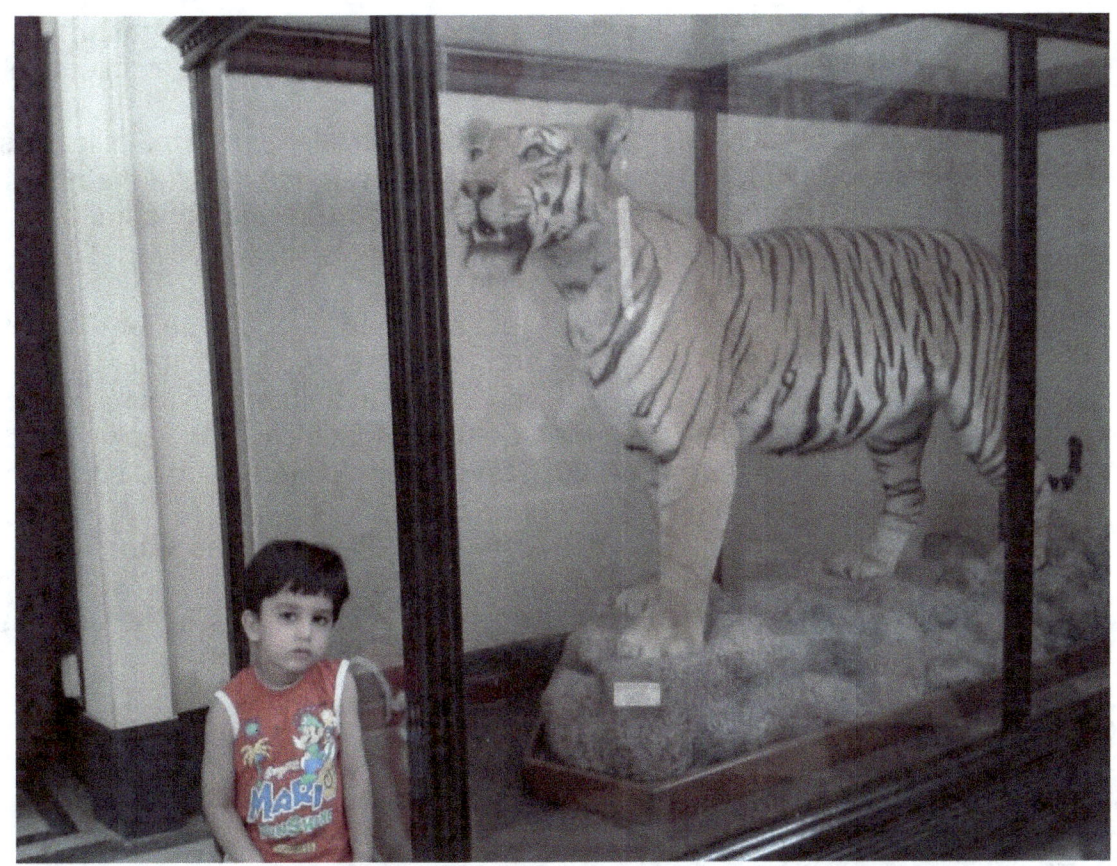

Jai Vilas Palace & Museum inside view

Jai Vilas Mahal Museum Details: -

Jai Vilas Mahal

Jai Vilas Mahal, a grand example of **European architectural influence**, was designed and built by **Lt. Col. Sir Michael Filose** (1832–1925), who served as the Chief Secretary and Director of Public Instruction of Gwalior. This magnificent palace showcases a **fusion of Mughal and European architectural styles**, particularly the Italian and Greek traditions.

Architectural Features:

- **Structure and Layout**:
    - The palace spans an area of **124,771 square feet**. The central building is double-storied, with wings and turrets rising up to **three** and **five stories**. The palace's total length is **106 feet**.

- The first floor is built in the **Tuscan style**, the second in the **Italian-Doric style**, and the third in the **Corinthian style**, creating a rich architectural diversity.
  - The **Durbar Hall**, the largest and most spectacular part of the palace, is **30 meters (100 feet)** long, **15 meters (50 feet)** wide, and **12 meters (41 feet)** high. The hall's ornate decor includes **gold furnishings** and **gigantic chandeliers**, with the entire interior lavishly embellished.
- **Design Details**:
  - The **Reception Room** spans **97 feet 8 inches** in length, **50 feet** in width, and is **41 feet** high. The **roof is arched with stone slabs** measuring **21 feet** long, which creates a prominent ribbed structure. The room is supported by **double Corinthian columns** forming a grand colonnade.
  - **Gold Leaf Decor**: Over **300,000 leaves of gold** were used to decorate the **Reception Hall**.
  - The **Grand Staircase Room** is roofed with **30-foot stone slabs** and serves as an expansive entryway to the palace's upper floors.
  - The **Grand Drawing Room**, considered one of the finest in the world, is adorned with magnificent **chandeliers** and **enormous mirrors**.

Unique Features and Furnishings:

- The **Prince's bedstead, washing service**, and **bath** were made from **solid silver**.
- The **cost of the palace** was around **1,100,000 rupees**, with an additional **500,000 rupees** spent on the garden, iron railings, chandeliers, and other interior elements.
- The **garden**, covering an area of about **one square mile**, features several **waterfalls** and **fountains**.

Museum Exhibits:

The **Jai Vilas Mahal** has been converted into a museum that preserves the opulence and history of the royal family. Notable items on display include:

- **Madhavrao Scindia's desk and photographs**, honoring his role as the Railway Minister of India.
- Preserved rooms, including **drawing rooms**, **bedrooms**, and **bathrooms**, maintaining the original **royal decor**.
- The **royal kitchen** remains intact with its **furnaces**, **pots**, **china**, and other utensils.
- **Unique items** such as **cut glass furniture**, **stuffed tigers**, and a **ladies-only swimming pool** with its own boat.
- A **model silver train** that carried after-dinner brandy and cigars around the table for the royal family.

Historical Significance:

- The palace also commemorates the **Scindia family's** humble origins. The family, originally from **Kanherkhed village** in Maharashtra, has preserved its **Maratha heritage**, often wearing the traditional **Shineshahi pagdi** turban on special occasions. The museum exhibits the detailed process of wrapping this distinctive **60-meter-long silk turban**.
- **Historical Memorabilia**: A significant piece is the **palanquin** gifted by **Mughal Emperor Shah Alam II** to **Mahadaji Scindia** in recognition of his assistance in restoring Shah Alam to the throne in **1787** after he was blinded and imprisoned by the Rohilla courtier **Ghulam Qadir**. The events are part of a tragic episode described by poet **Allama Iqbal** and symbolize **Mahadji Scindia's** crucial role in **Maratha history** and his contribution to the Mughal Empire.

Jai Vilas Mahal is not just a remarkable architectural marvel but a symbol of the cultural and political legacy of the **Scindia family**, serving as a museum that houses the rich history of Gwalior and the Maratha Empire.

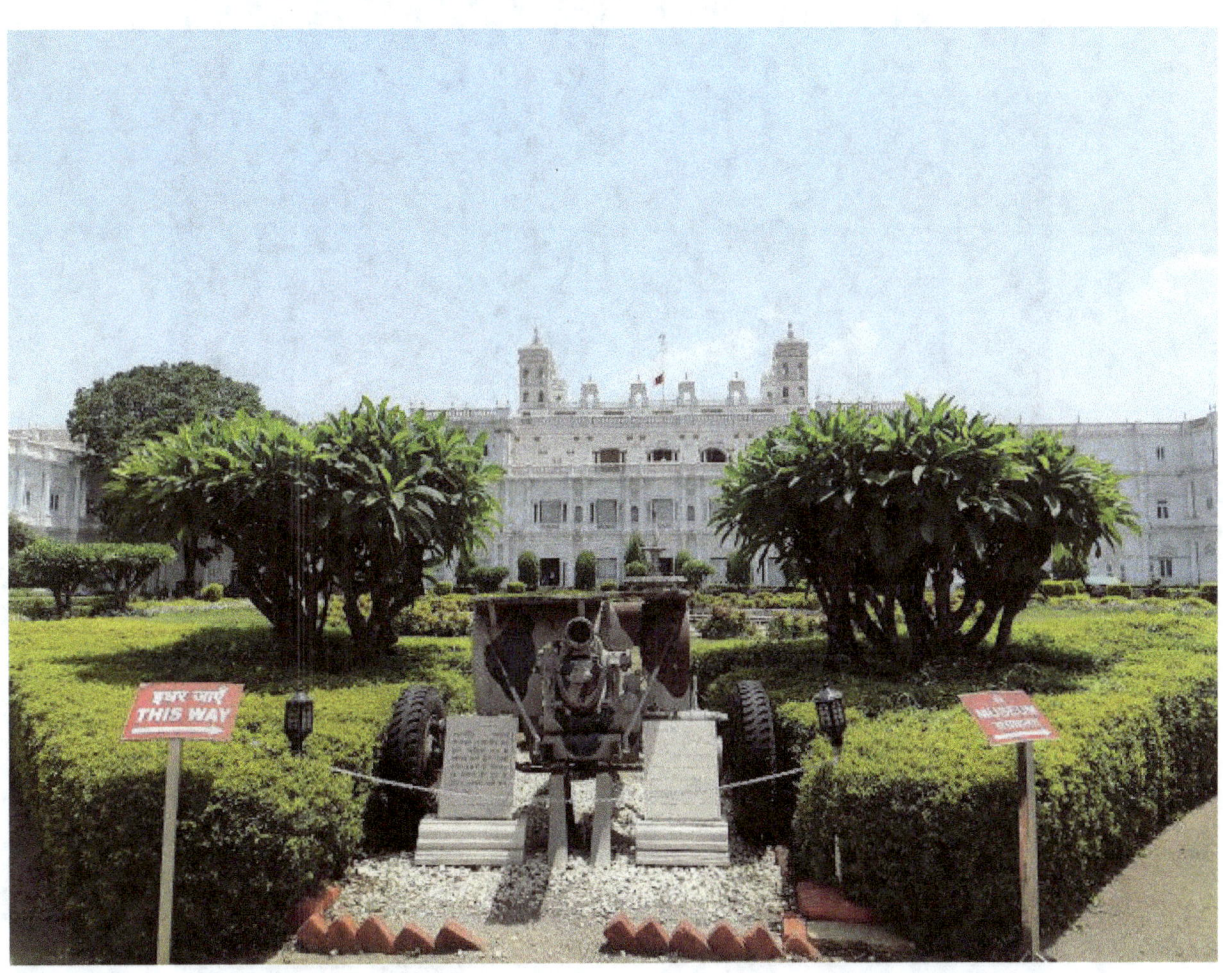

Jai Vilas Palace & Museum outside view

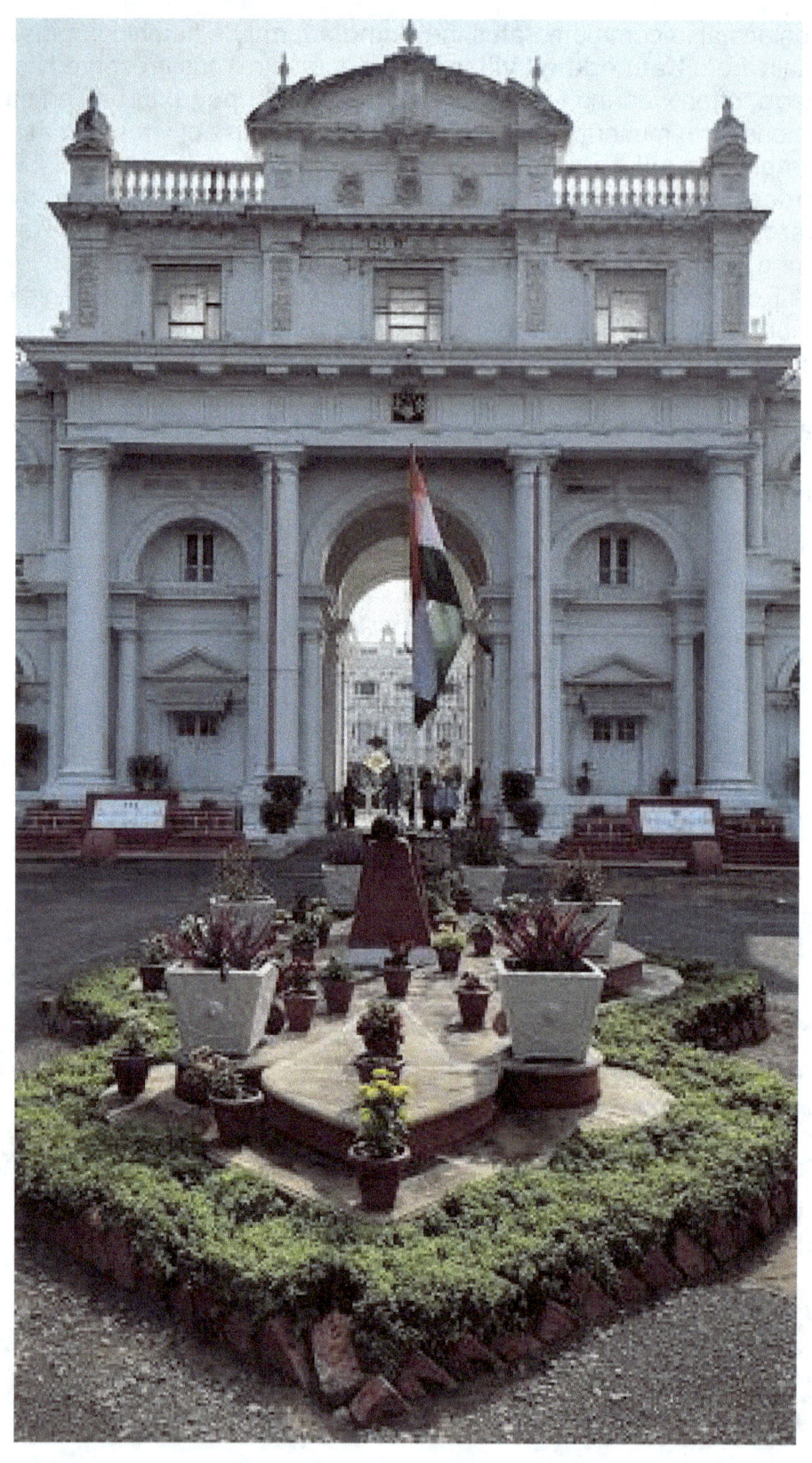

Jai Vilas Palace & Museum outside view

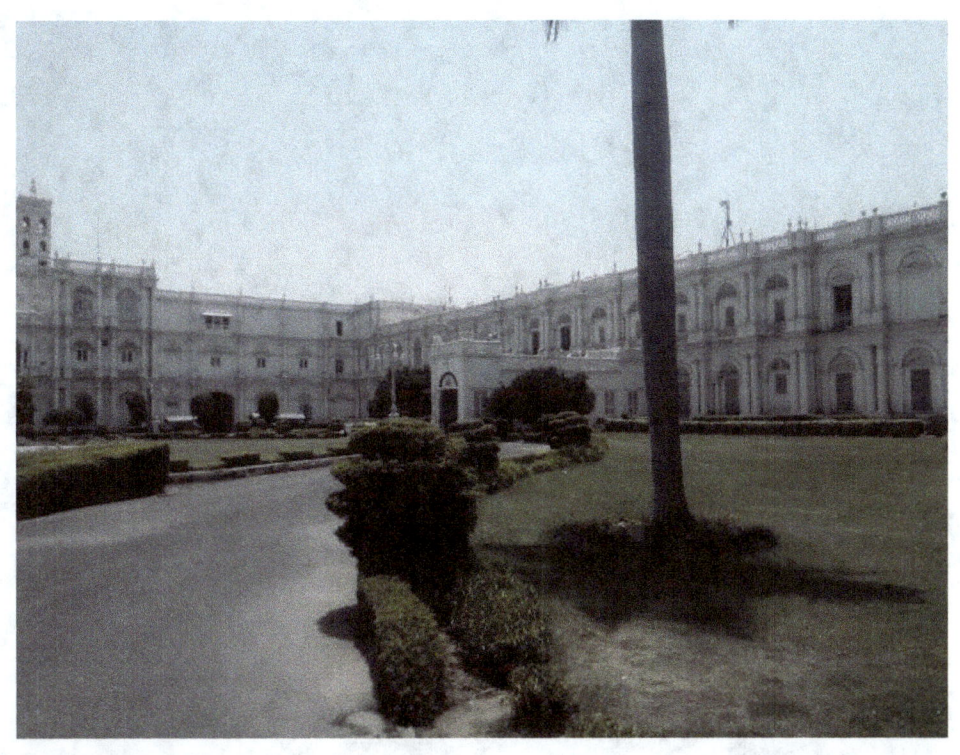
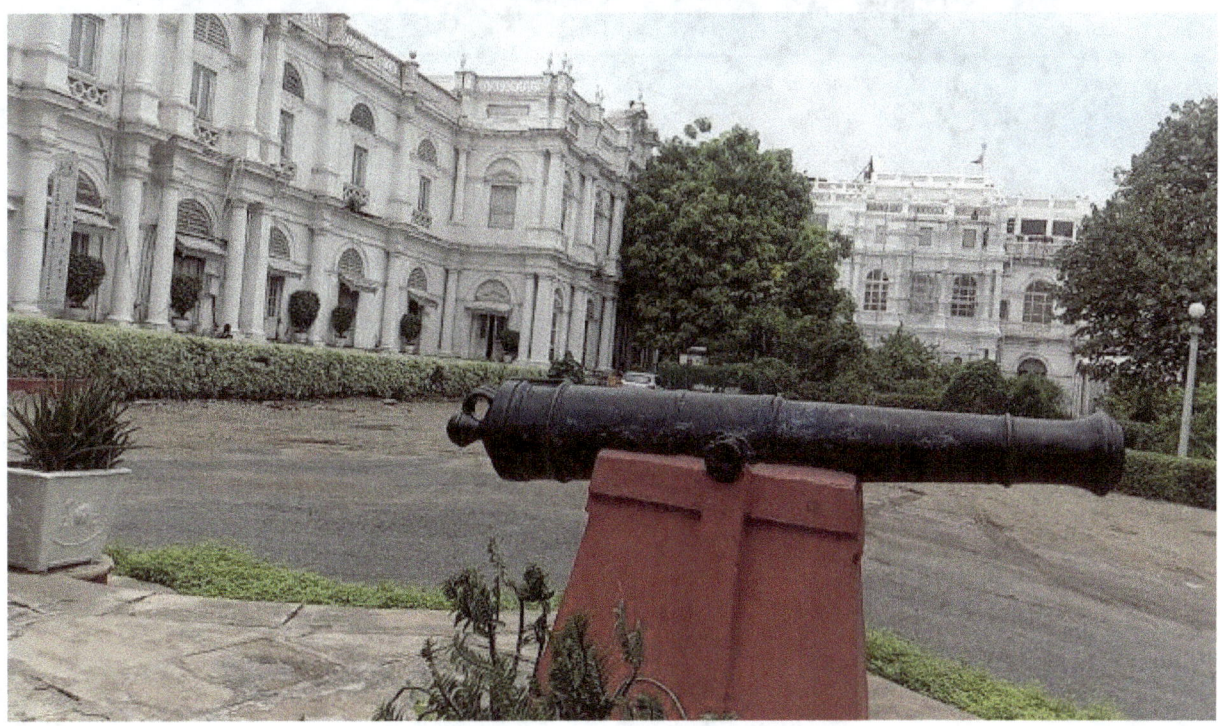

Jai Vilas Palace & Museum outside view with Canon

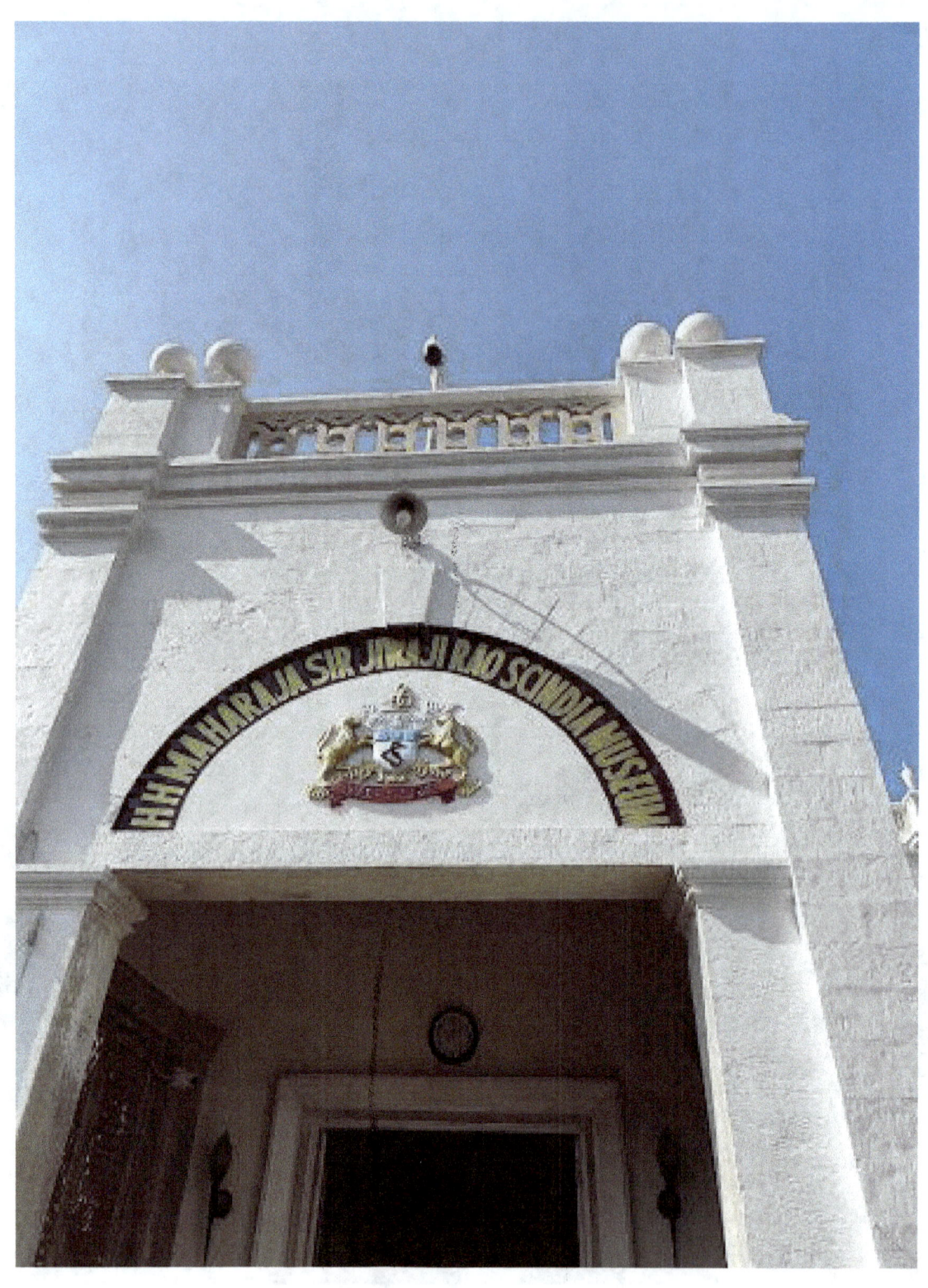

Jai Vilas Palace & Museum Entrance Gate outside view

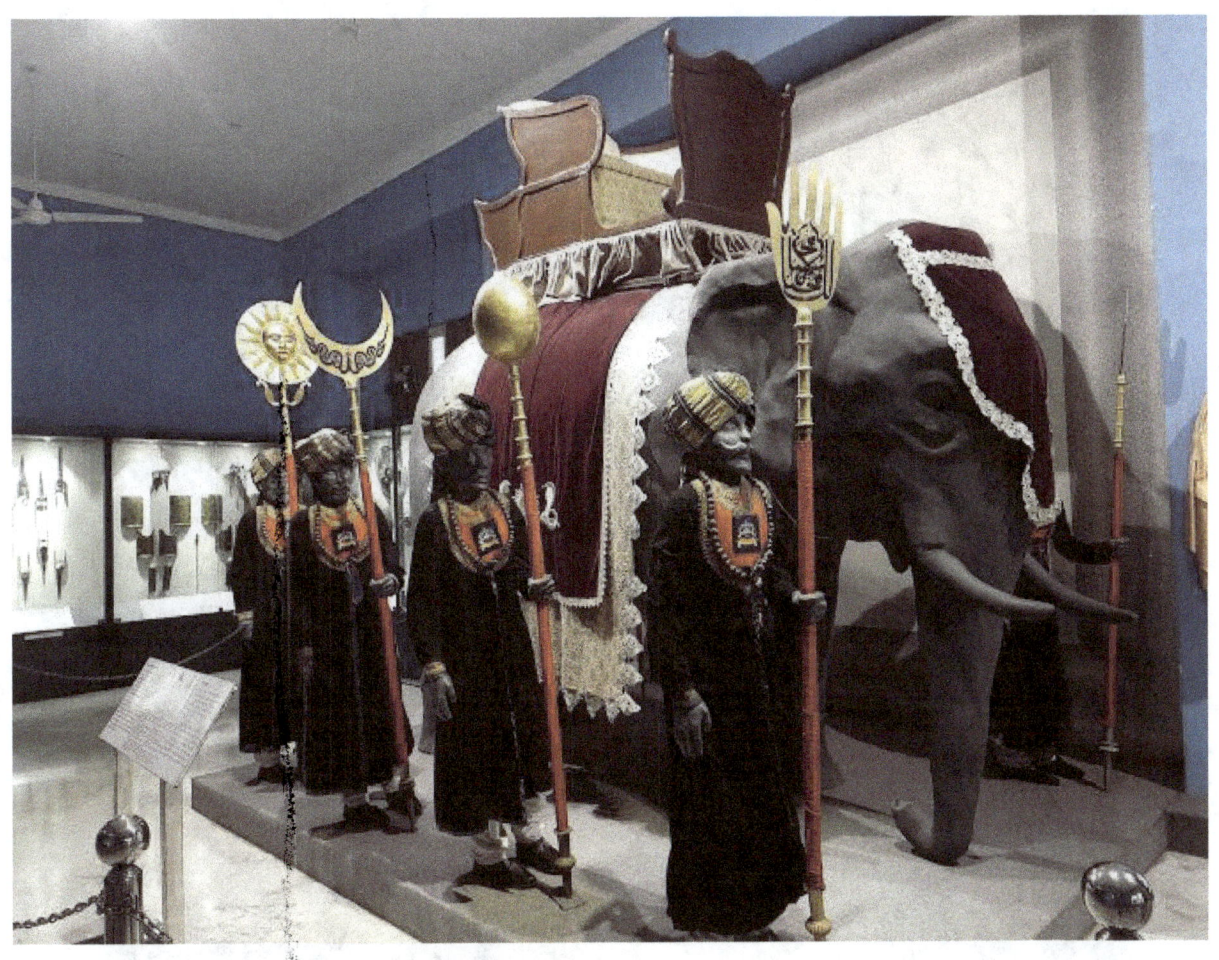

Jai Vilas Palace & Museum inside view- Royal King's Elephant Seat with Guards

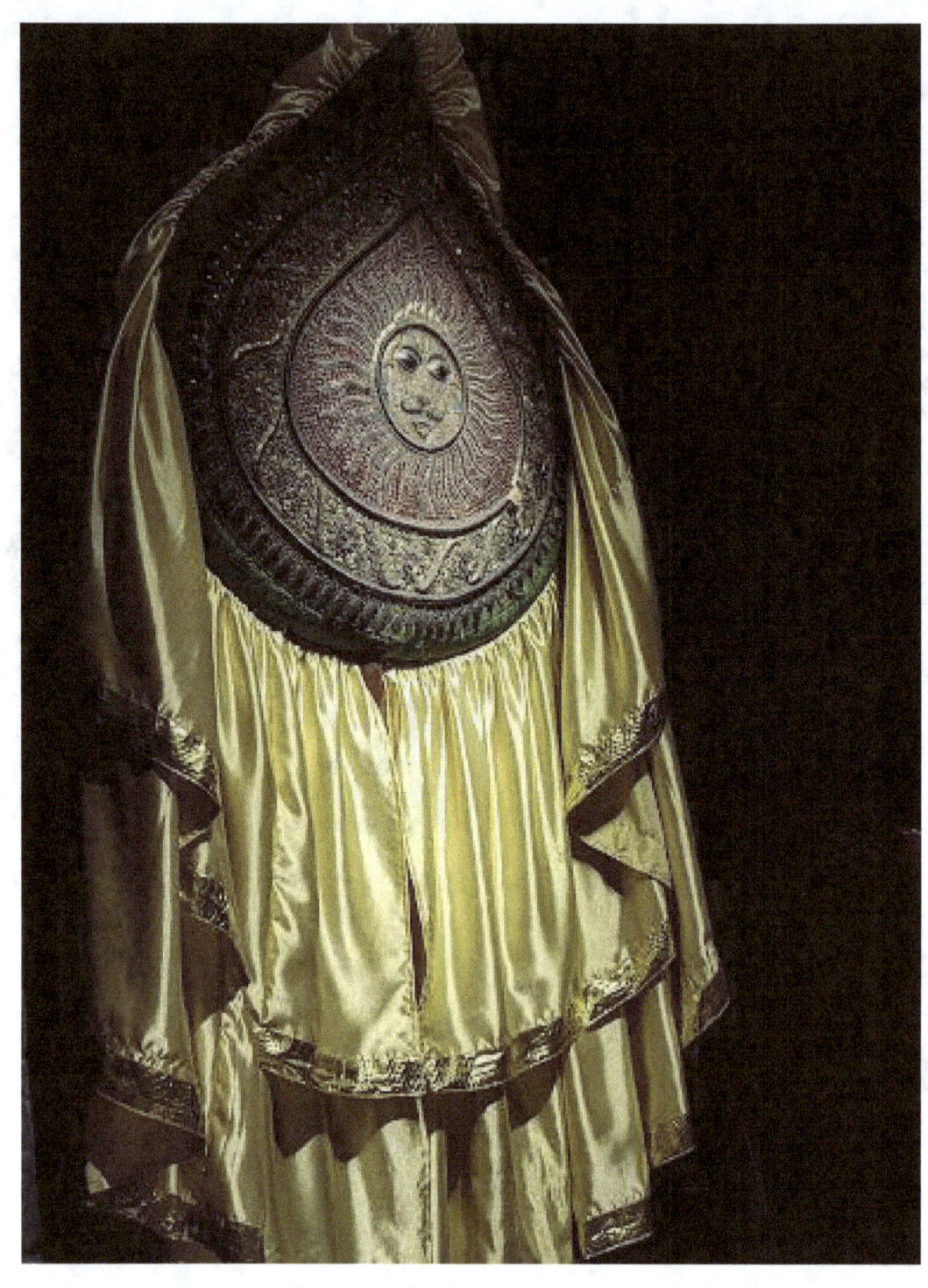
Jai Vilas Palace & Museum inside view- Royal King's Costume

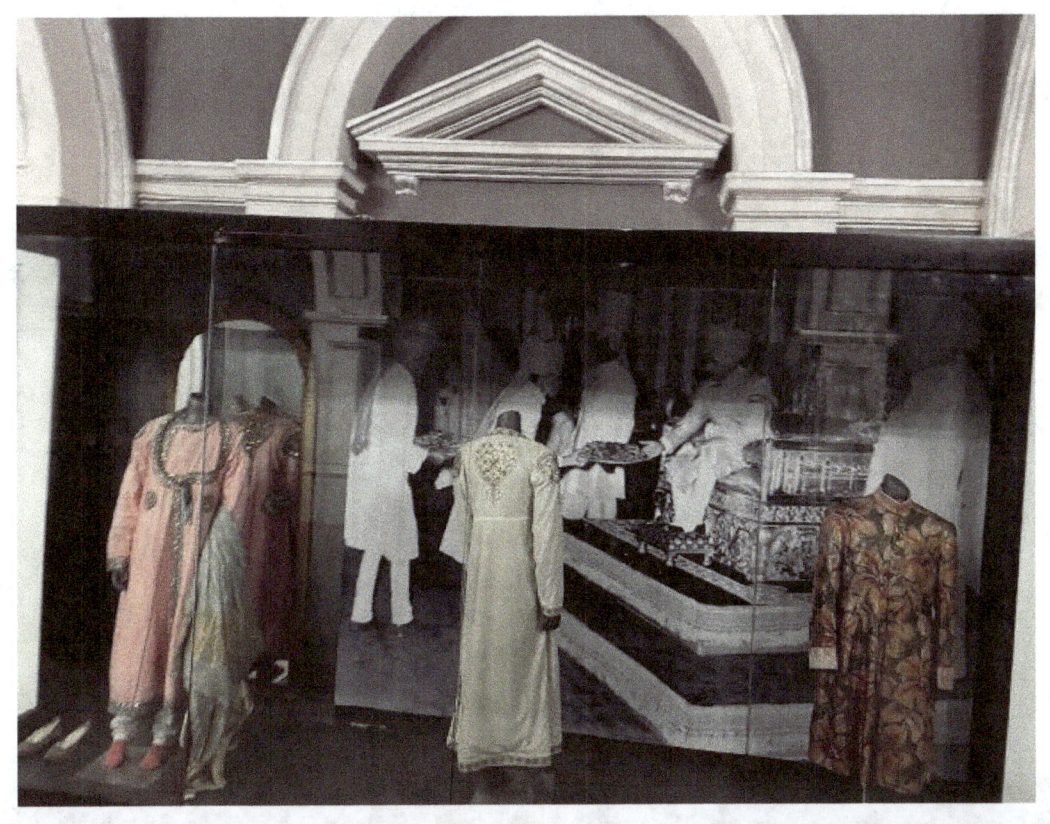
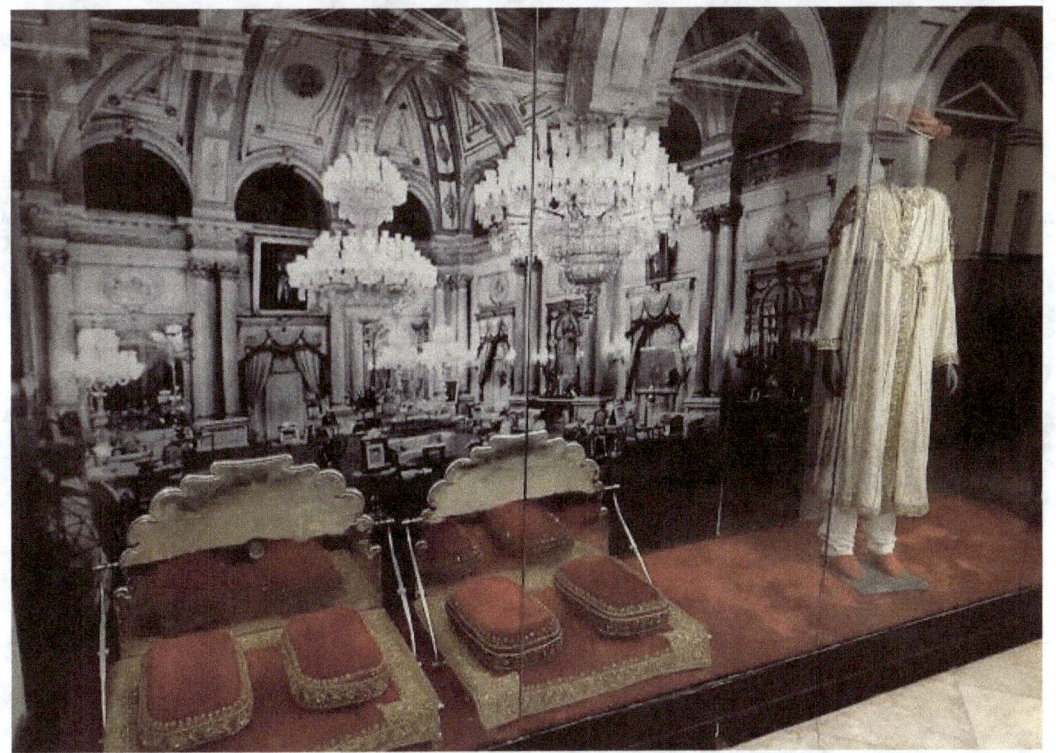

Jai Vilas Palace & Museum inside view- Royal King's Costume

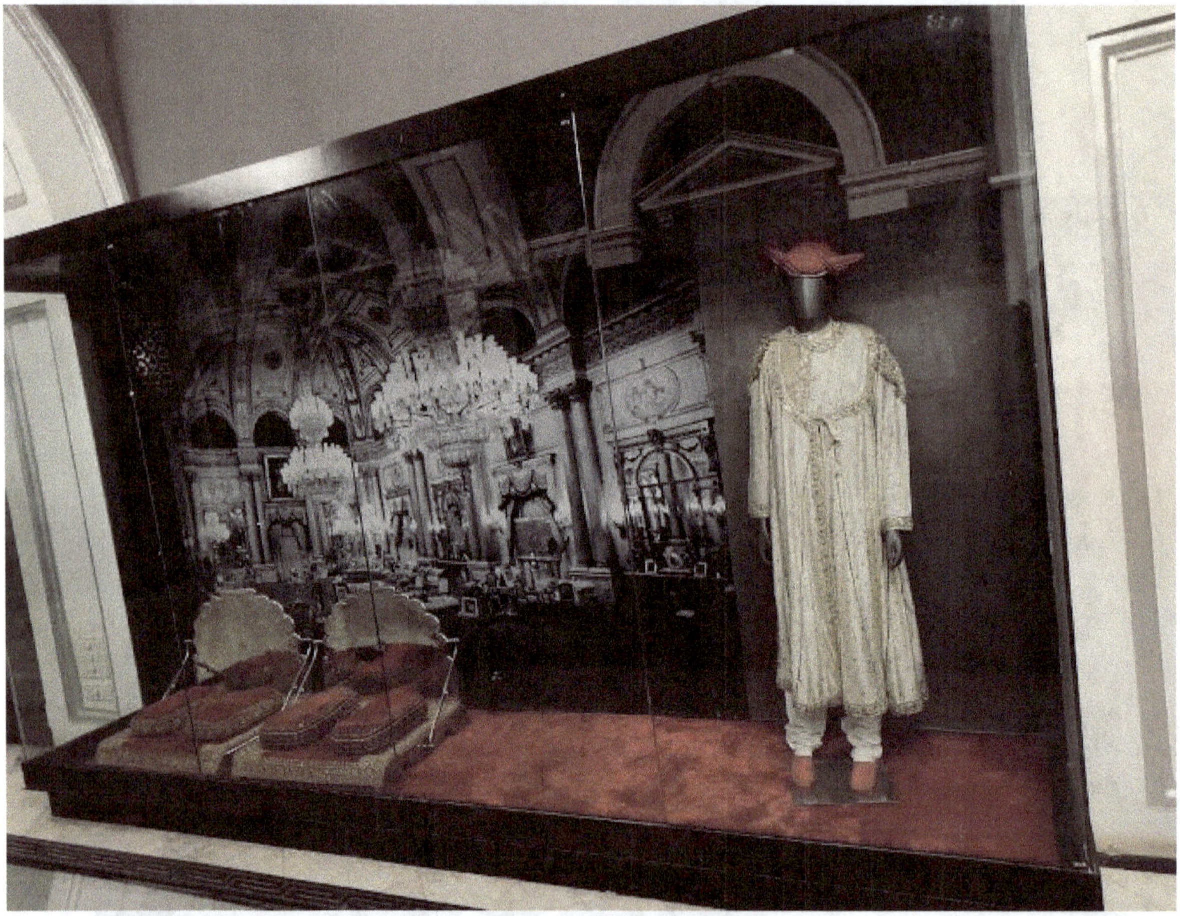

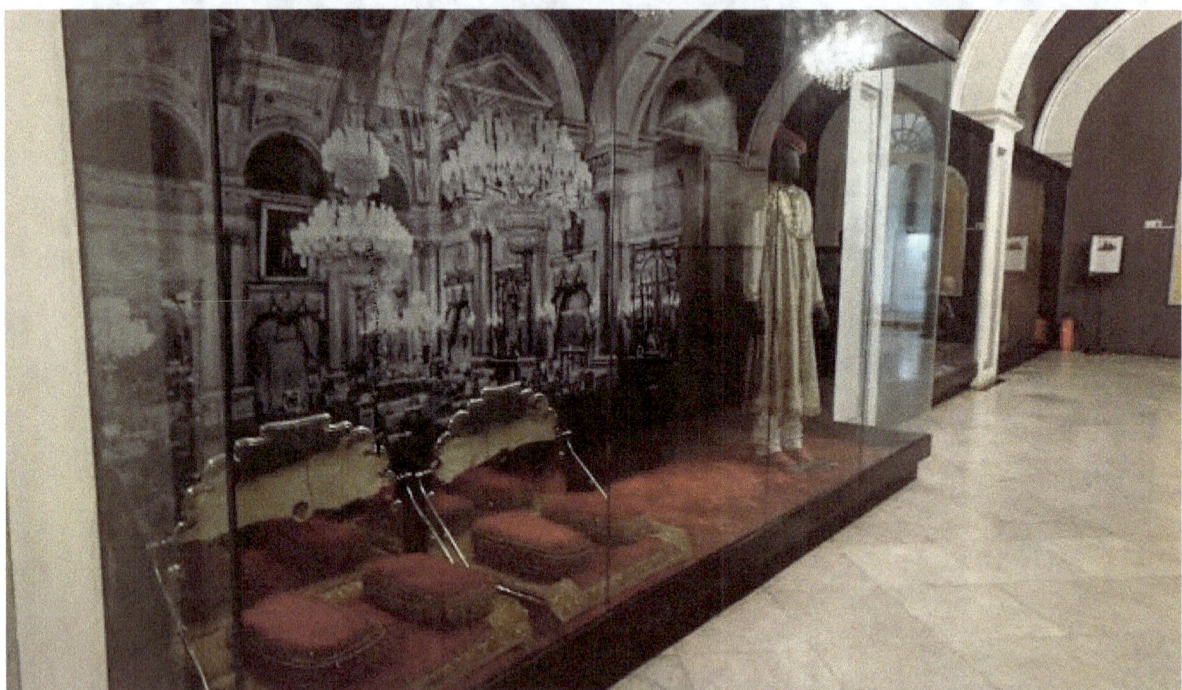

Jai Vilas Palace & Museum inside view- Royal King's Costume

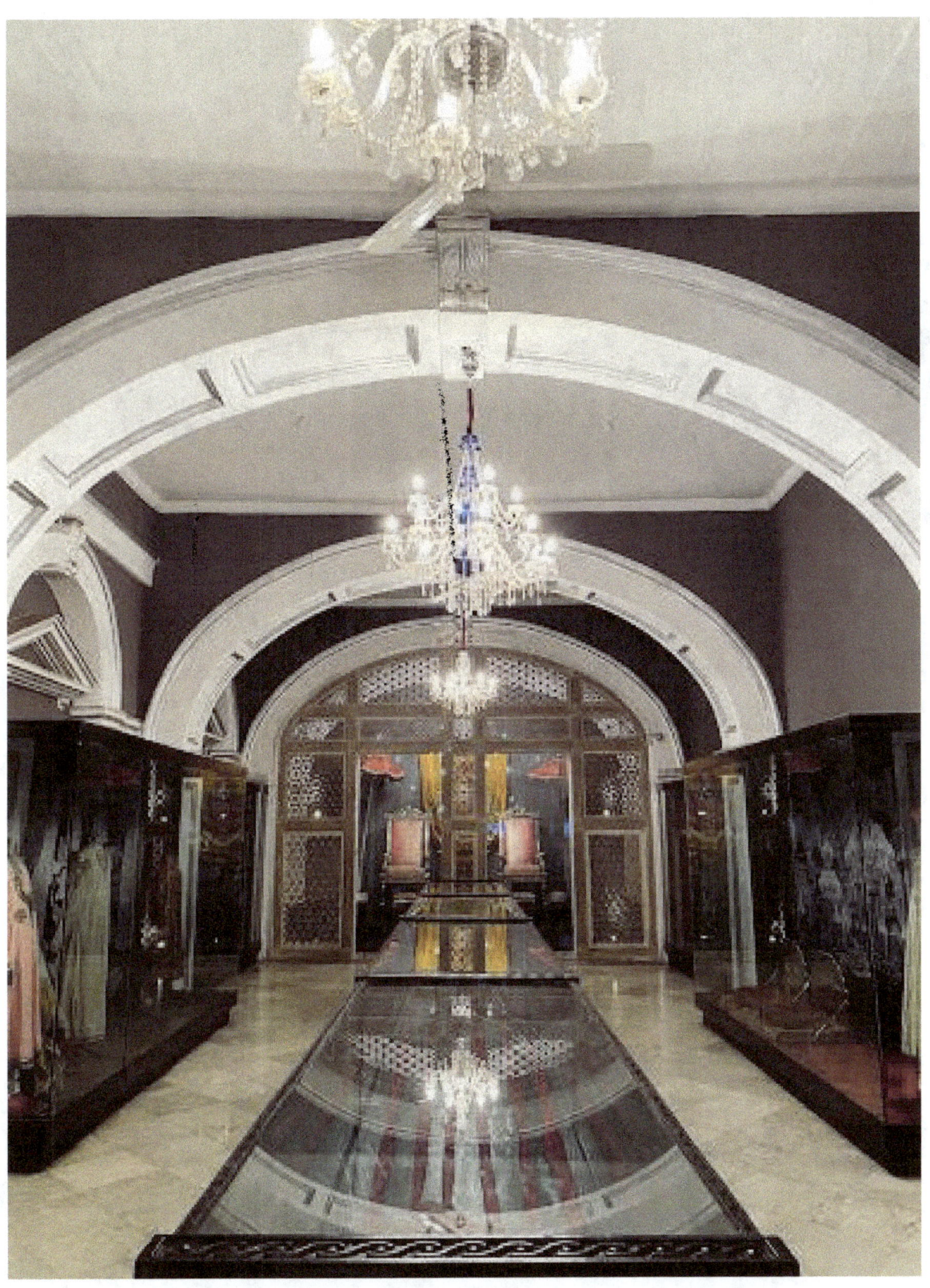

Jai Vilas Palace & Museum inside view- Royal Costume

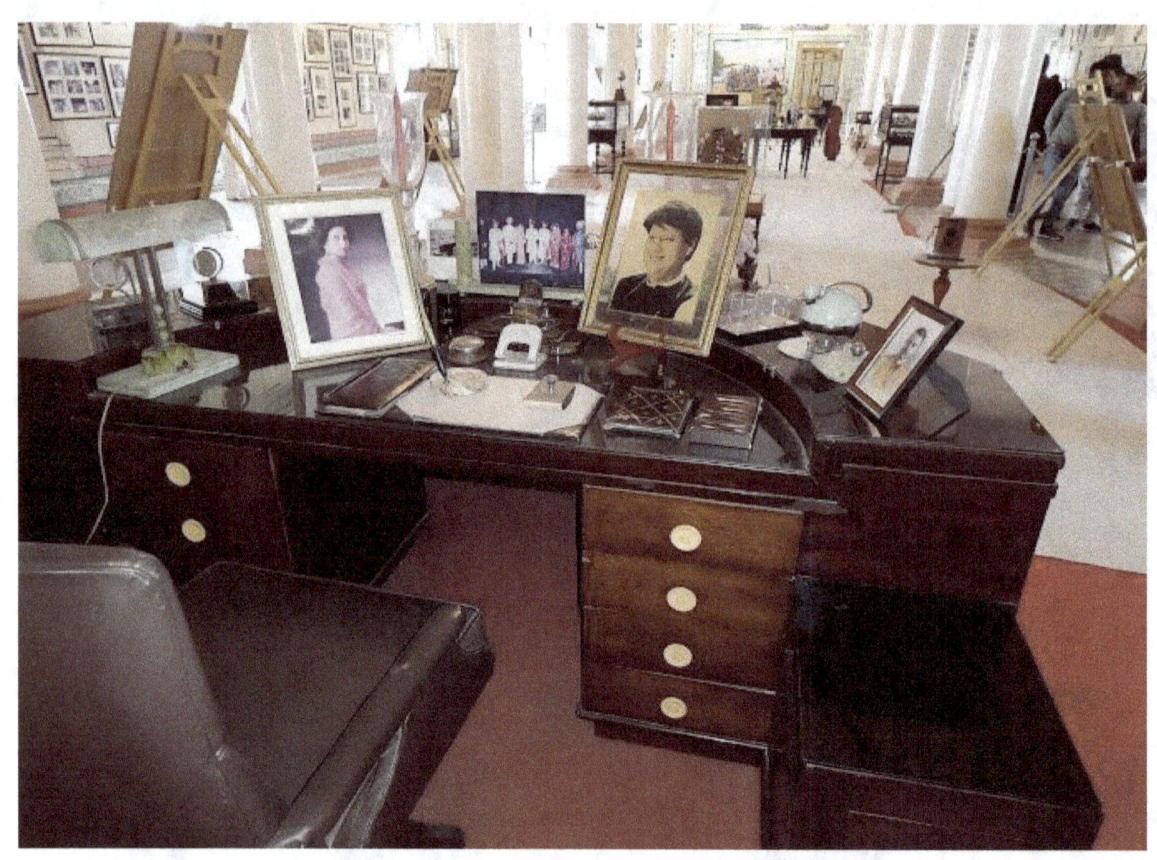

Jai Vilas Palace & Museum inside view- Royal Family Photos on Table

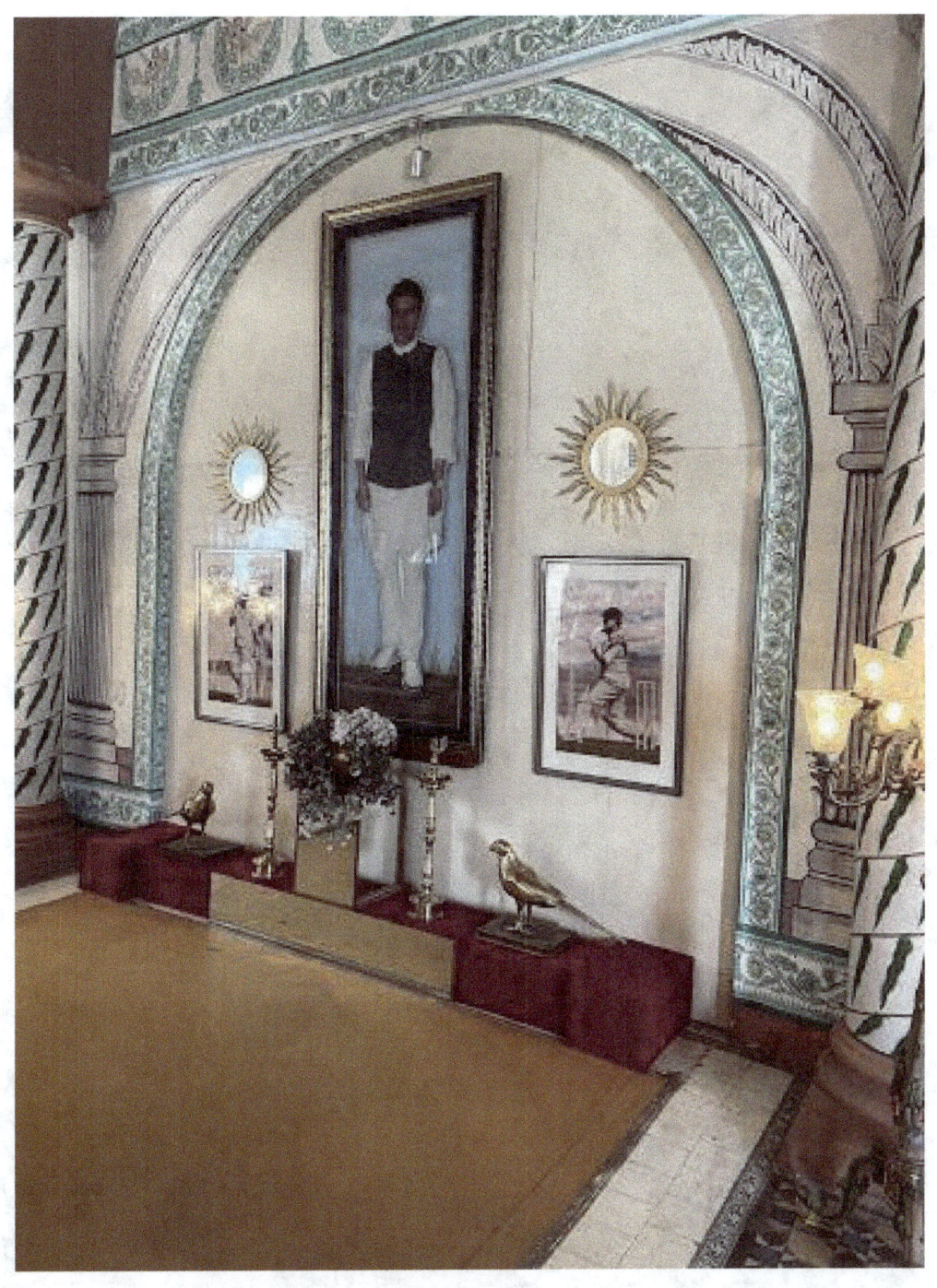

Jai Vilas Palace & Museum inside view- Royal Family Photos on wall

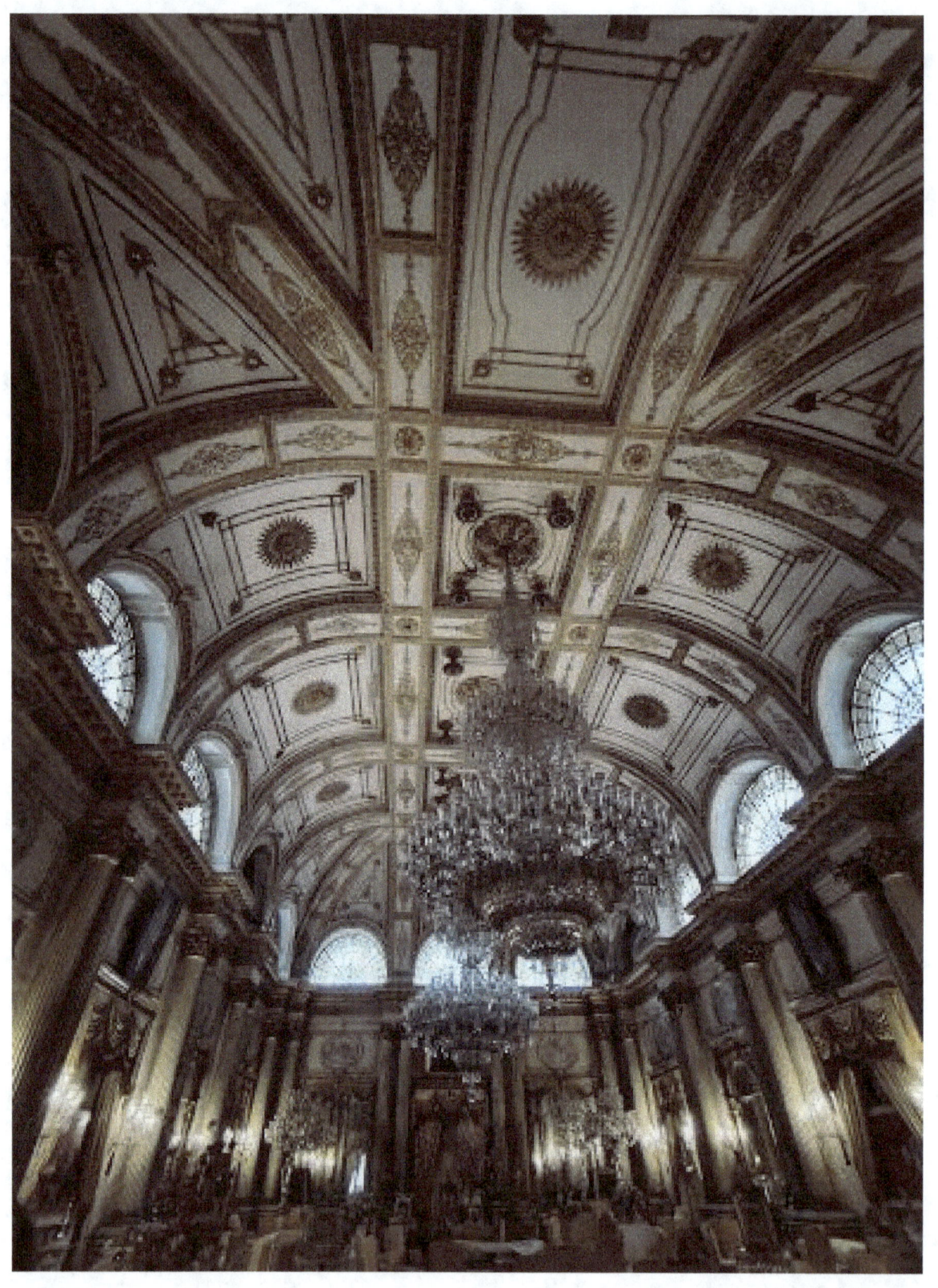

Jai Vilas Palace & Museum inside view-Royal Hall with Gold Paintings on wall & Roof

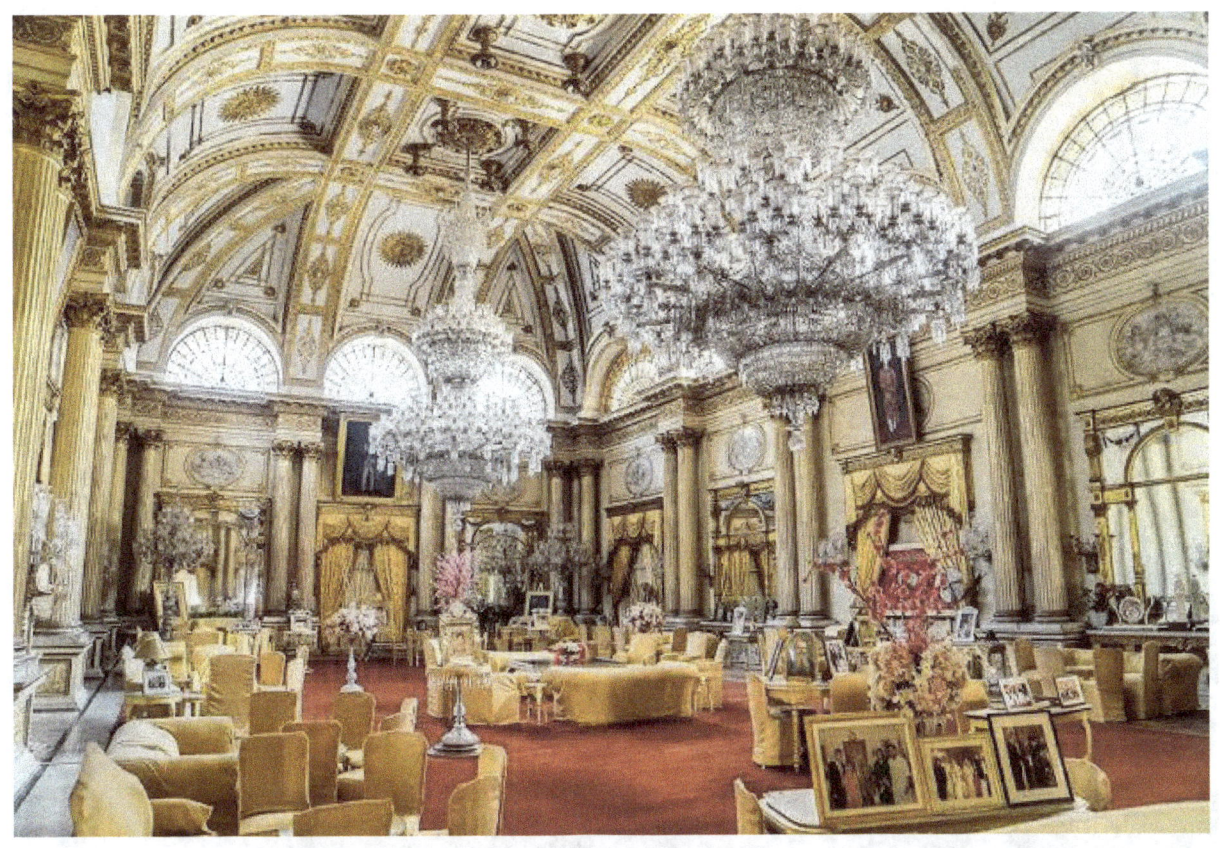

Jai Vilas Palace & Museum inside view-Royal Hall with Gold Paintings on wall & Roof

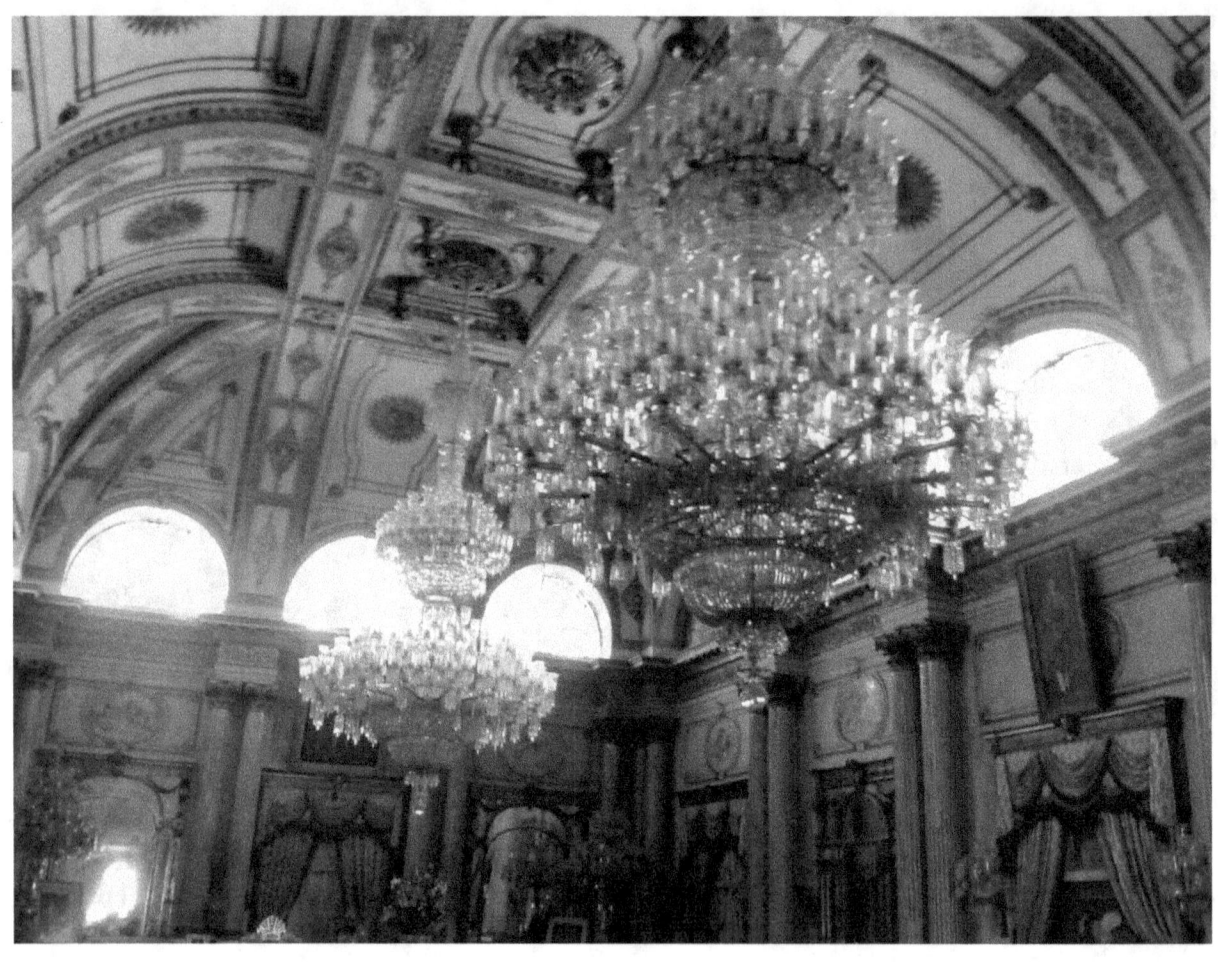
Jai Vilas Palace & Museum inside view-Royal Hall with Gold Paintings on wall & Roof

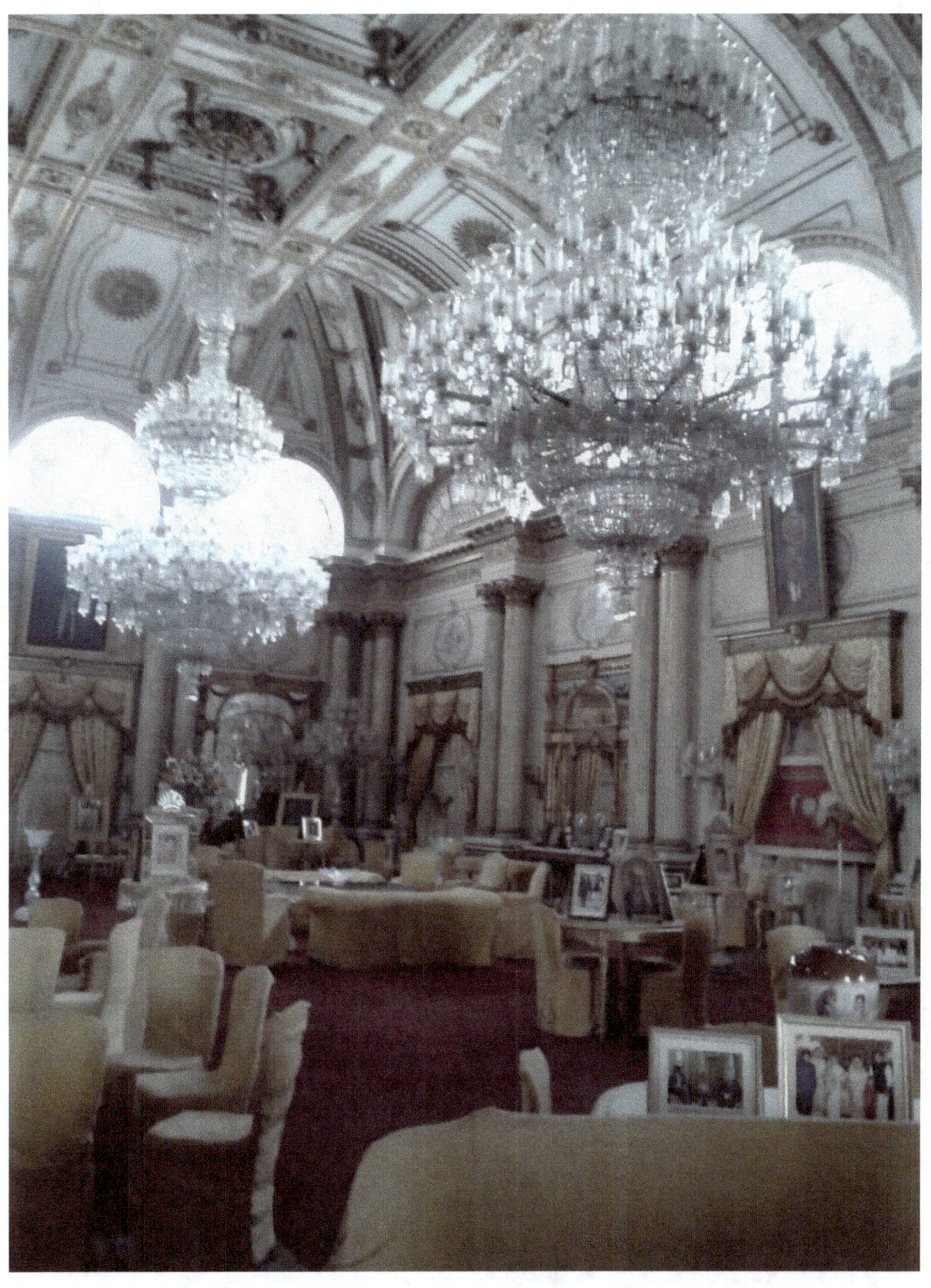

Jai Vilas Palace & Museum inside view-Royal Hall with Gold Paintings on wall & Roof

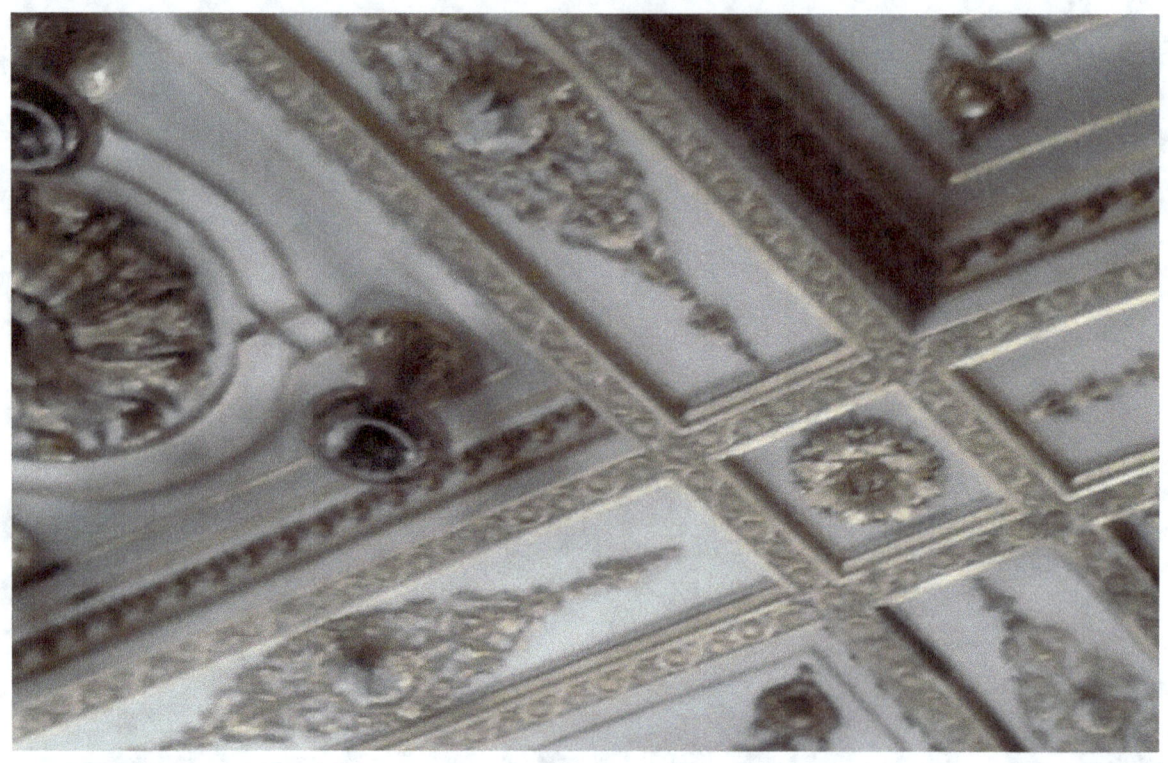

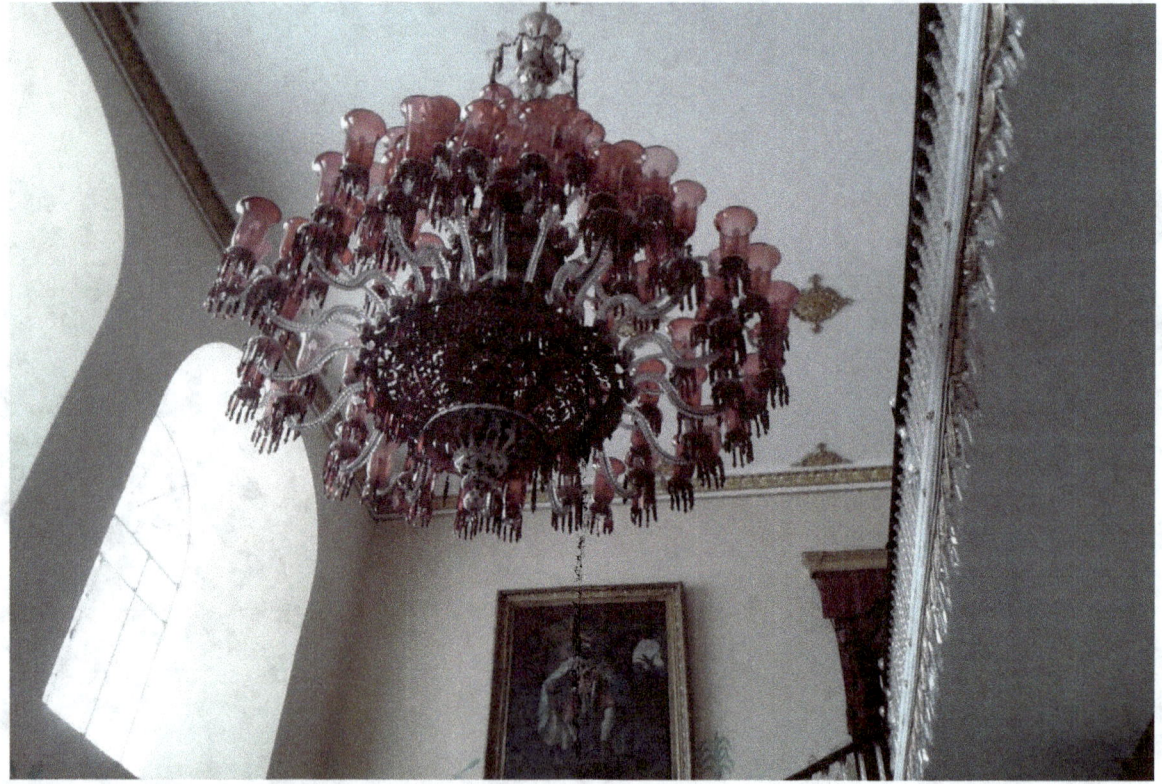

Jai Vilas Palace & Museum inside view-Royal Hall with Gold Paintings on wall & Roof

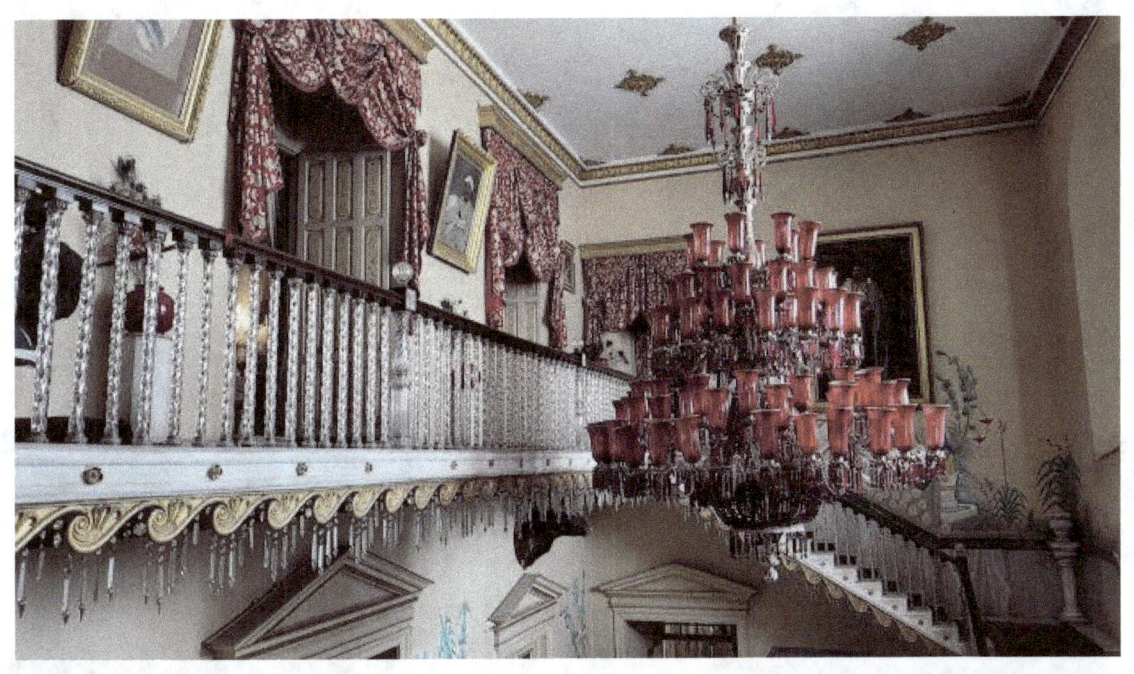
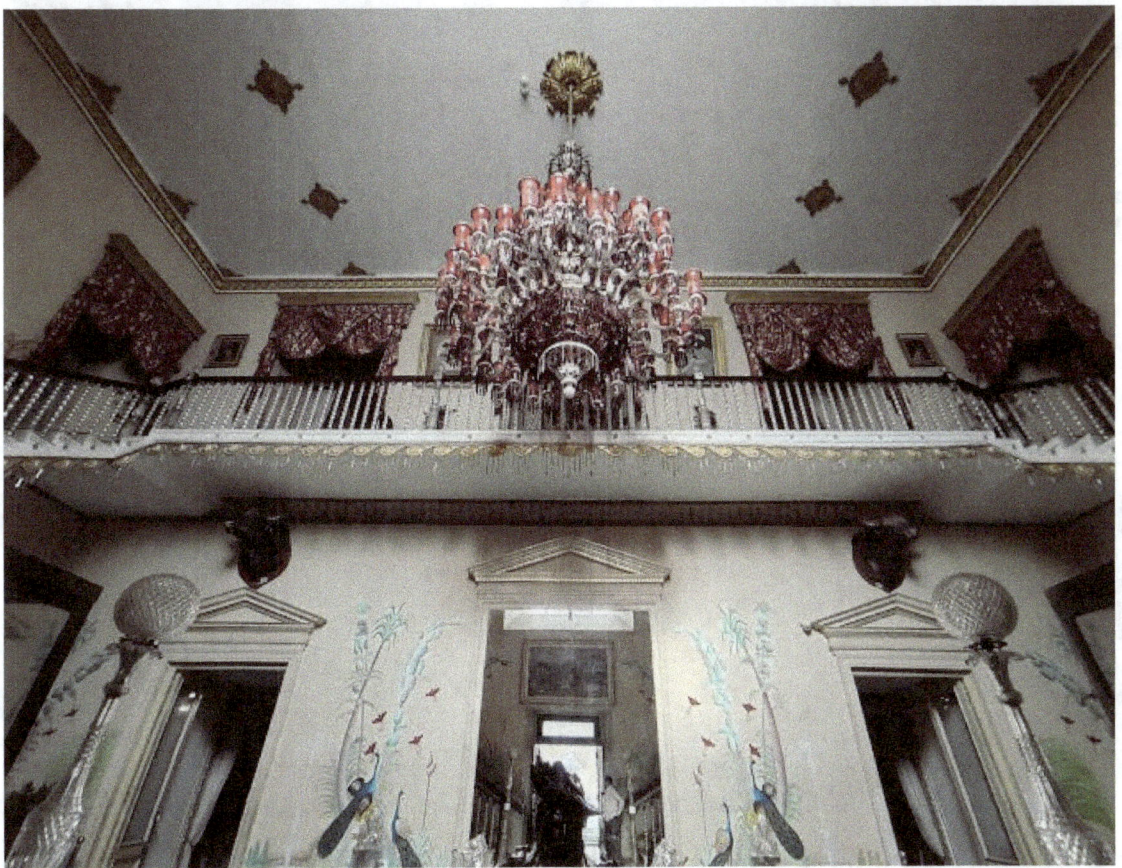

Jai Vilas Palace & Museum inside view-Royal Hall with Gold Paintings on wall & Roof

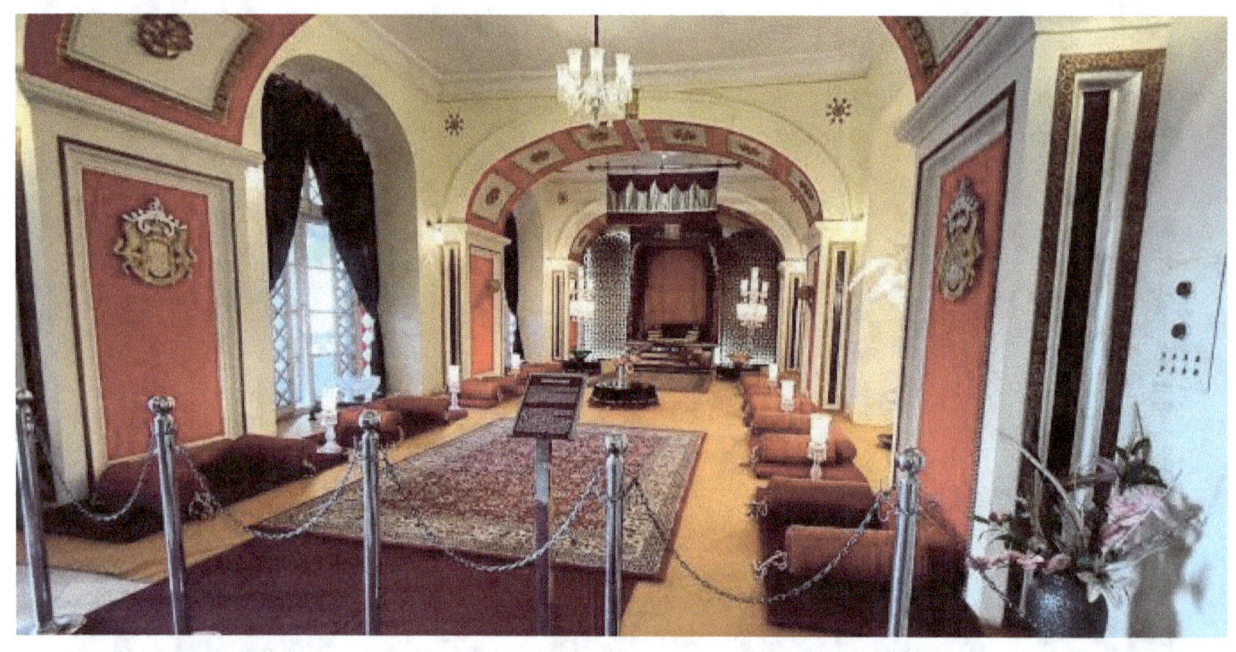
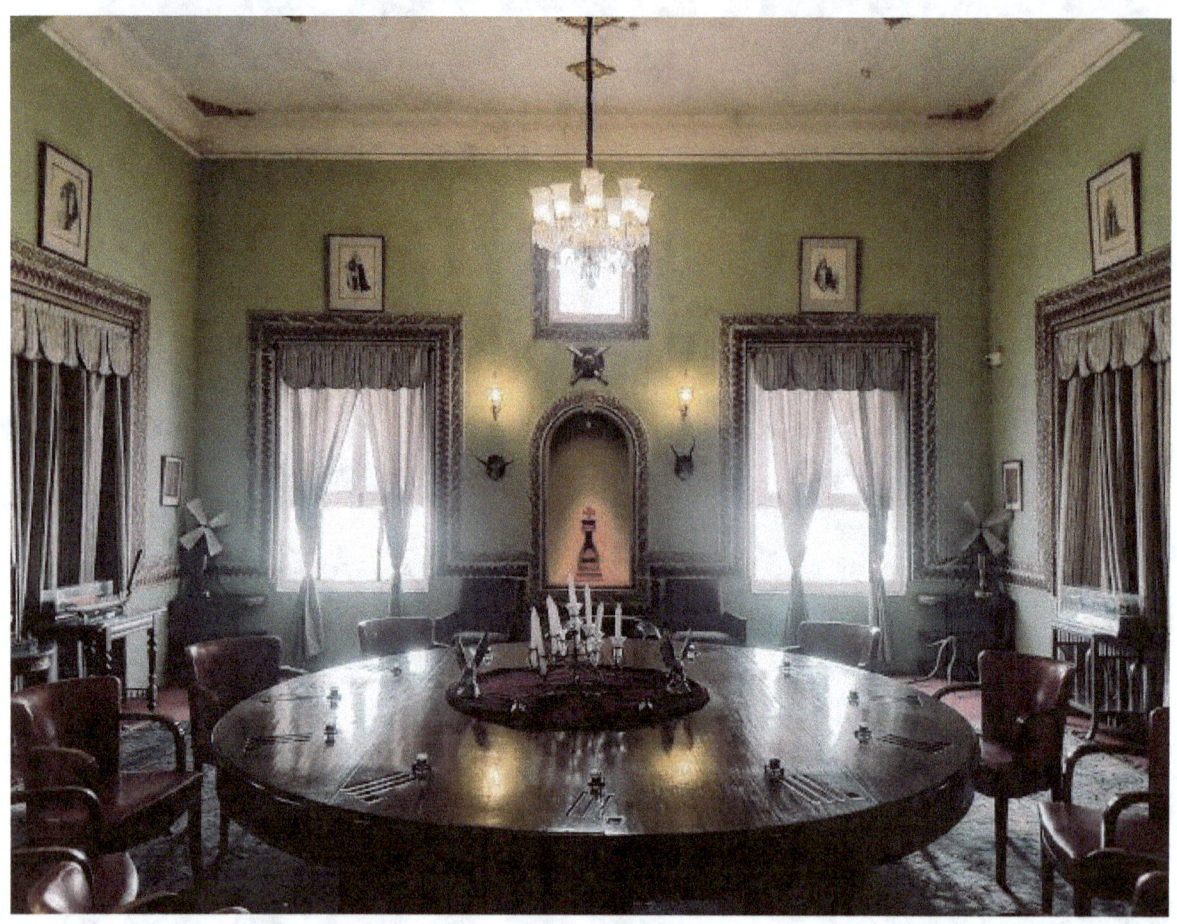

Jai Vilas Palace & Museum inside view-Royal Rooms

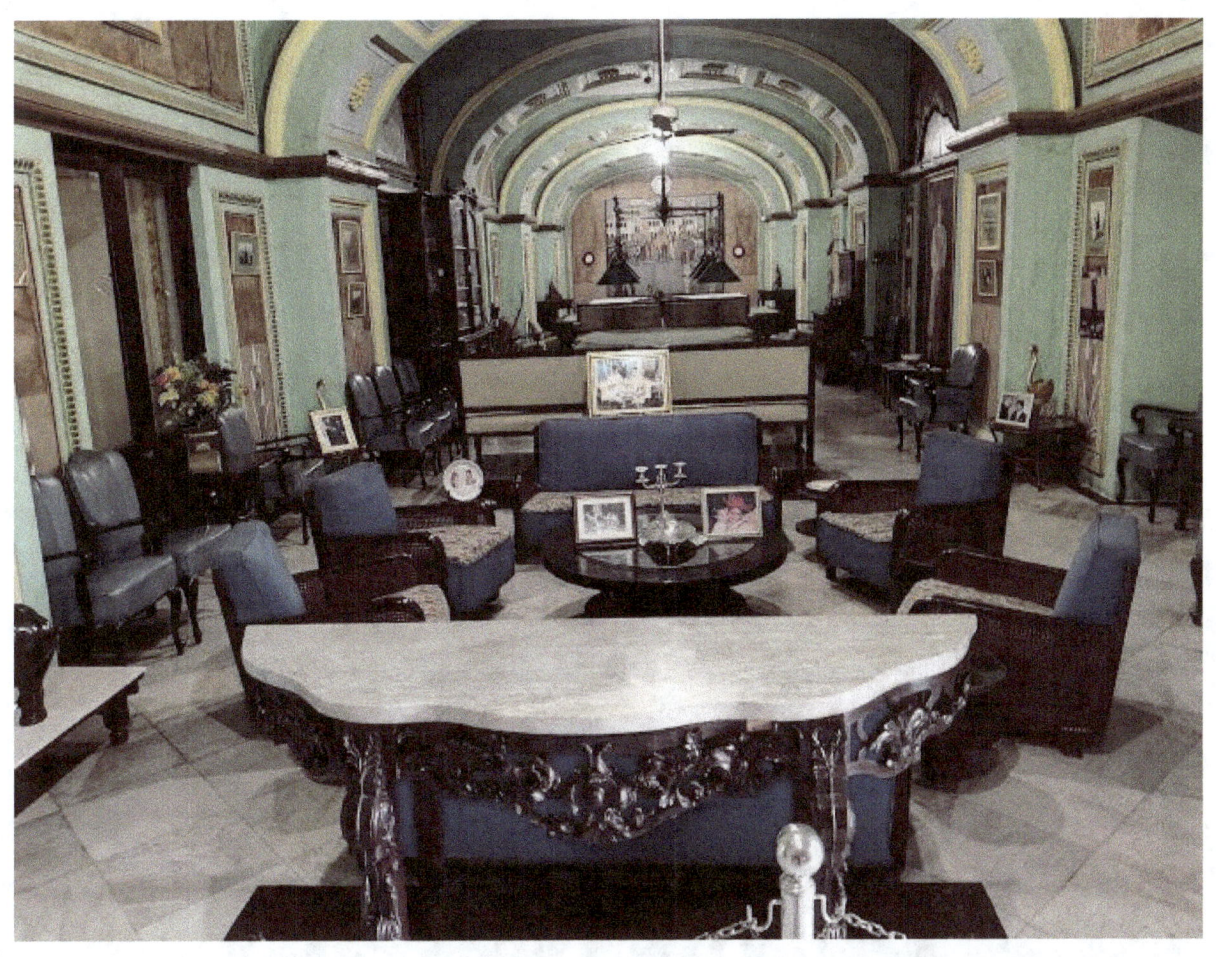
Jai Vilas Palace & Museum inside view-Royal Rooms

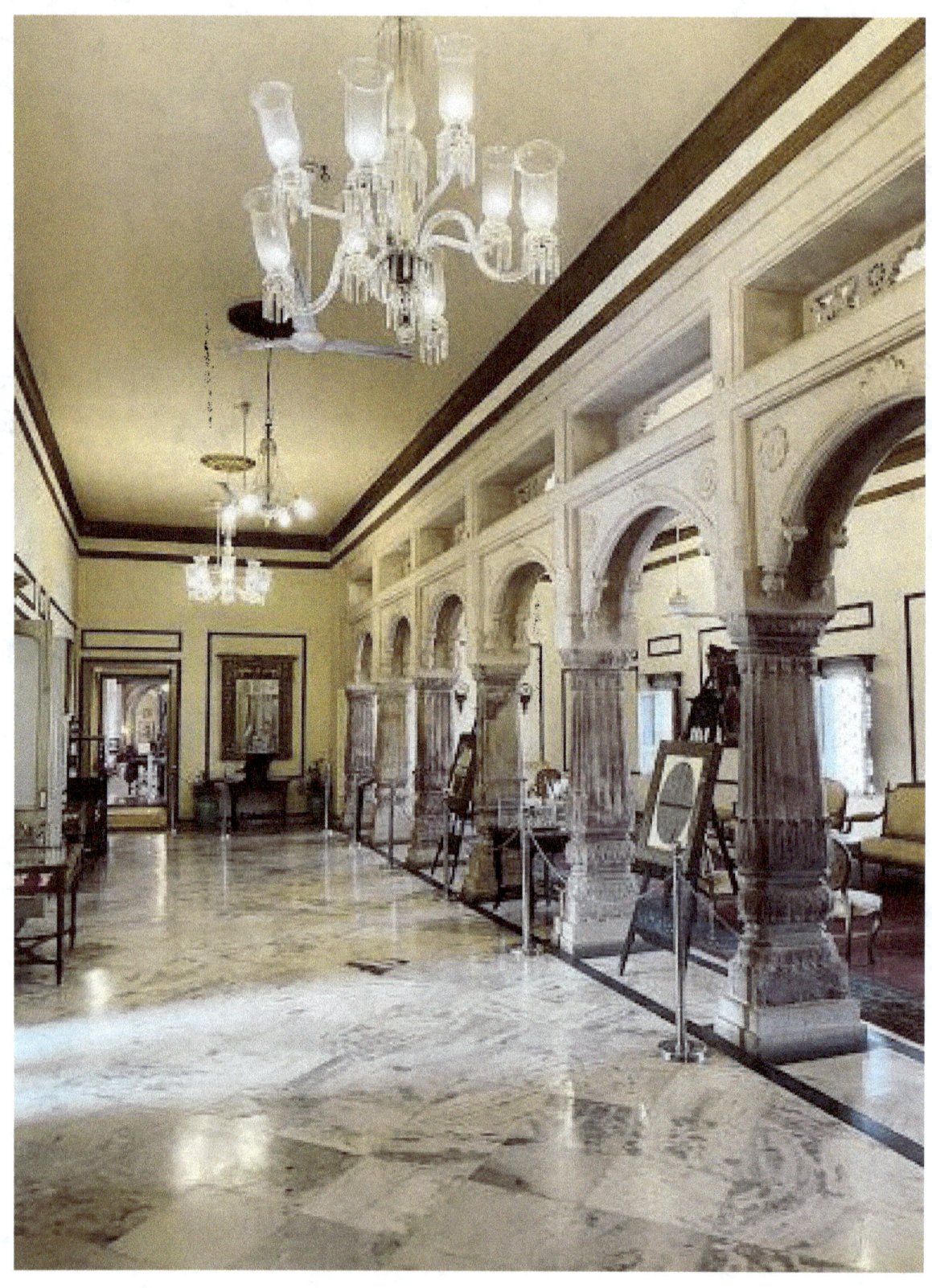

Jai Vilas Palace & Museum inside view-Royal Rooms

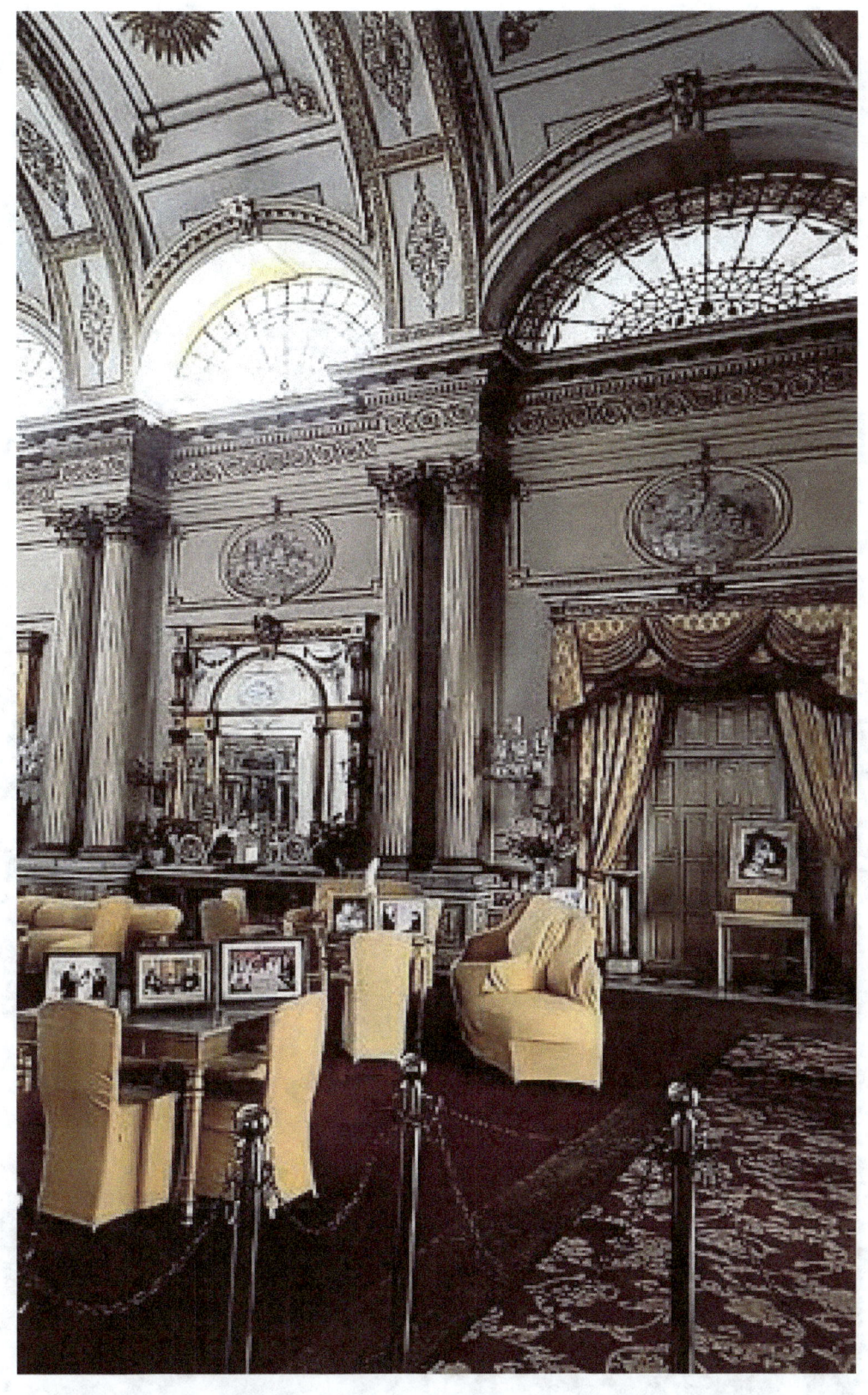

Jai Vilas Palace & Museum inside view-Royal Rooms

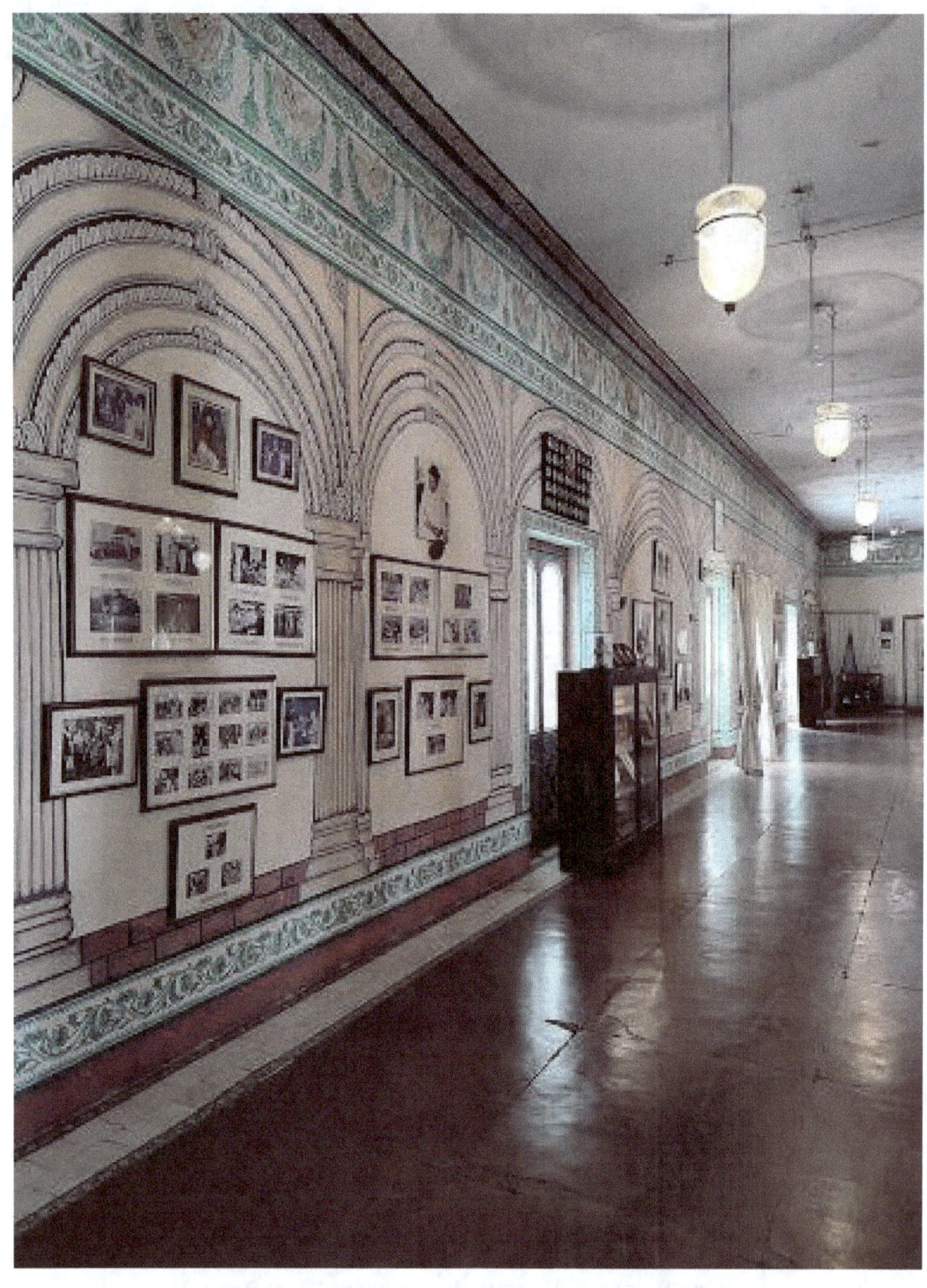

Jai Vilas Palace & Museum inside view-Picture Gallery in Royal Rooms

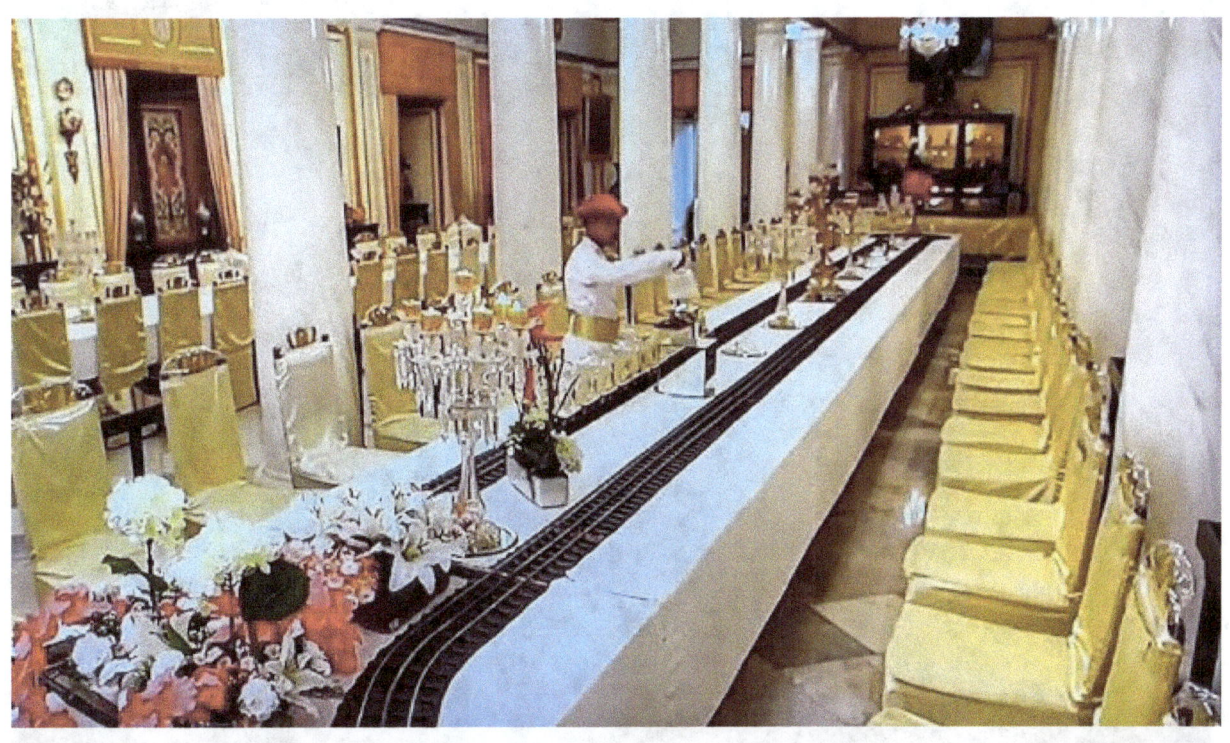

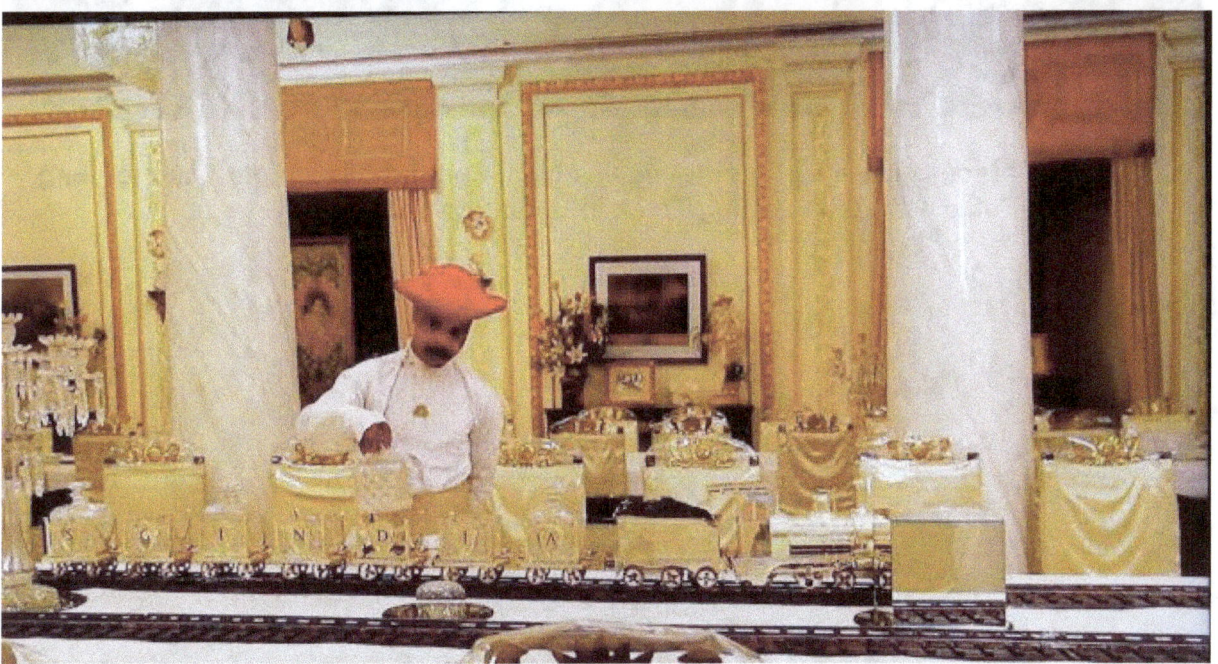

Jai Vilas Palace & Museum inside view - Royal Dining Hall for many Guests with Serving Silver Pots Train on long Table with Rail Running Track

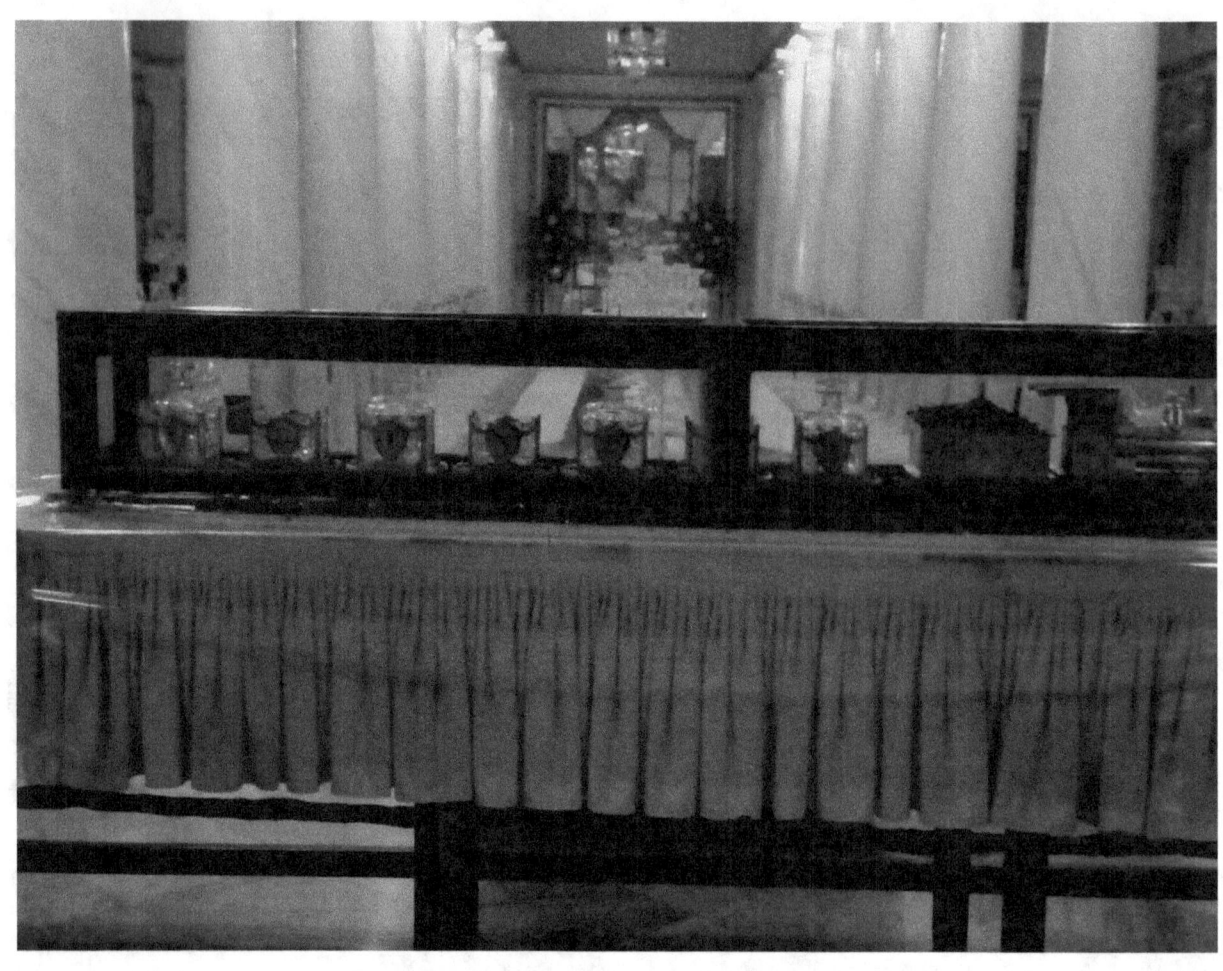

Jai Vilas Palace & Museum inside view - Royal Serving Silver Pots Train for long Table with Rail Running Track in Dining Hall for many Guests

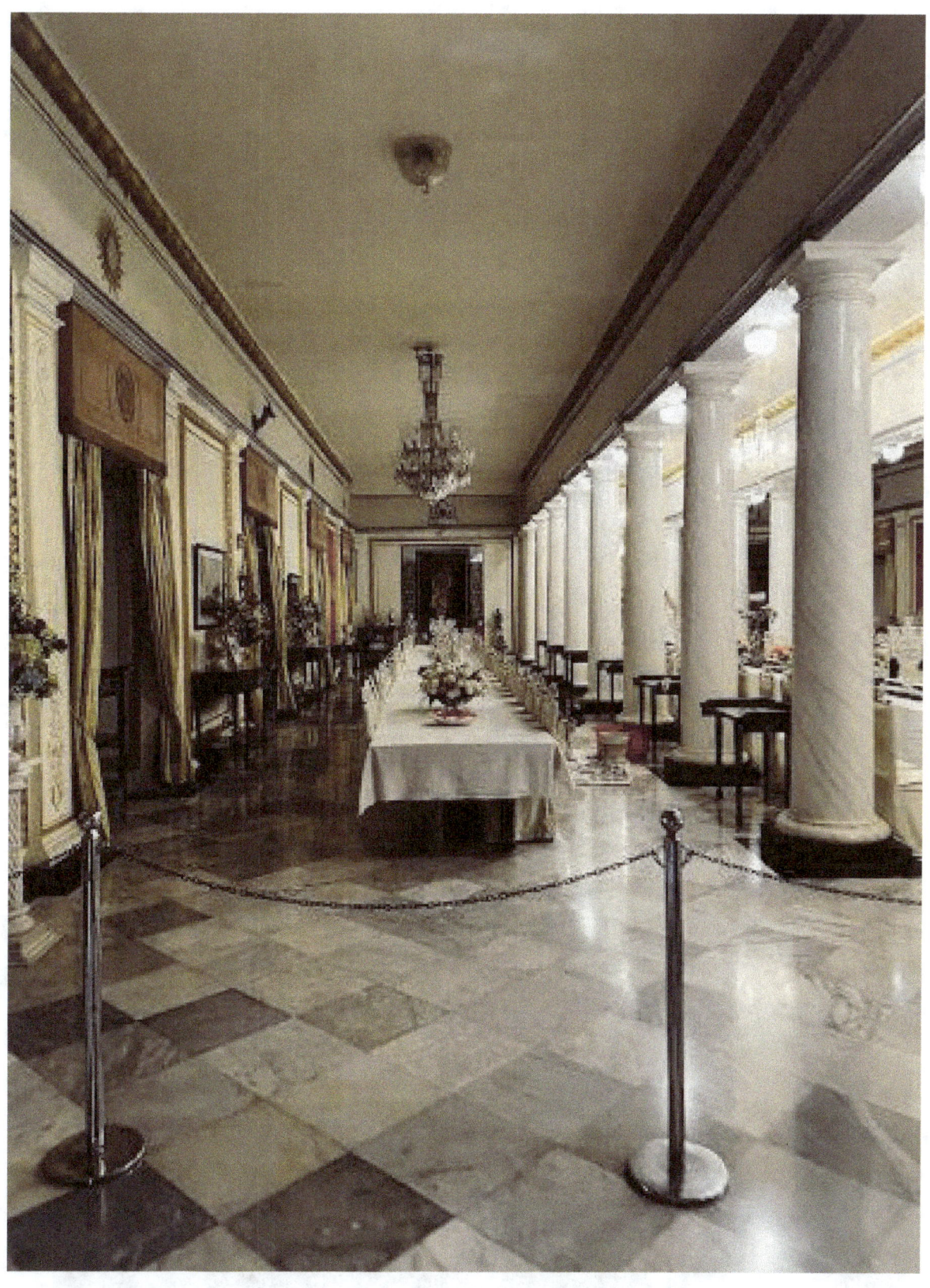

Jai Vilas Palace & Museum inside view - Royal long Table Dining Hall for many Guests

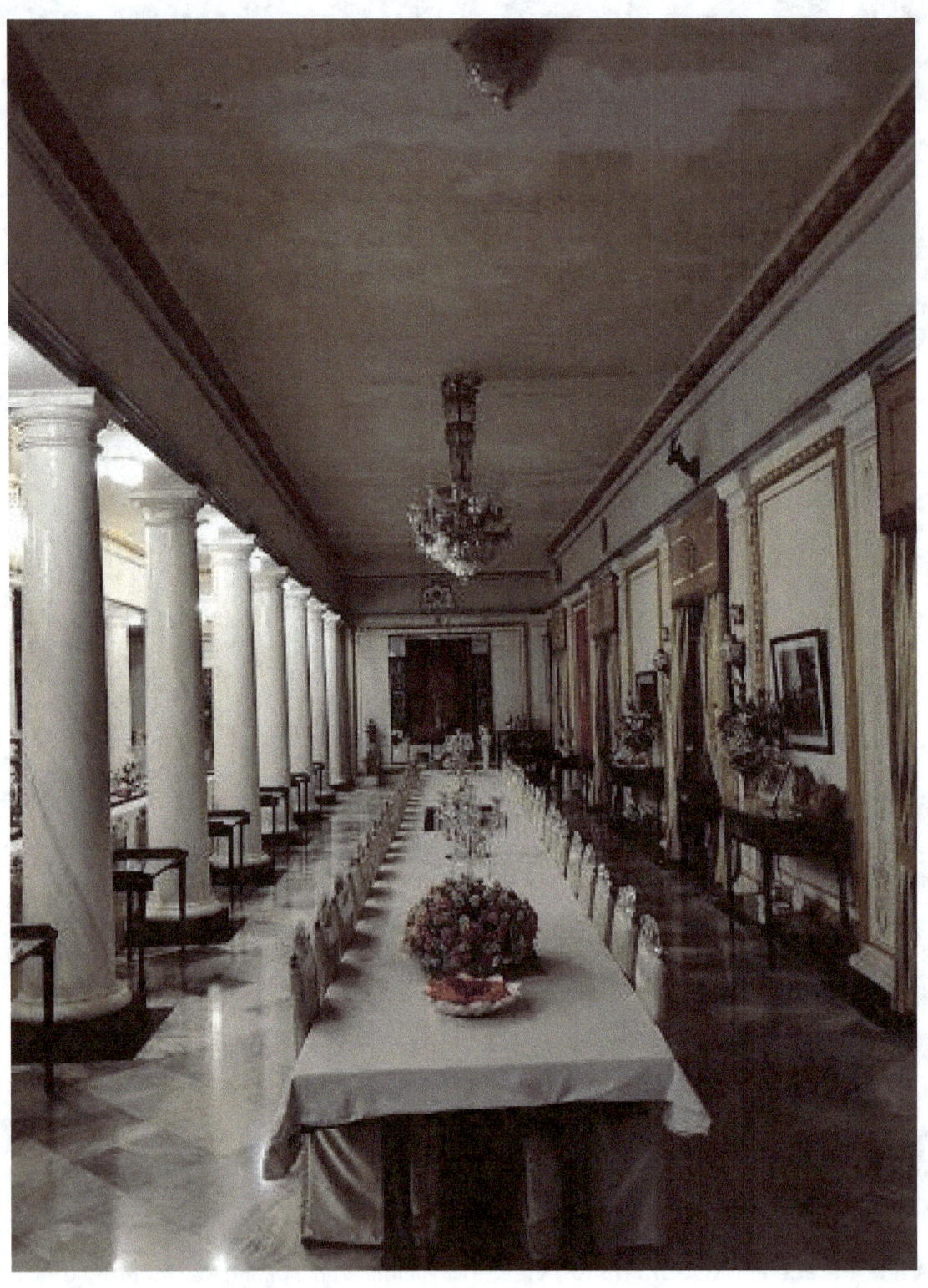

Jai Vilas Palace & Museum inside view - Royal long Table Dining Hall for many Guests

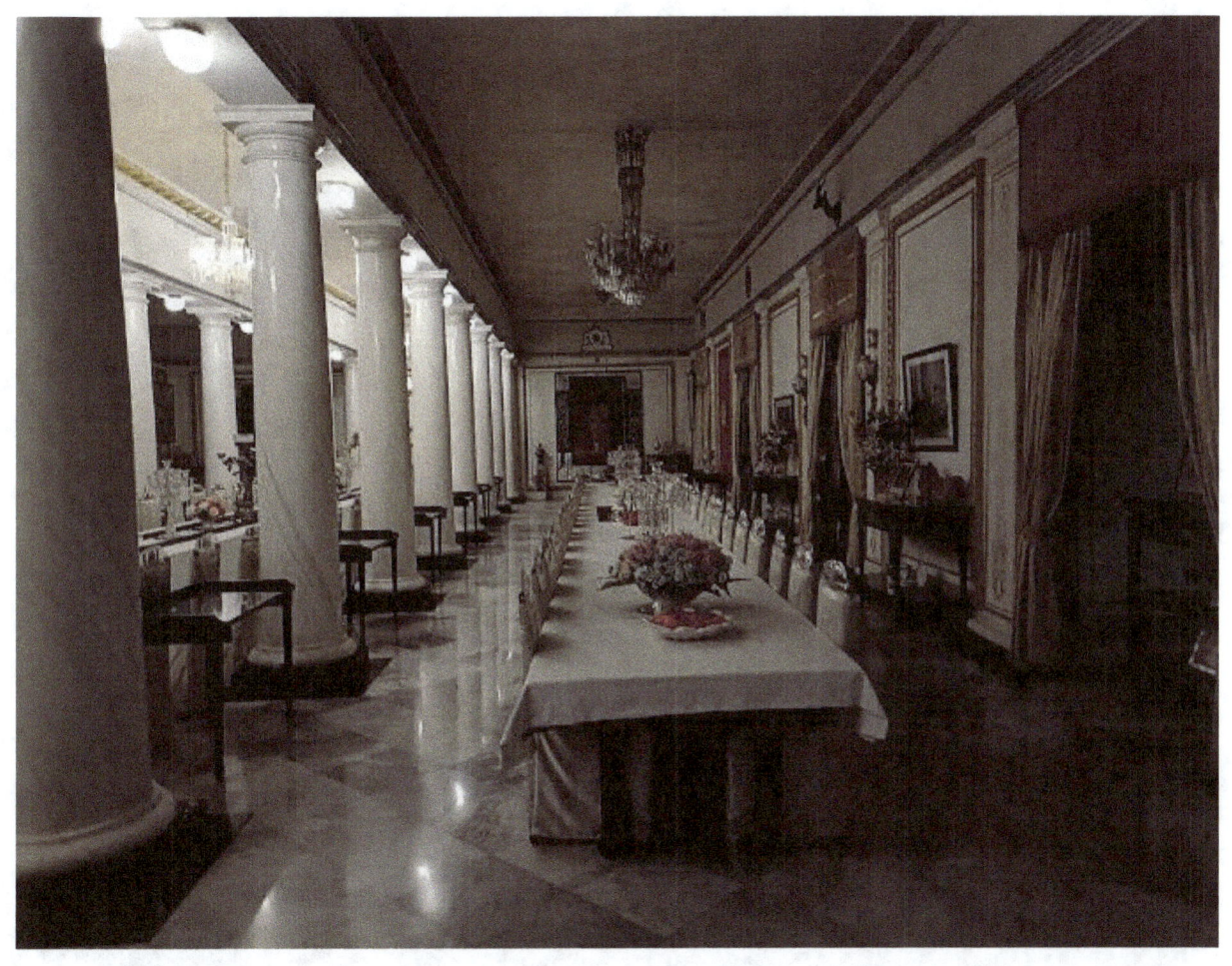
Jai Vilas Palace & Museum inside view - Royal long Table Dining Hall for many Guests

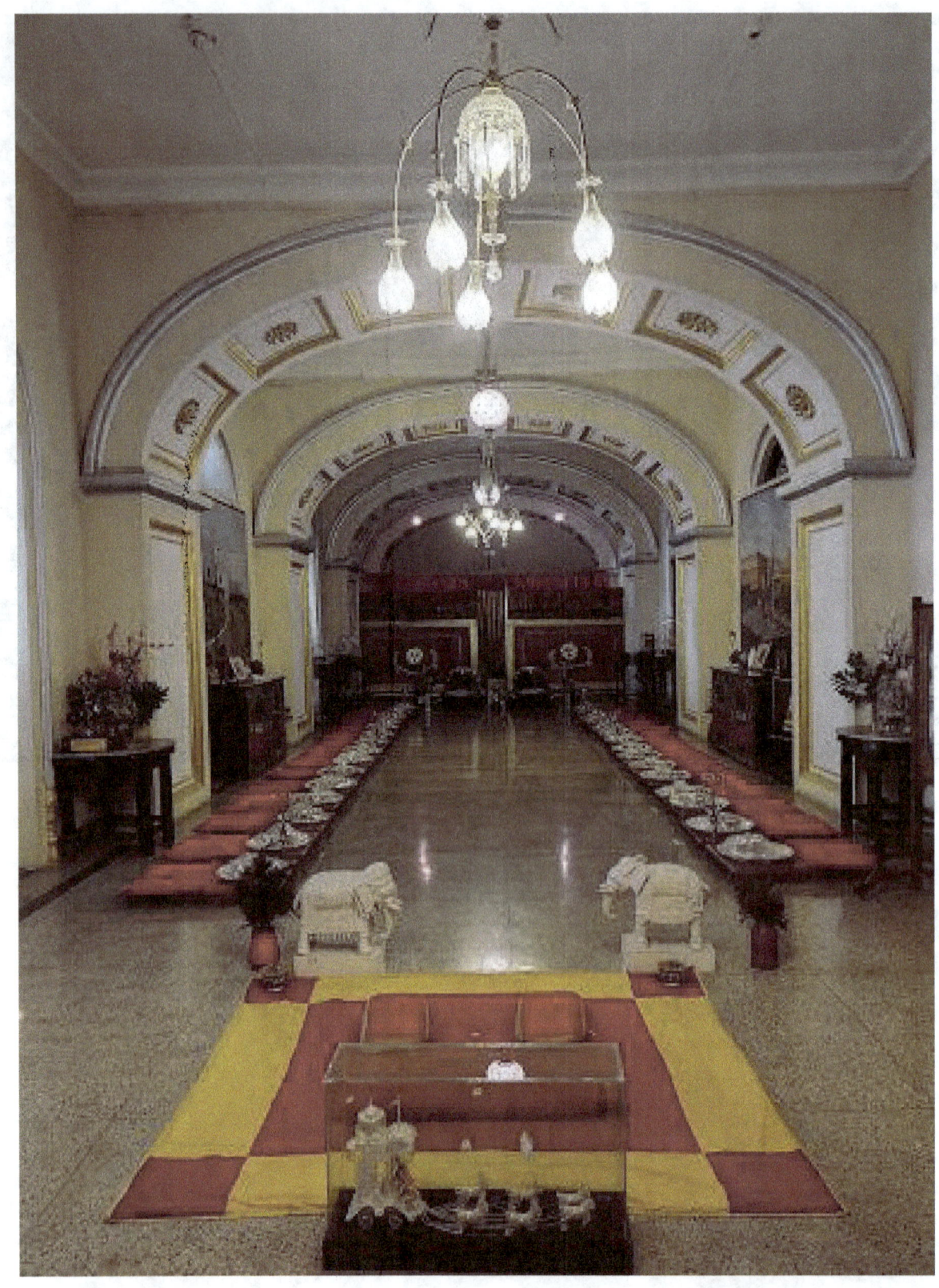

Jai Vilas Palace & Museum inside view - Royal long ground sitting Dining Hall for many Guests

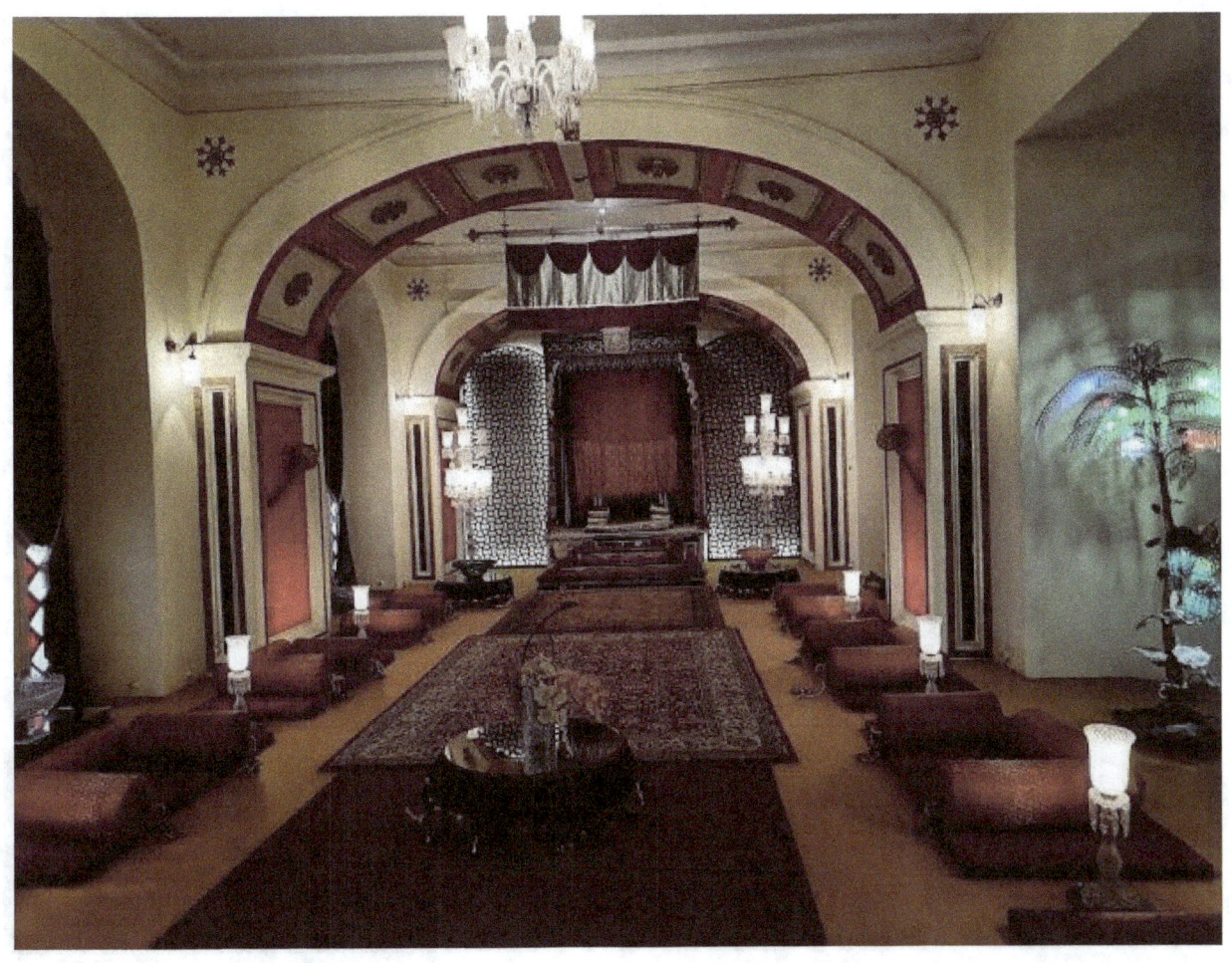
Jai Vilas Palace & Museum inside view - Royal long ground sitting Dining Hall for many Guests

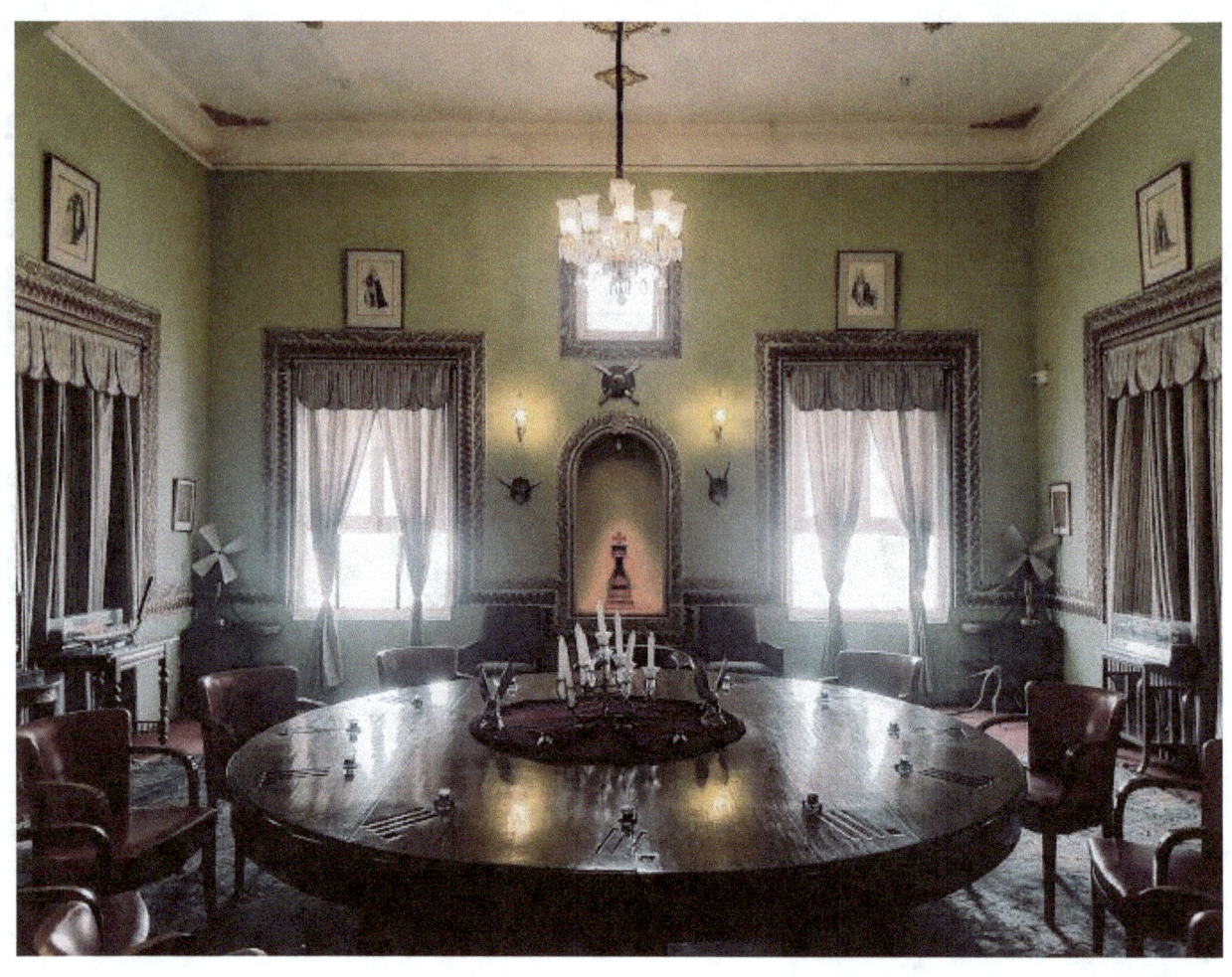

Jai Vilas Palace & Museum inside view - Royal round Table Dining Hall for many Guests

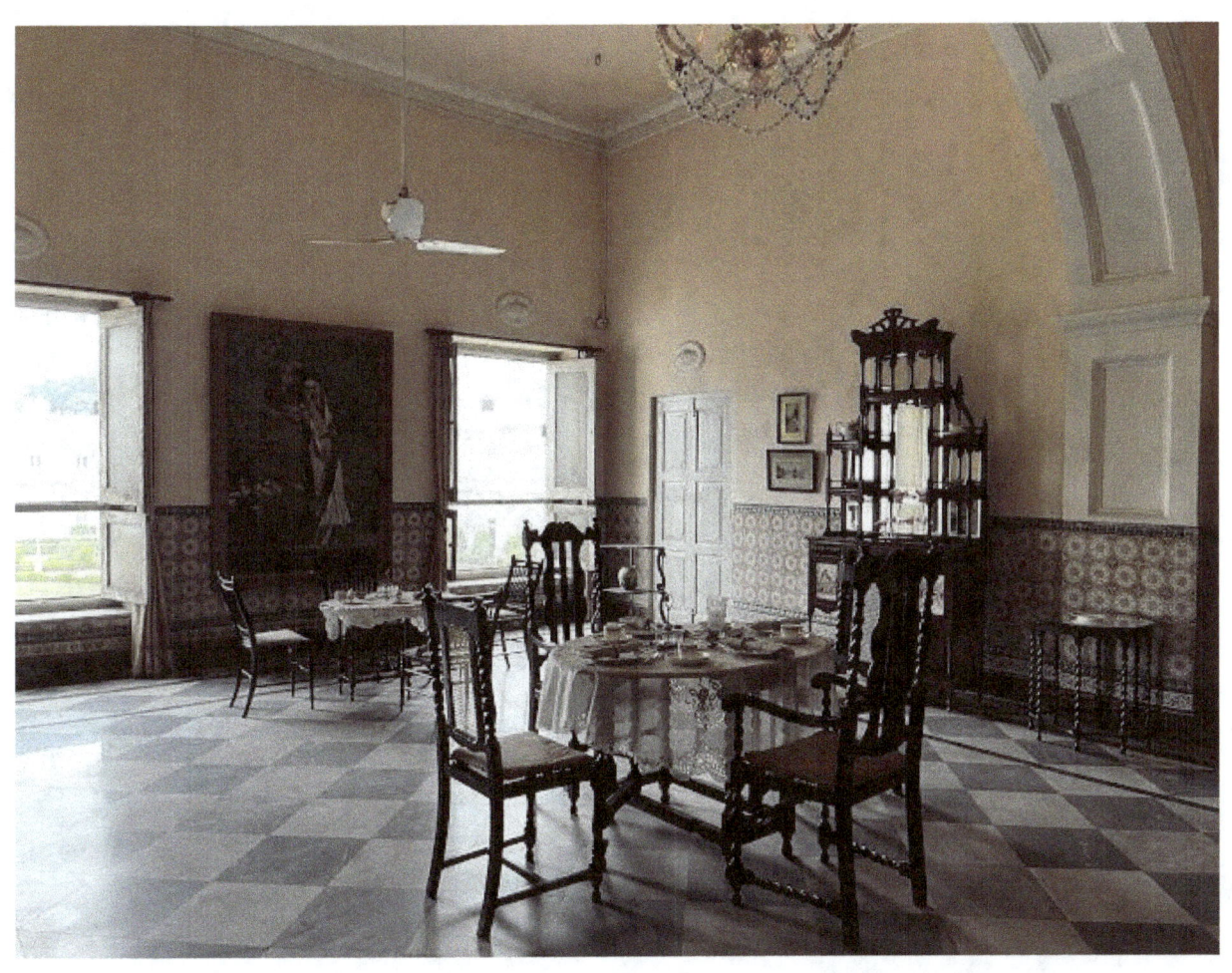

Jai Vilas Palace & Museum inside view - Royal round Table Dining Hall for family

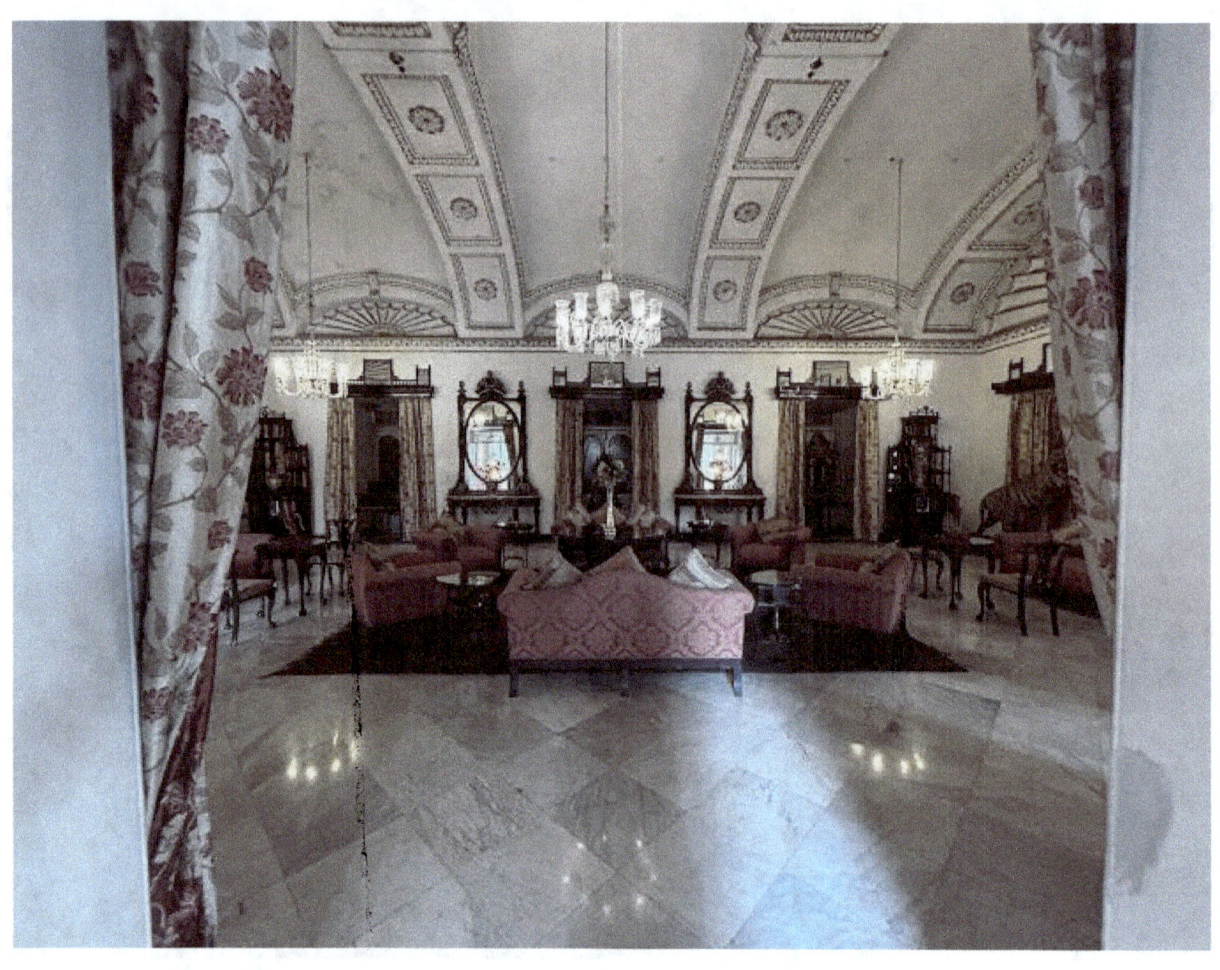

Jai Vilas Palace & Museum inside view - Royal Room

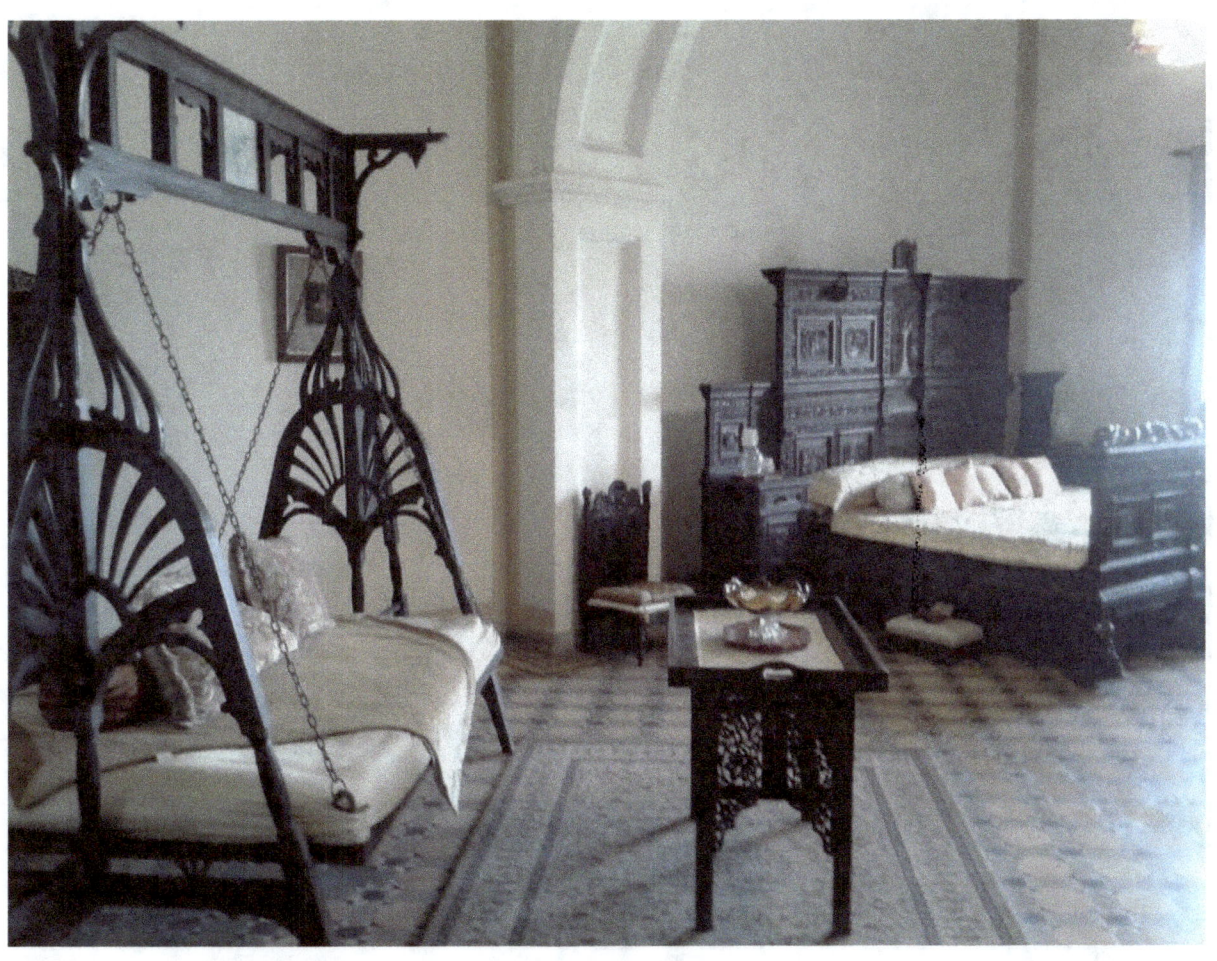
Jai Vilas Palace & Museum inside view - Royal Room

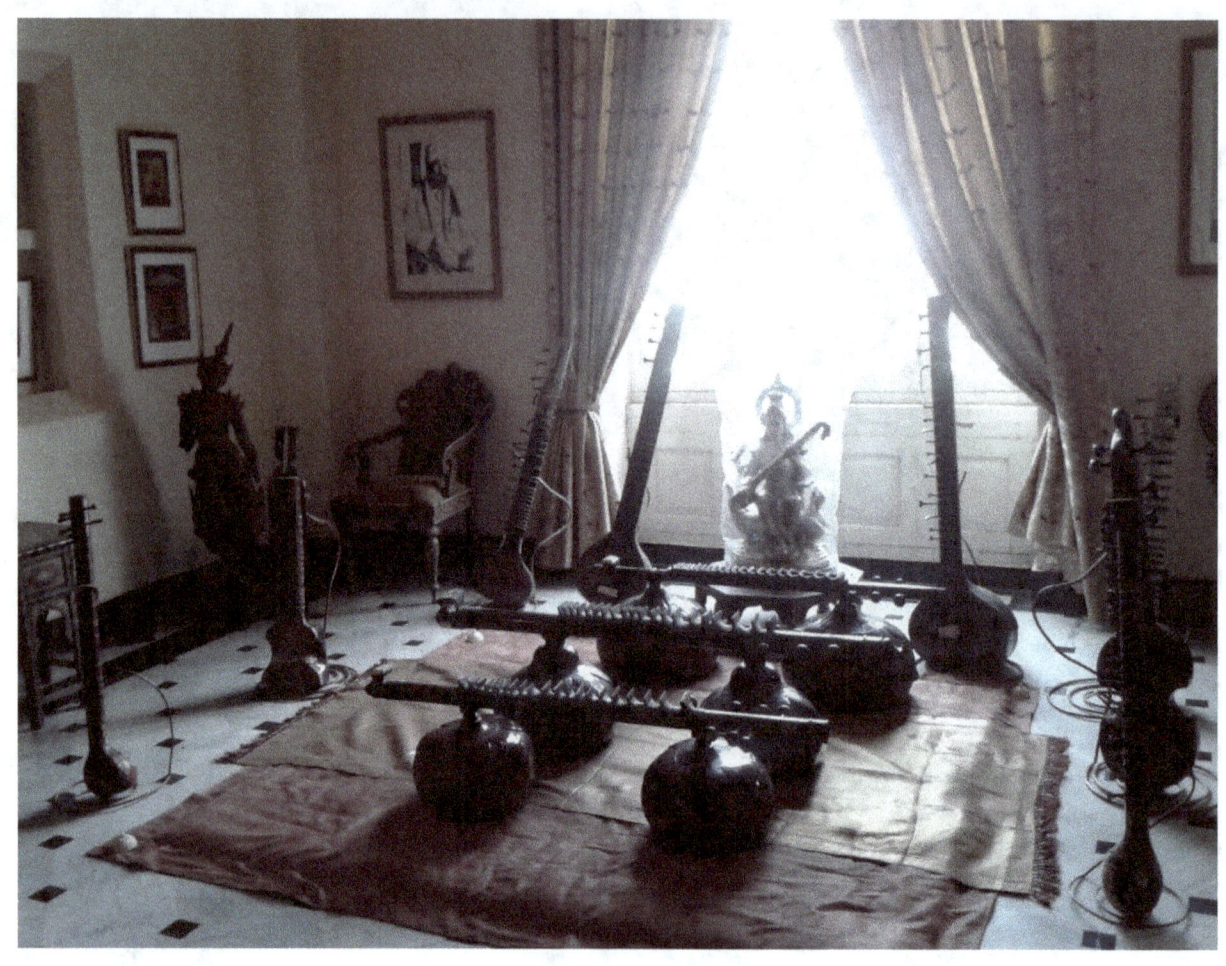

Jai Vilas Palace & Museum inside view - Royal Music Instruments Room

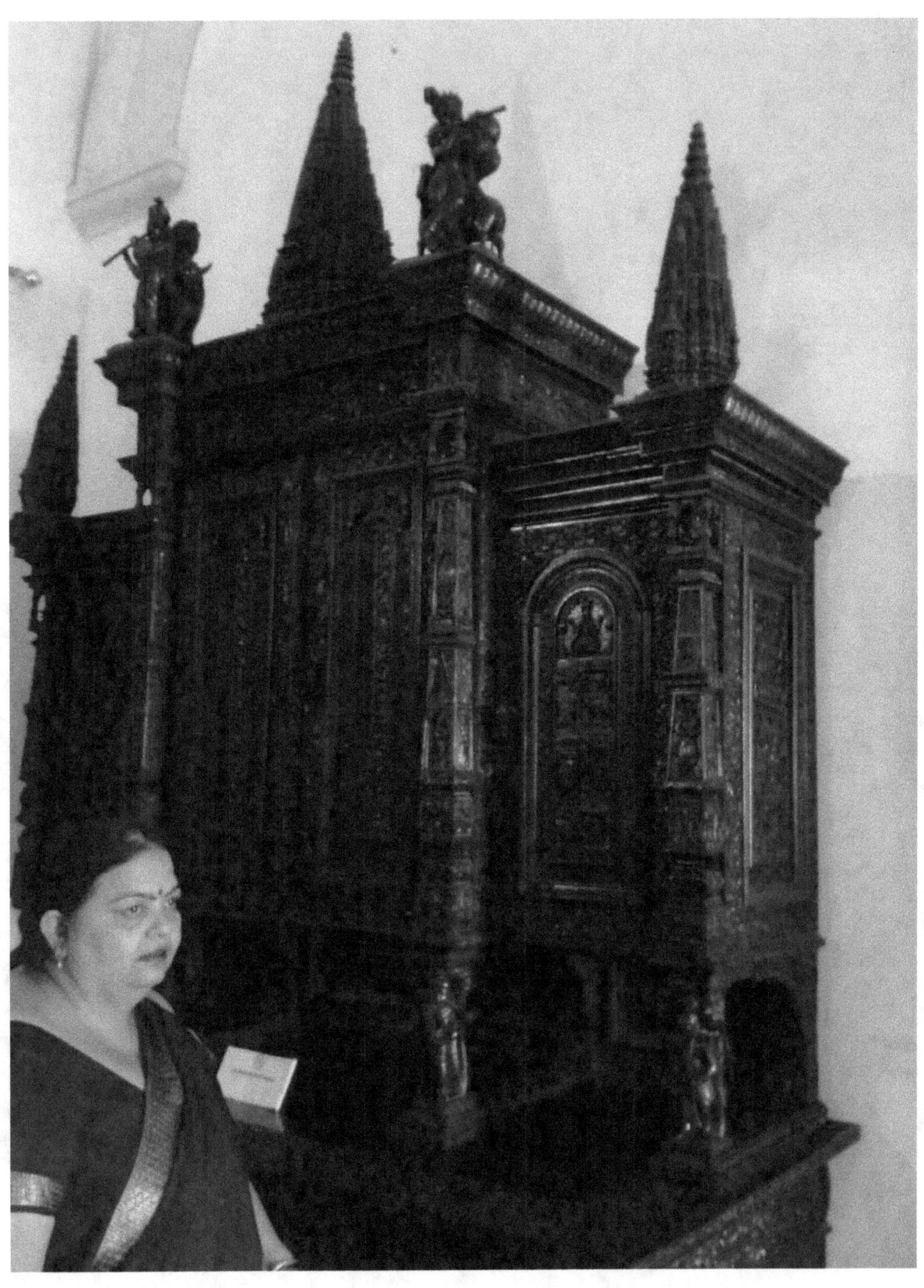

Jai Vilas Palace & Museum inside view – Big Almirah in Royal Room

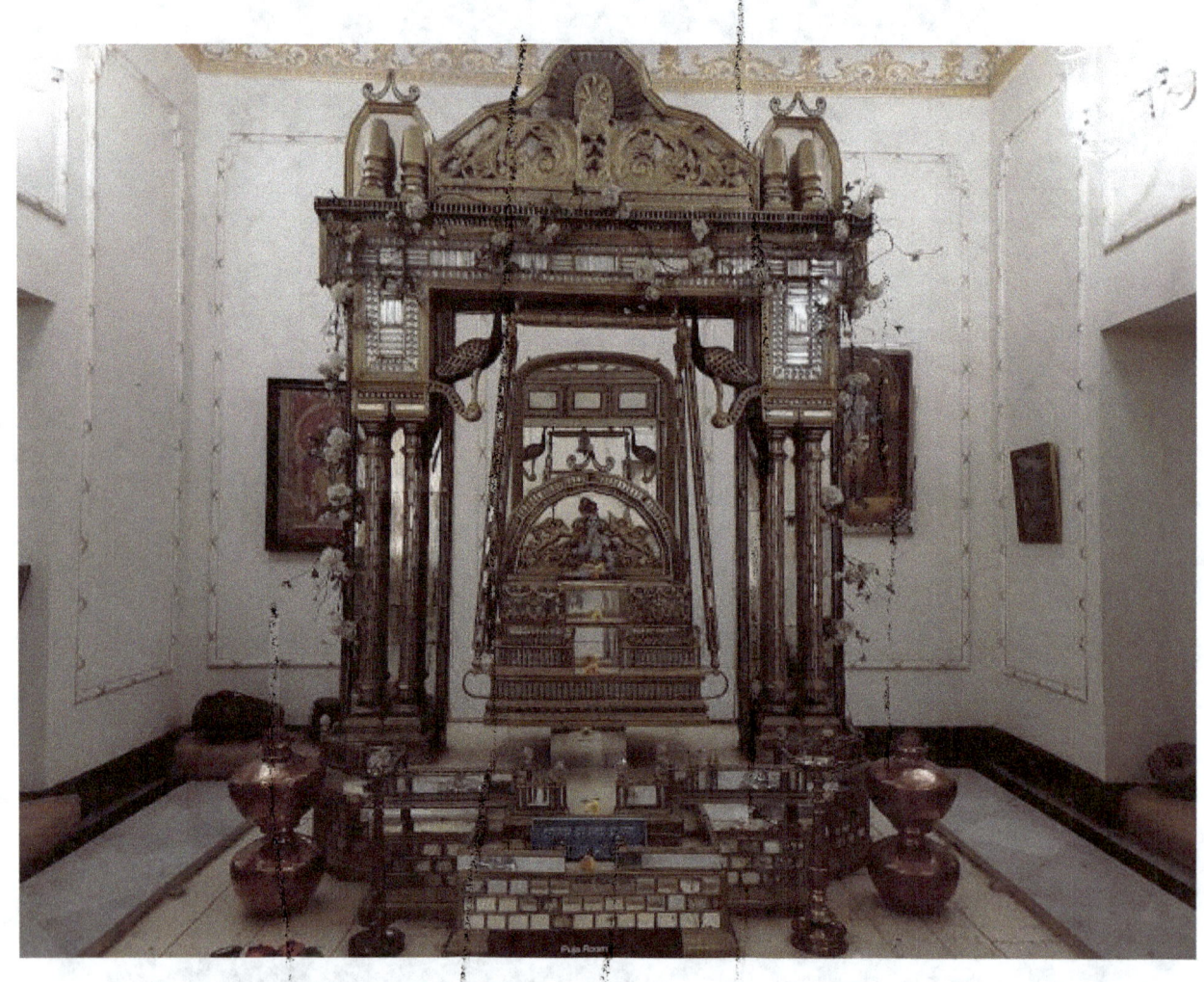

Jai Vilas Palace & Museum inside view – Big Jhoola in Royal Room

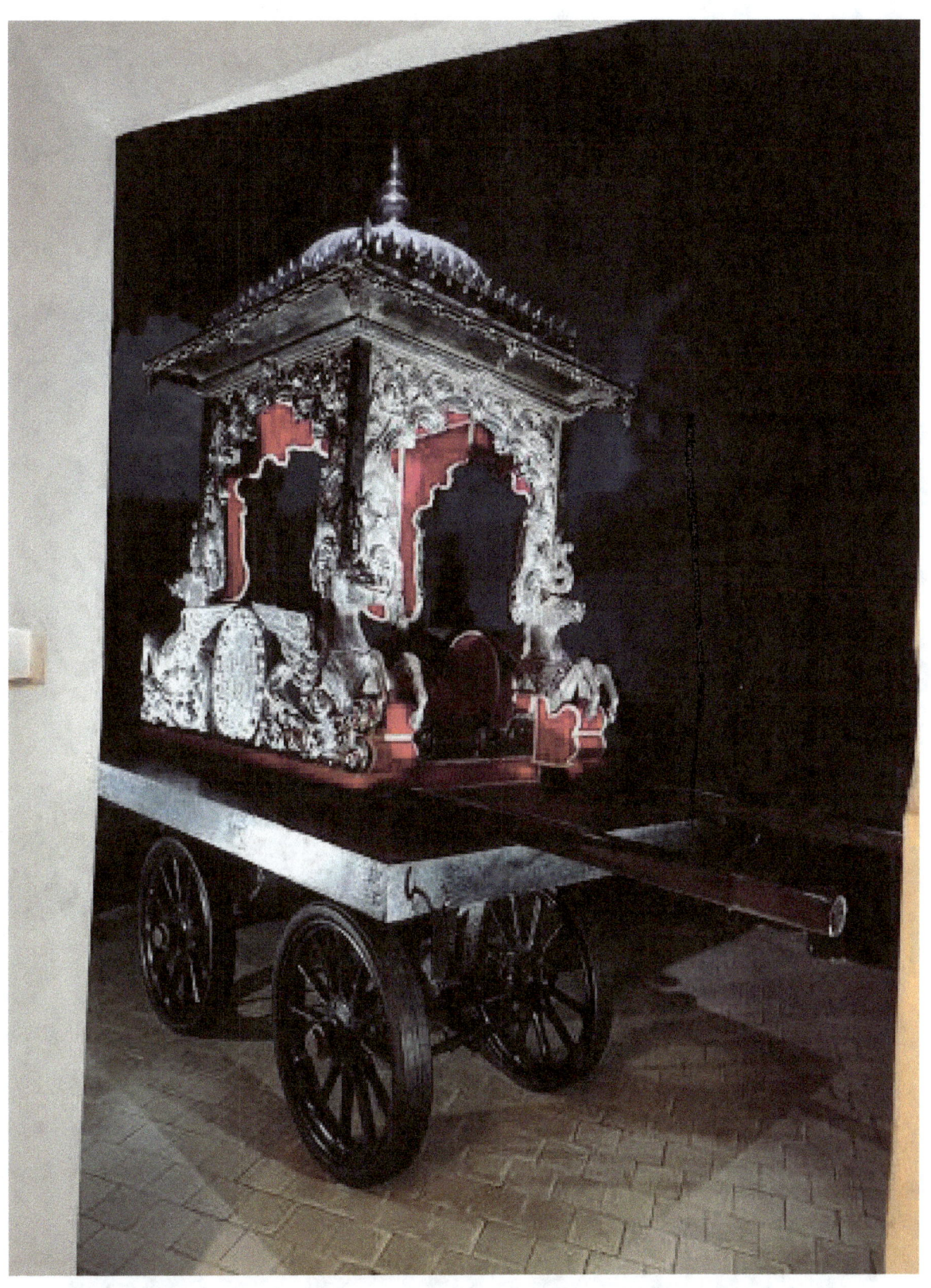

Jai Vilas Palace & Museum inside view – Doly - Palanquin

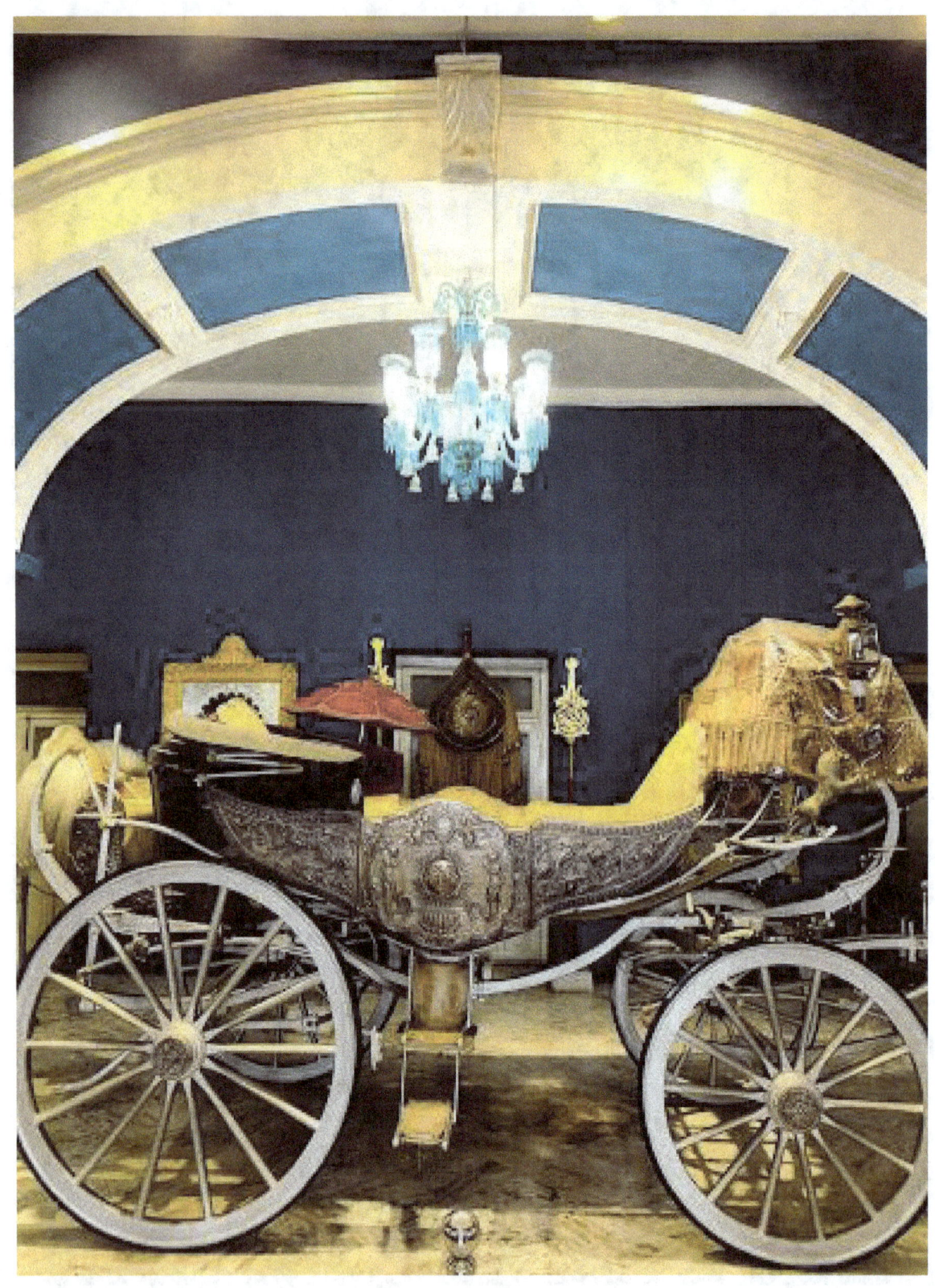

Jai Vilas Palace & Museum inside view –Horse Driven Baggi

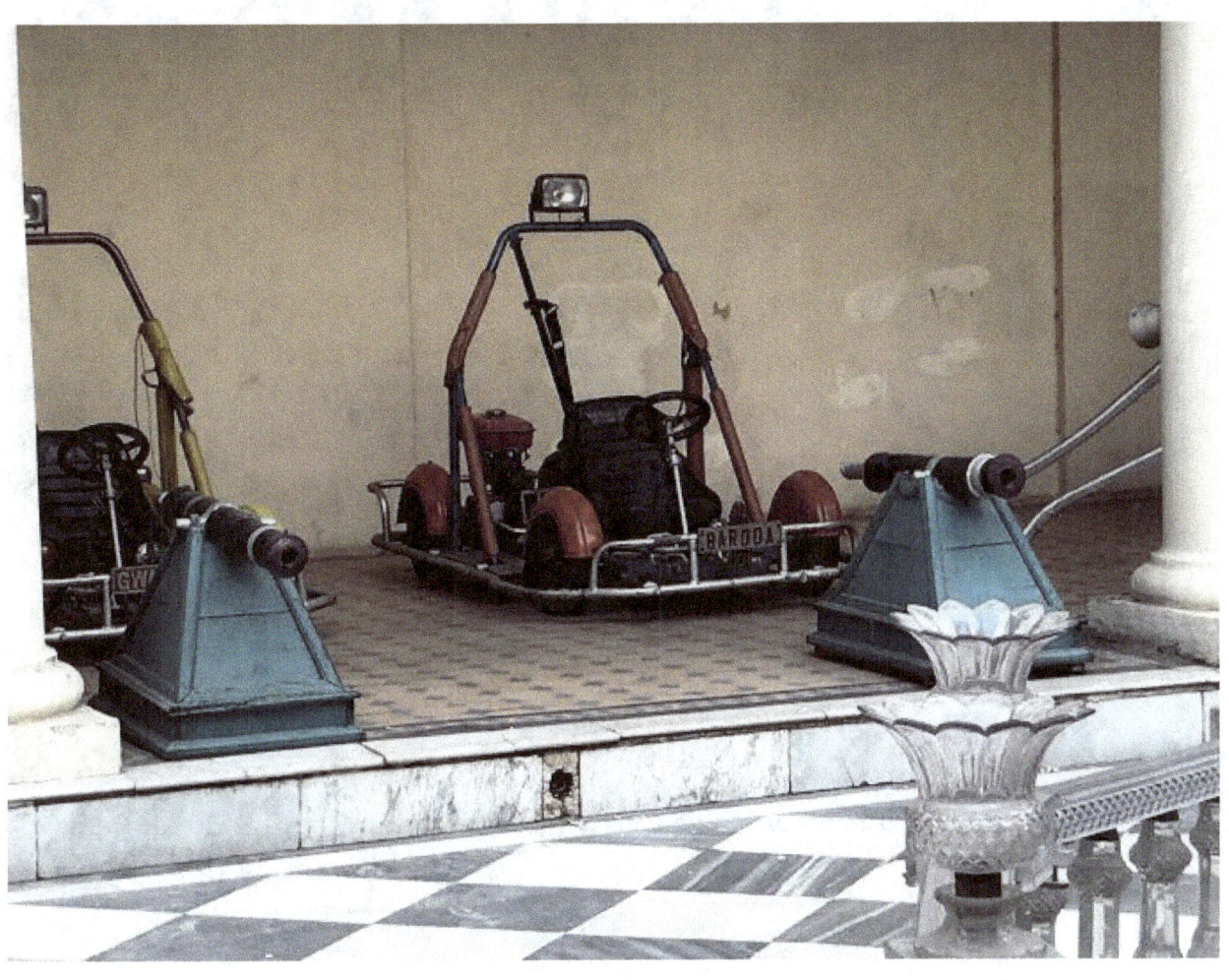

Jai Vilas Palace & Museum inside view – Transport Carts

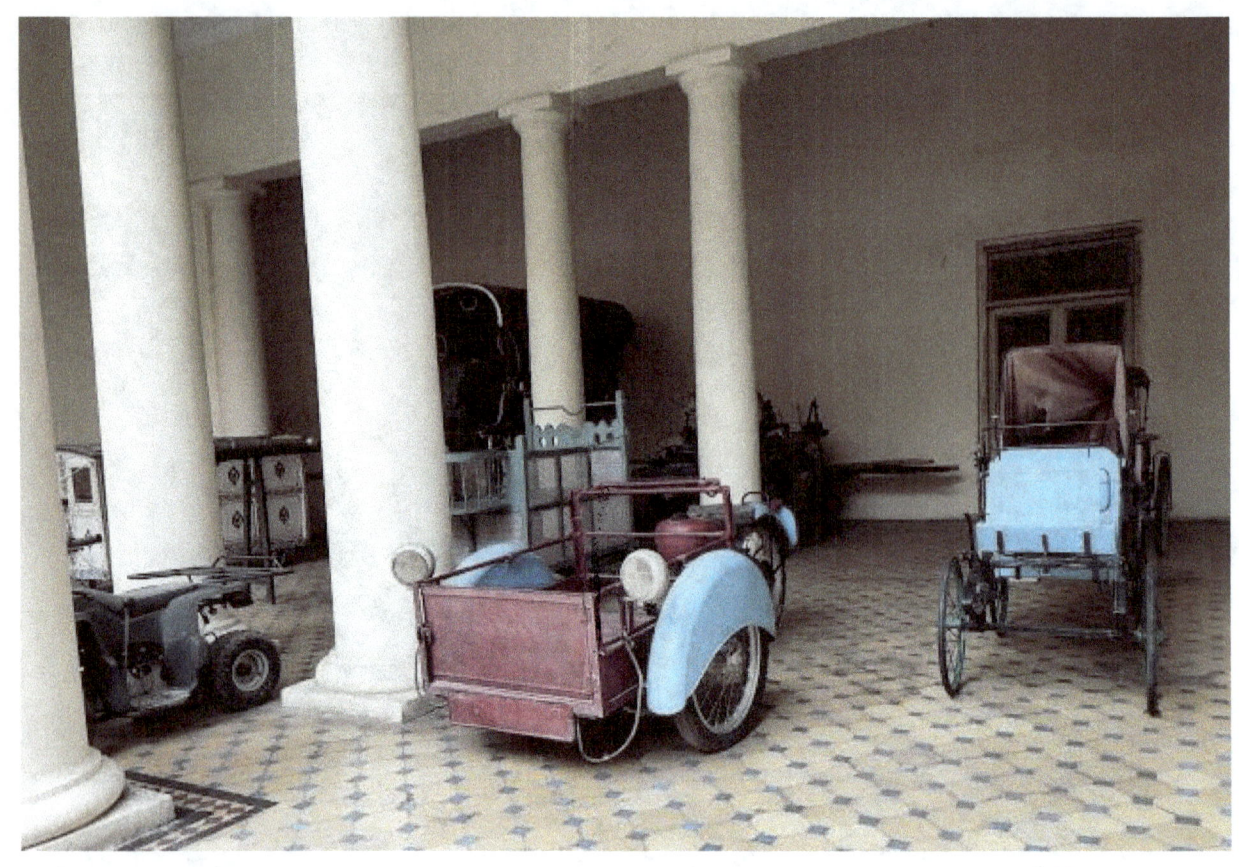
Jai Vilas Palace & Museum inside view –Horse Driven Baggi & Small Cars

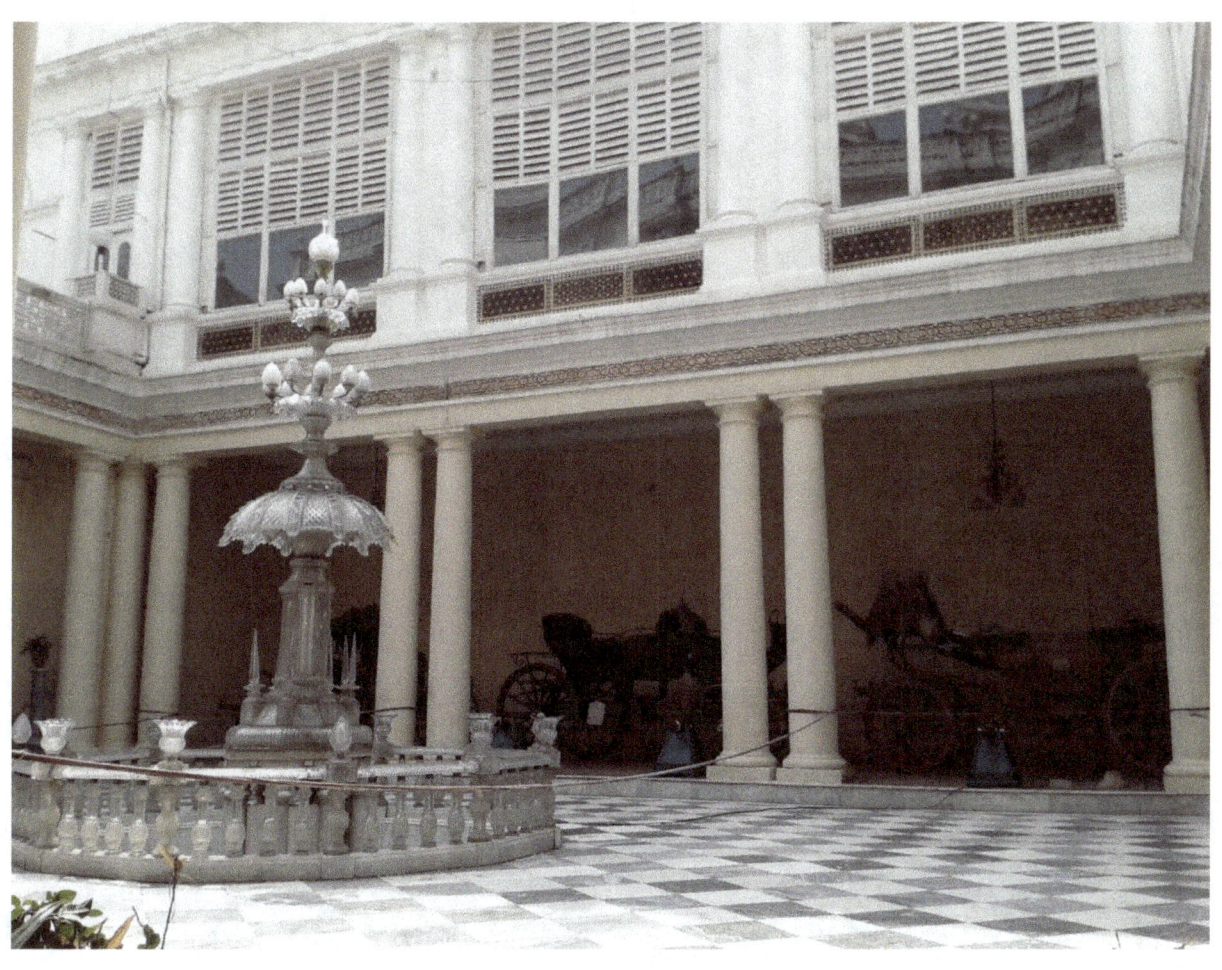

Jai Vilas Palace & Museum inside view –Horse Driven Baggi

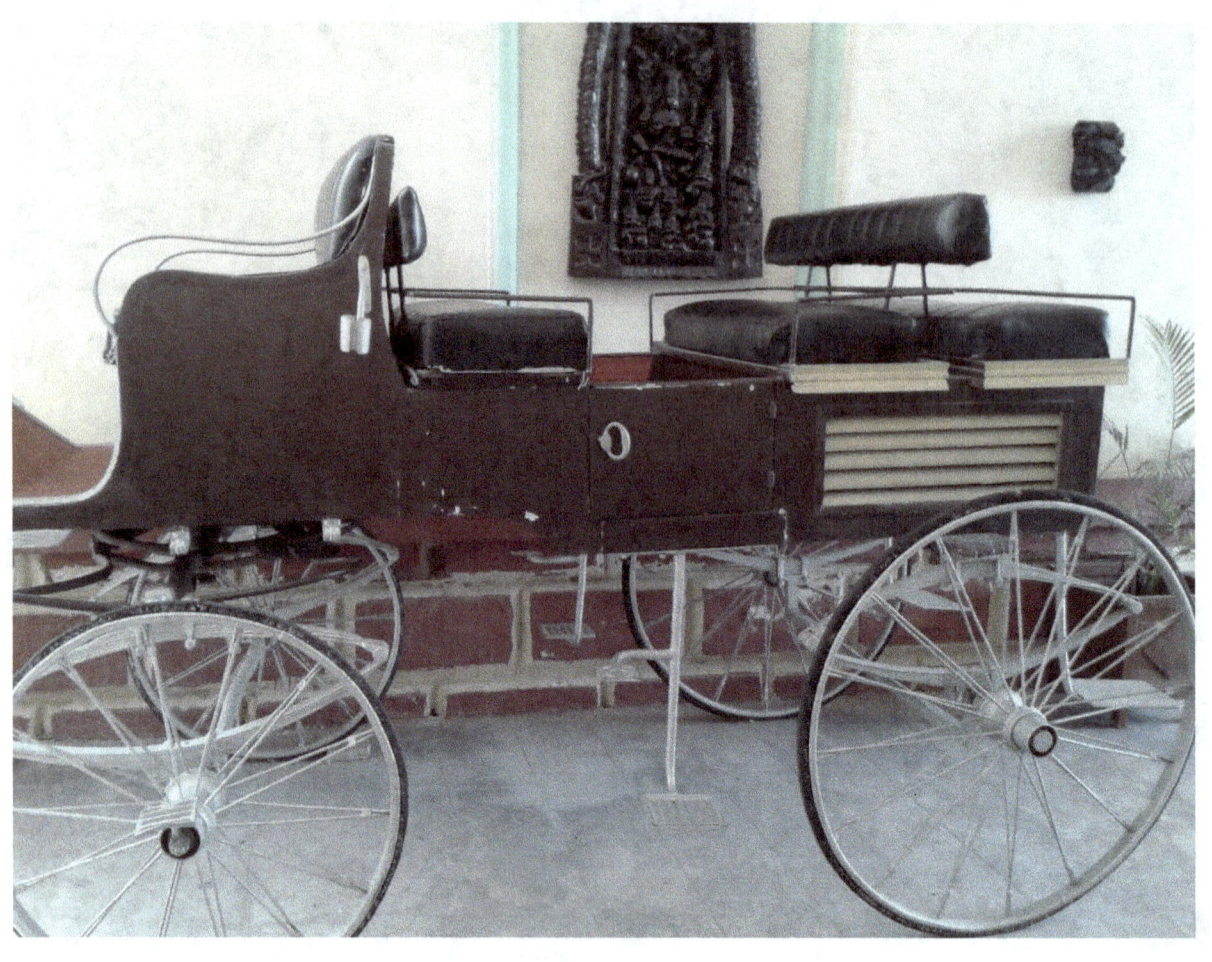

Jai Vilas Palace & Museum inside view –Horse Driven Baggi

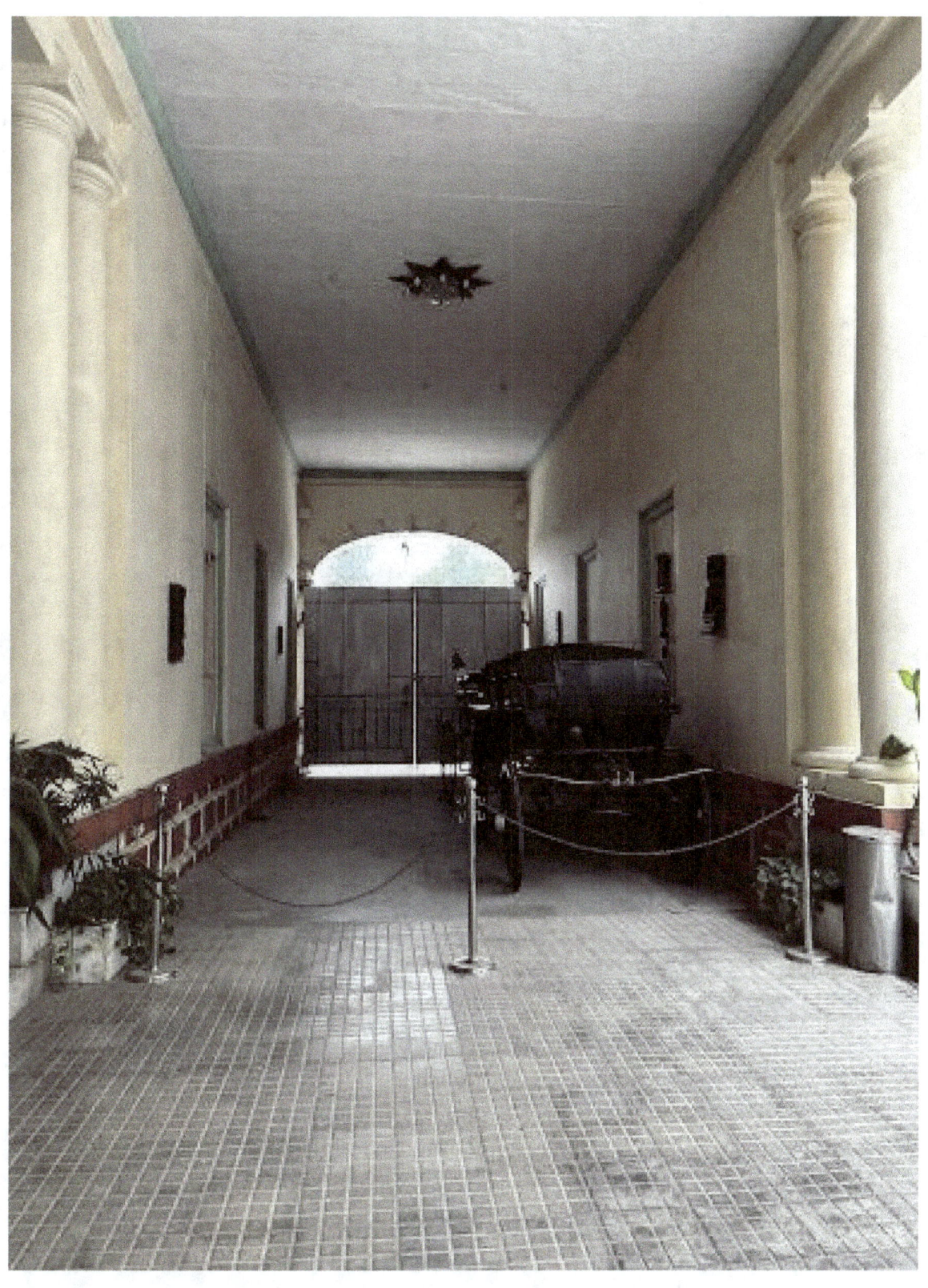

Jai Vilas Palace & Museum inside view –Horse Driven Baggi

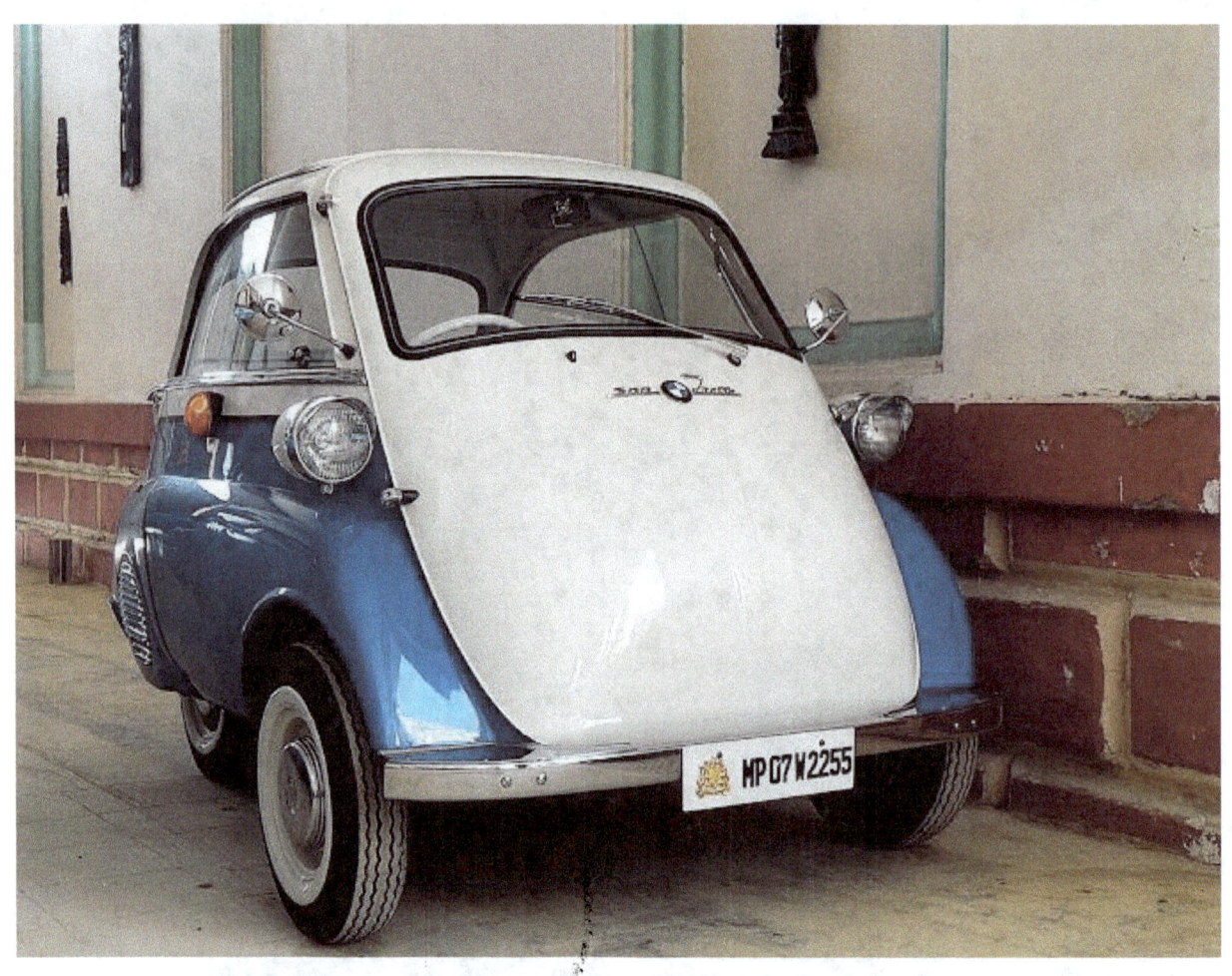

Jai Vilas Palace & Museum inside view – Three-wheel Small Car

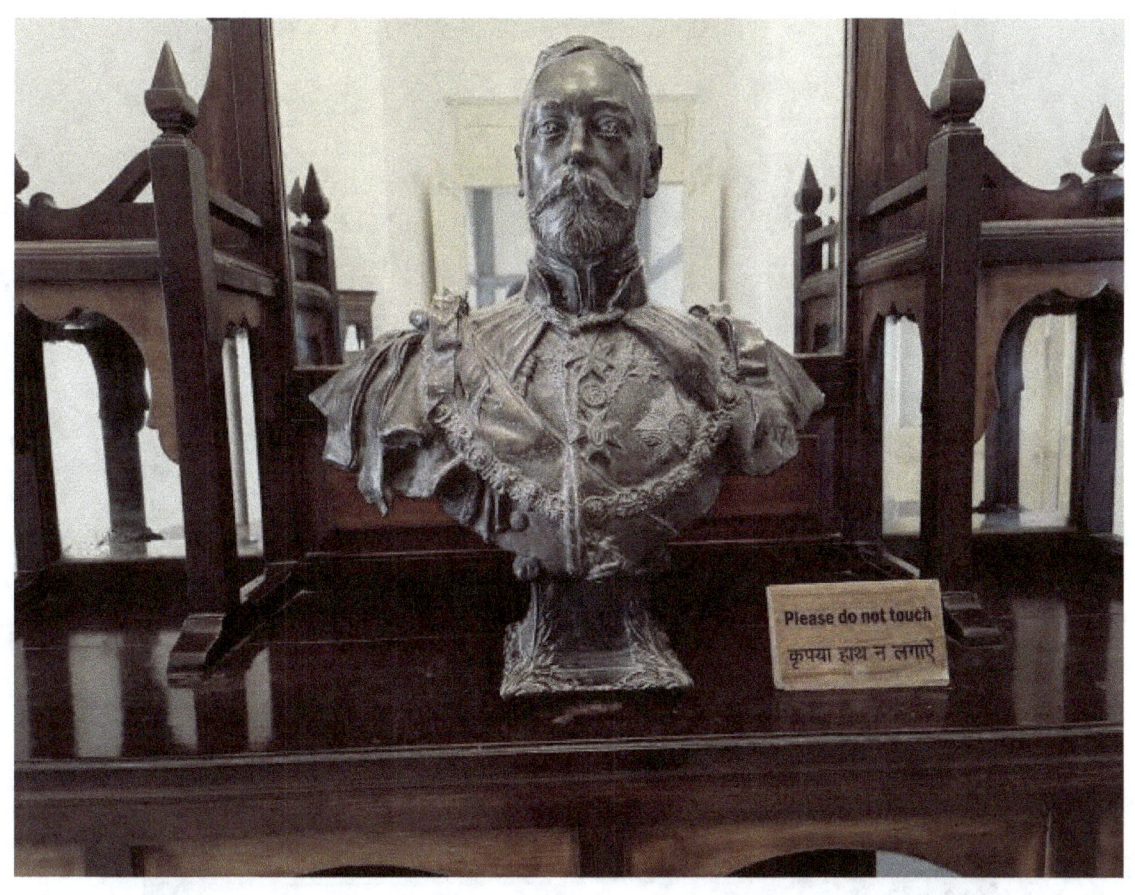

Jai Vilas Palace & Museum inside view – British Emperor Statue

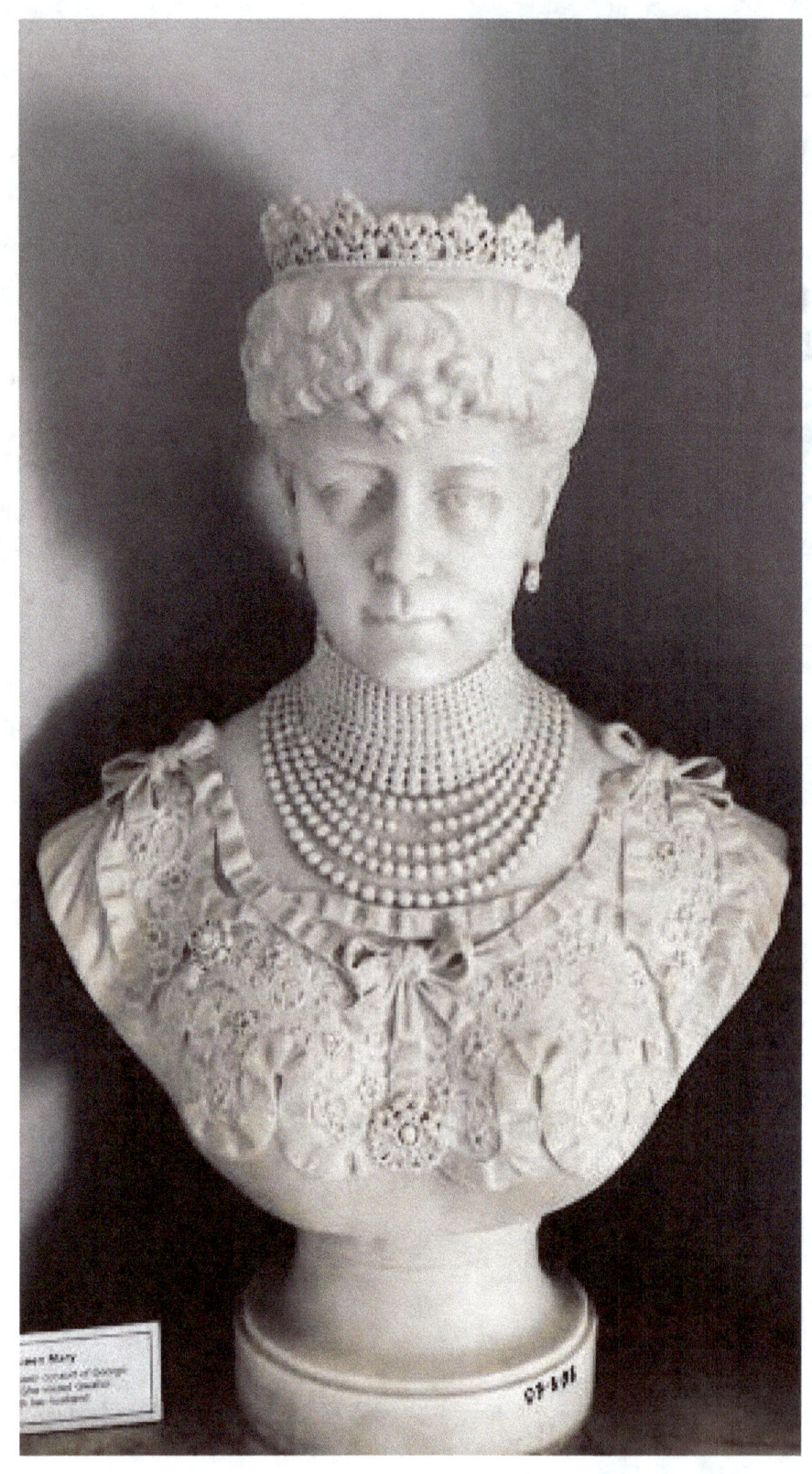

Jai Vilas Palace & Museum inside view – British Queen Statue

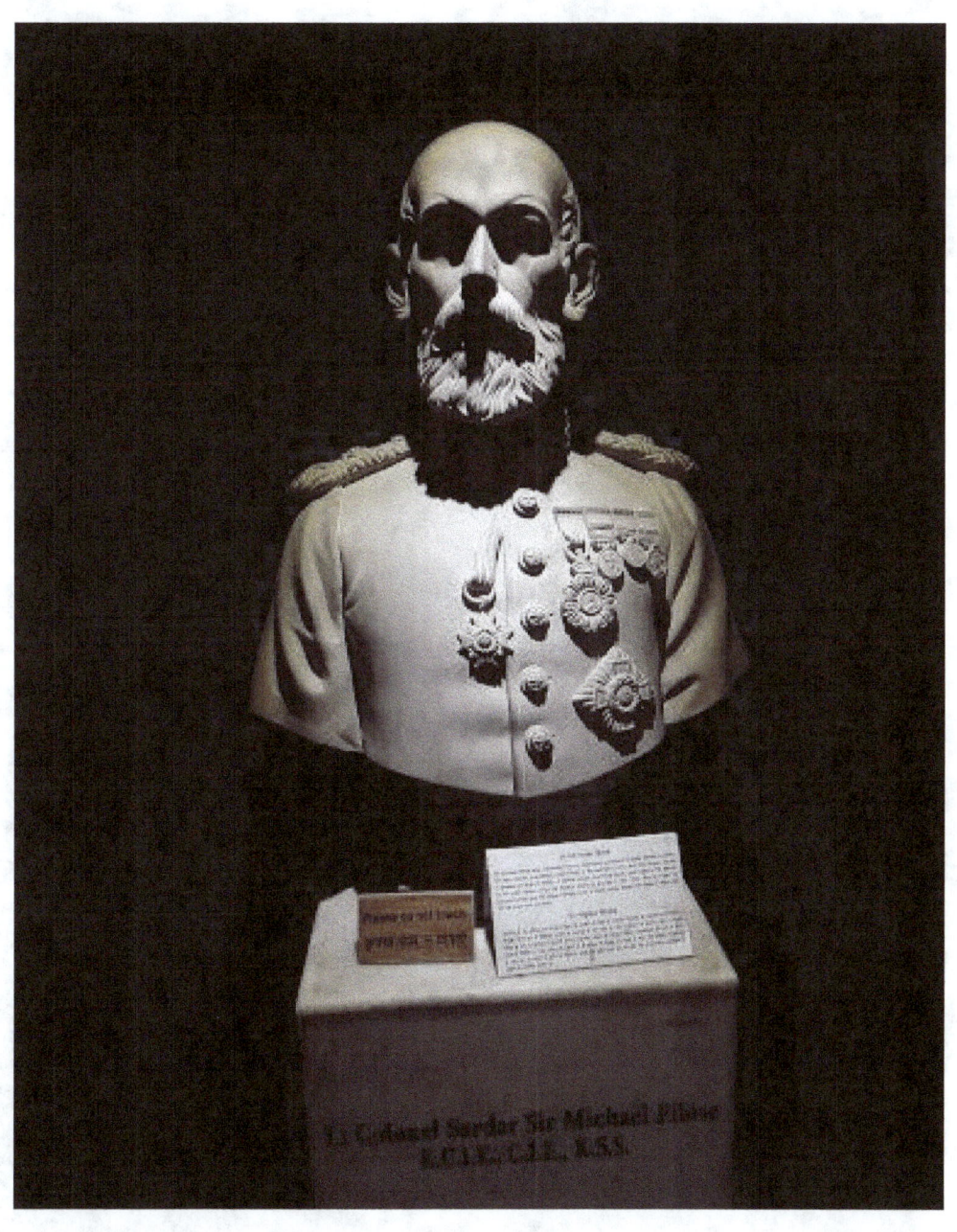

Jai Vilas Palace & Museum inside view – British Colonel Statue

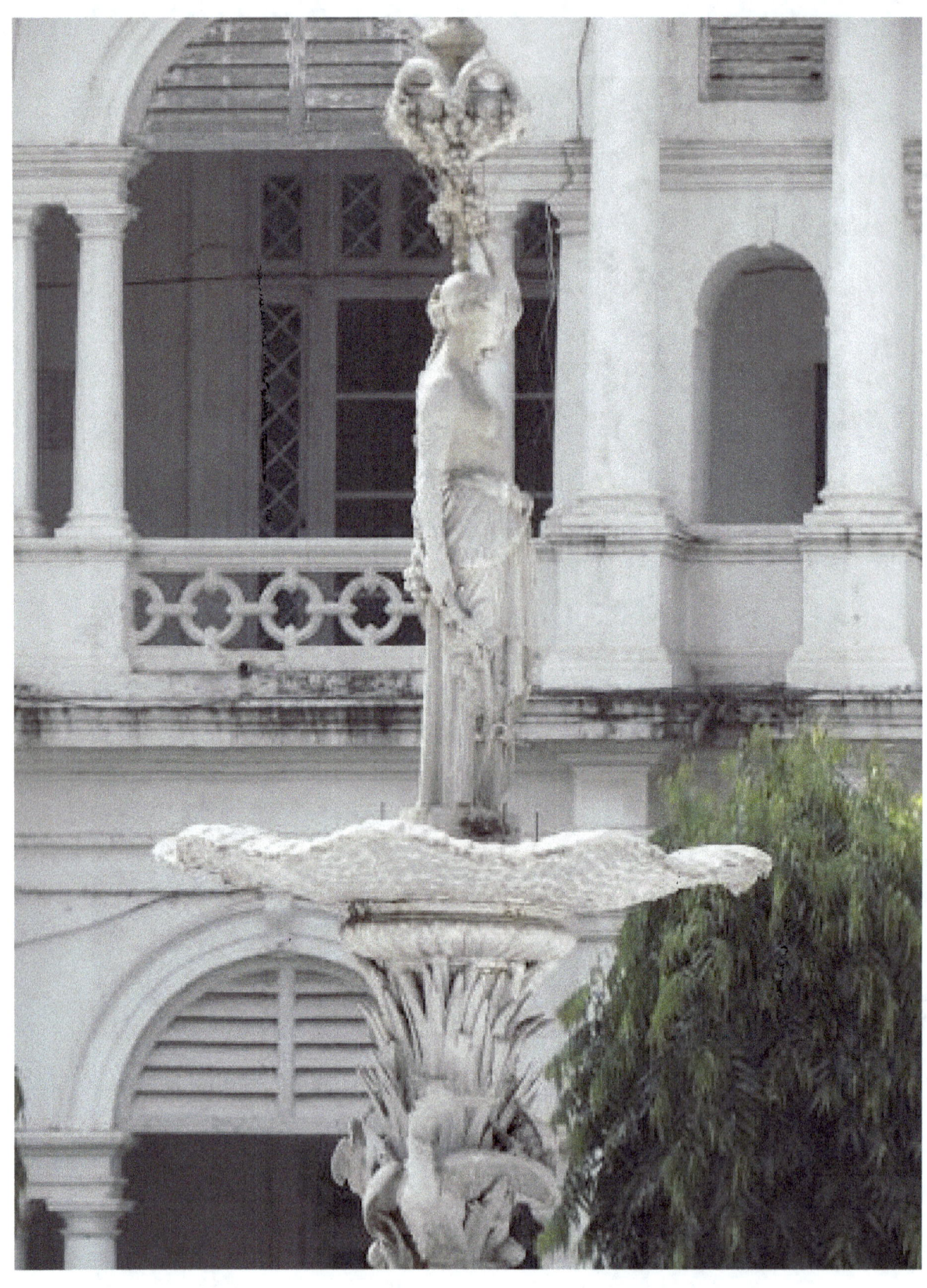

Jai Vilas Palace & Museum outside view – British Lady Statue

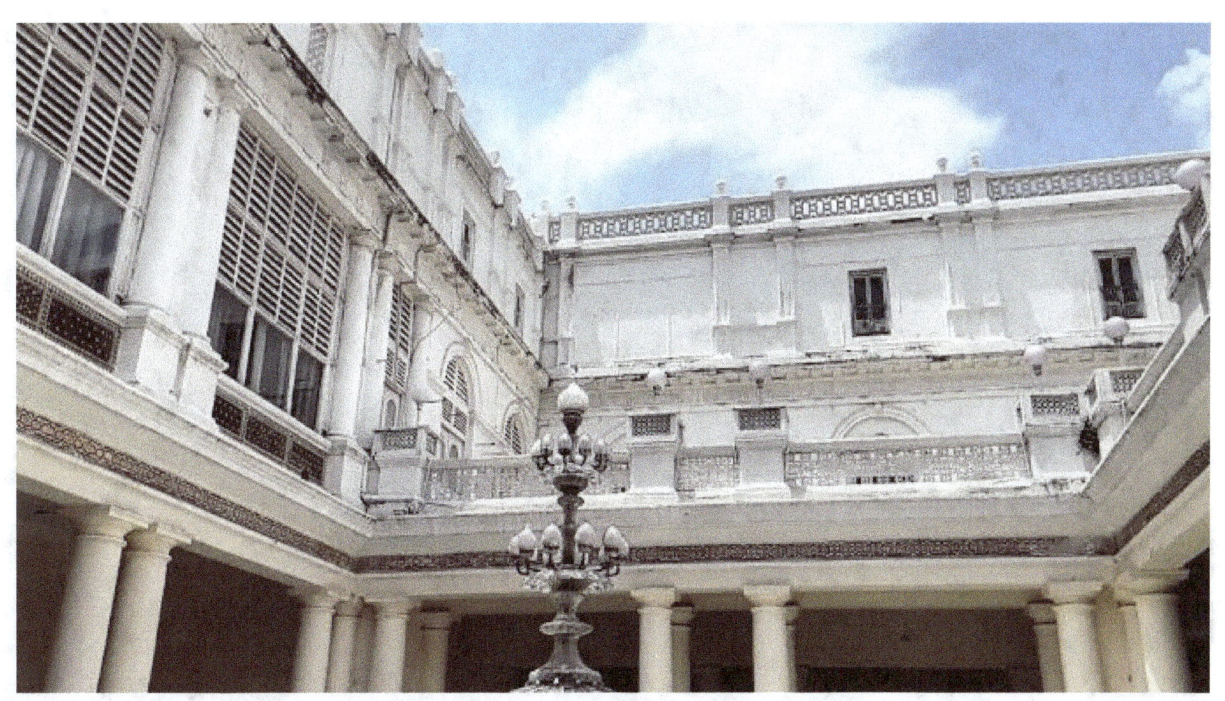

Jai Vilas Palace & Museum outside view

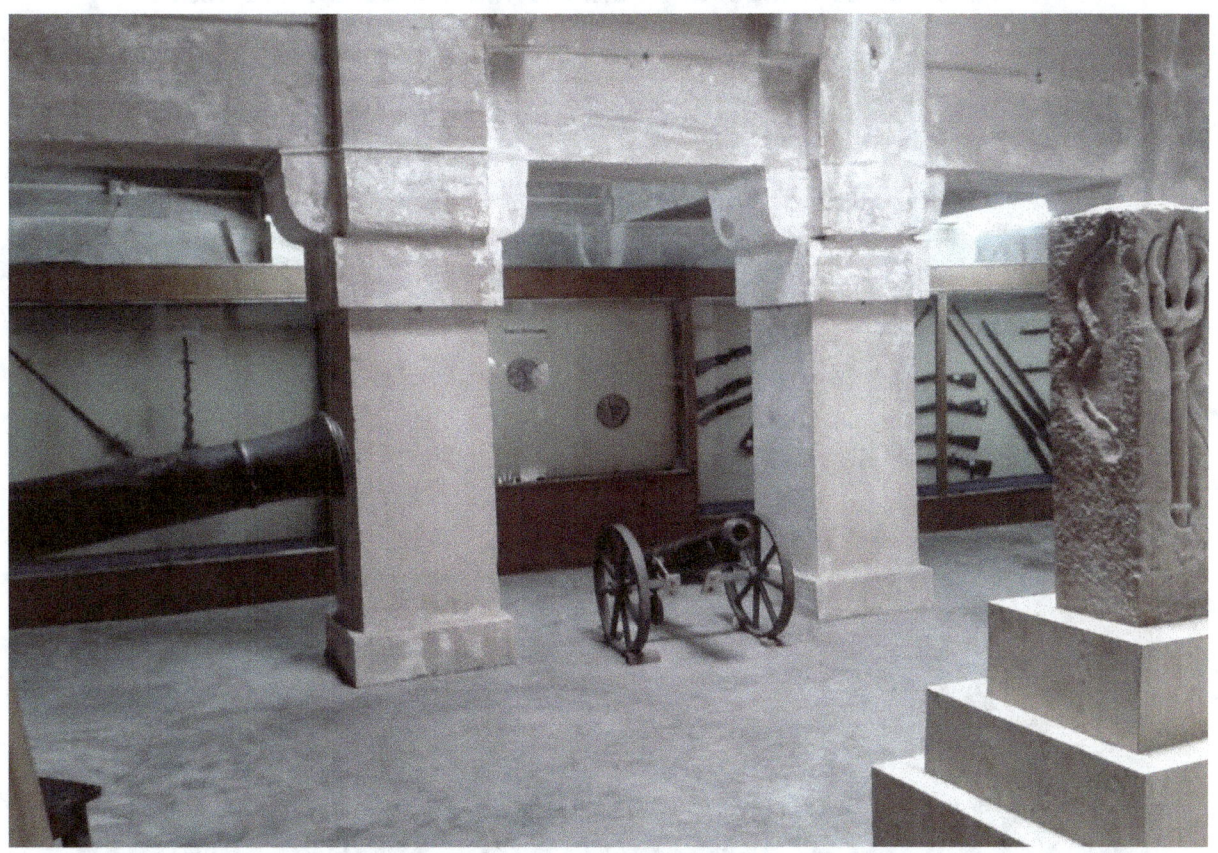

Jai Vilas Palace & Museum Guns & Canons

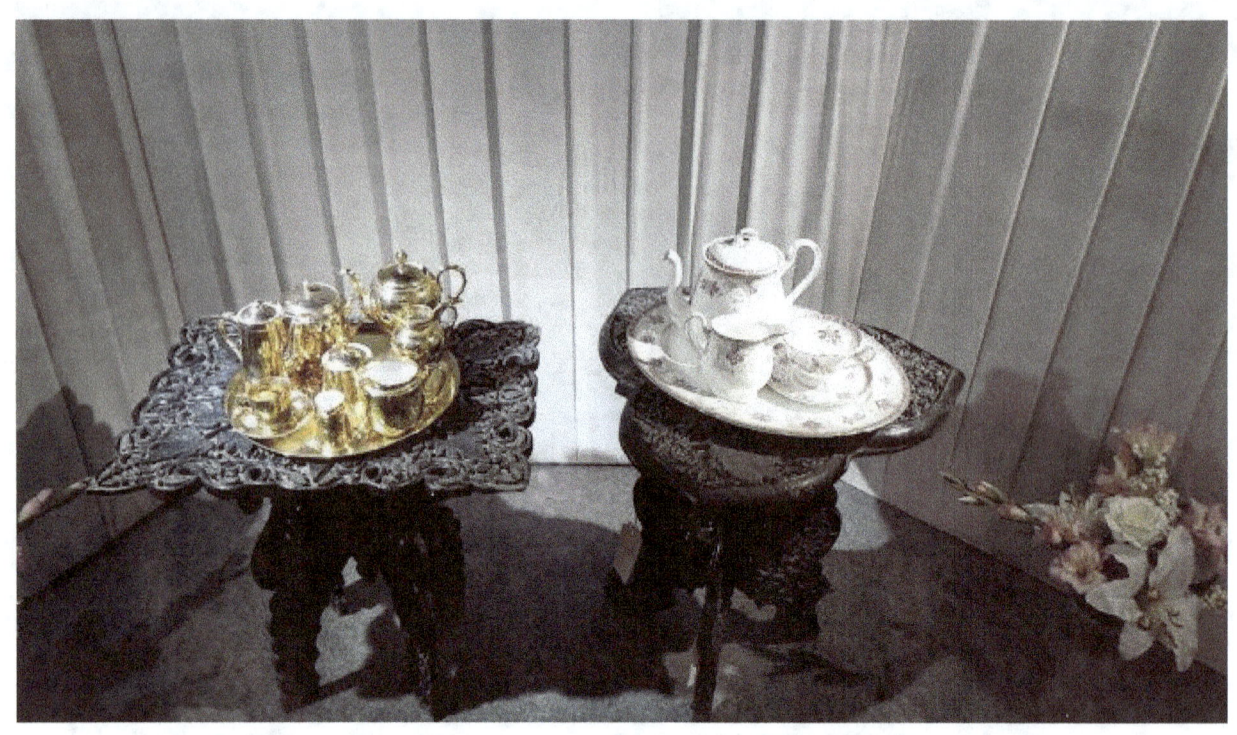

Jai Vilas Palace & Museum Gold & White Porcelain Tea Sets

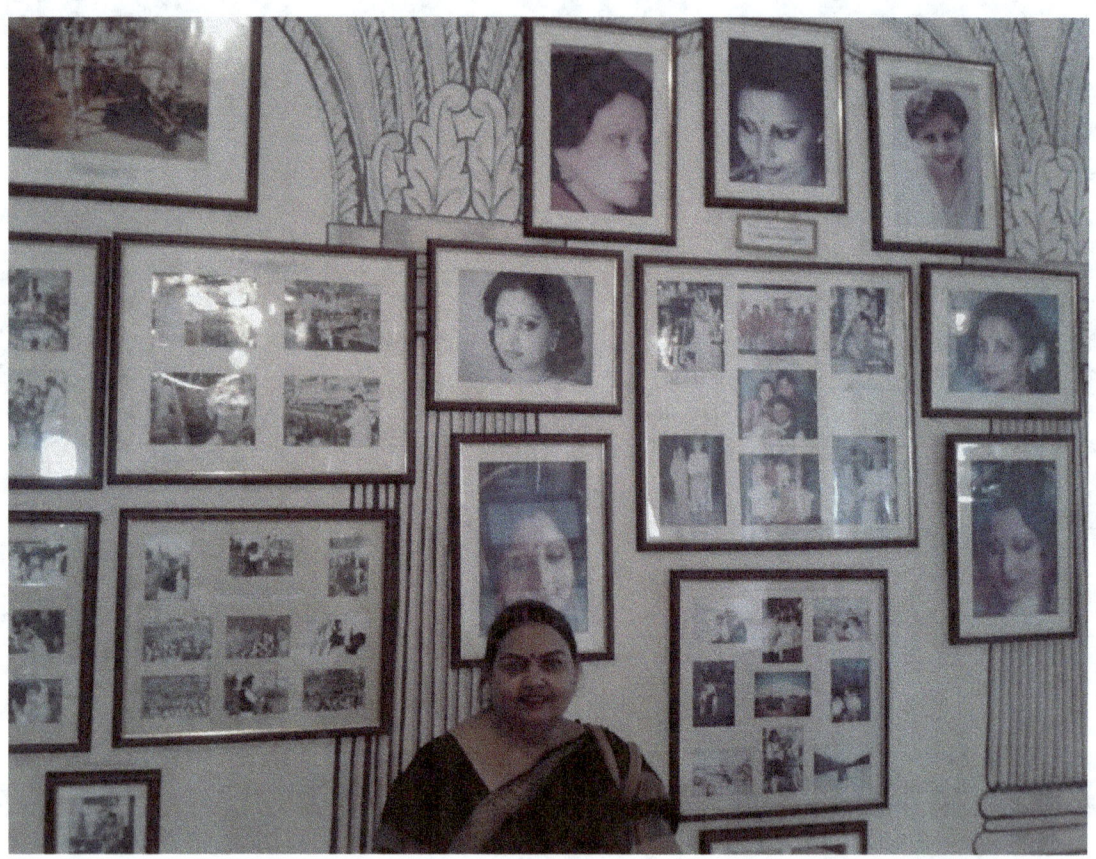

Jai Vilas Palace & Museum inside Picture Gallery view

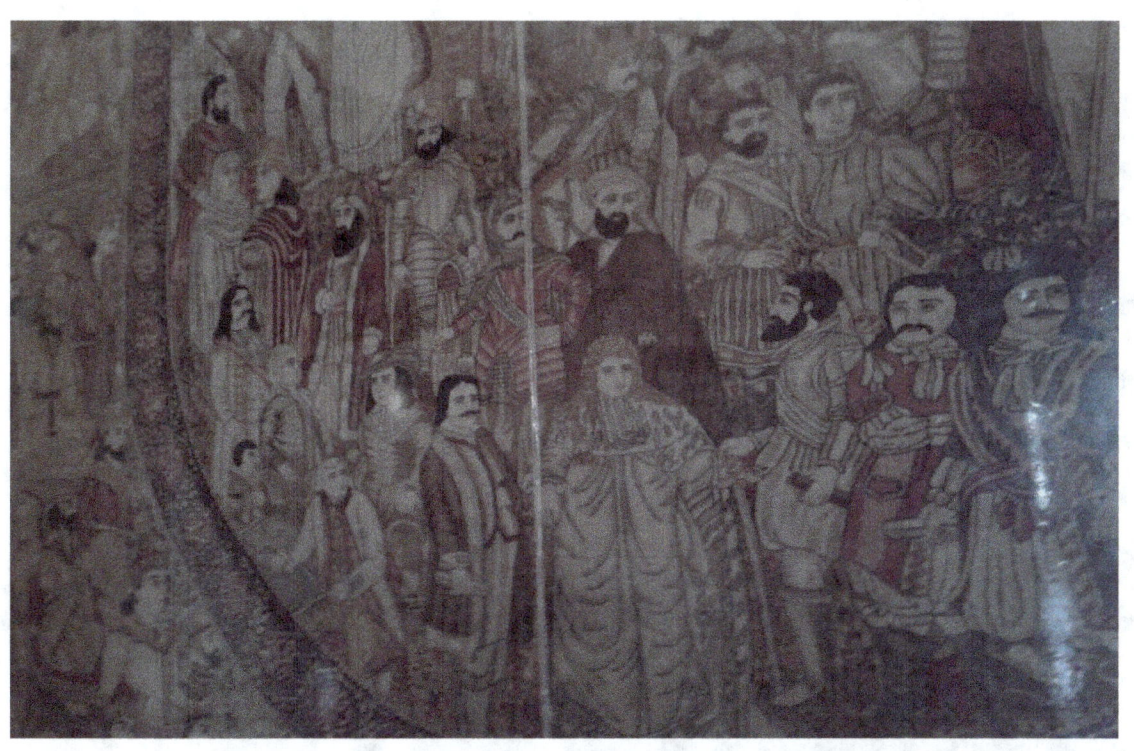

Jai Vilas Palace & Museum inside Picture Gallery Painting view

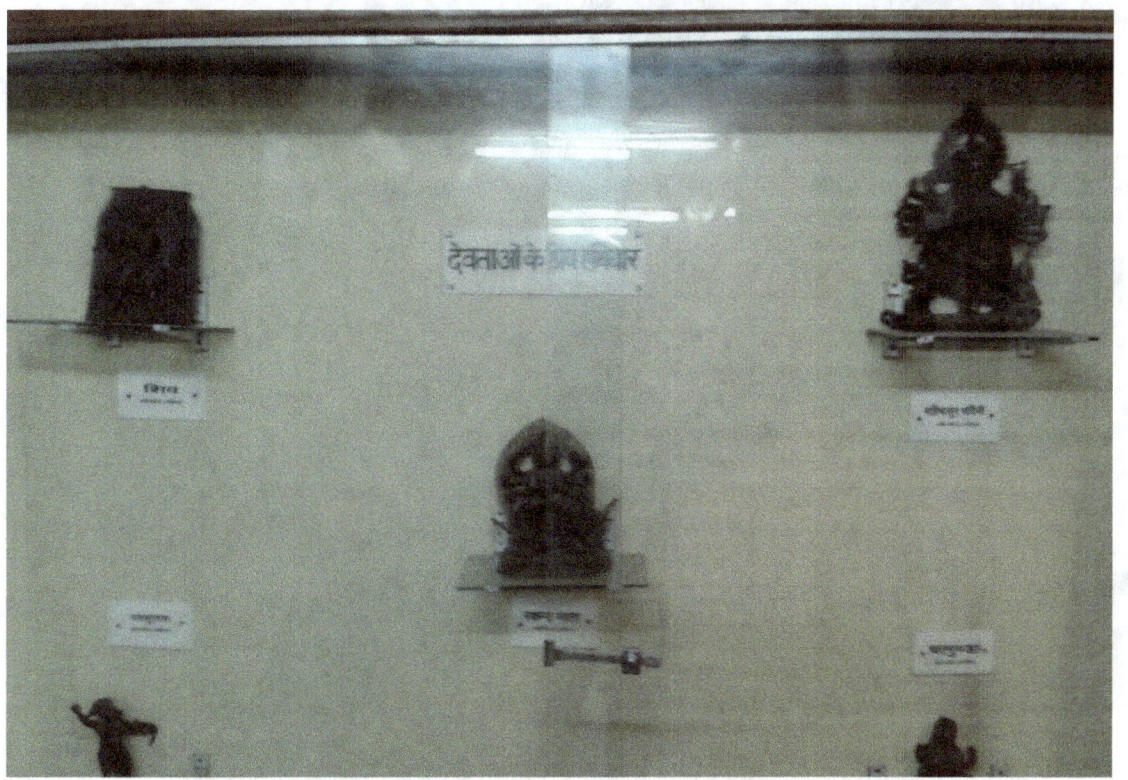

Jai Vilas Palace & Museum inside Idols view

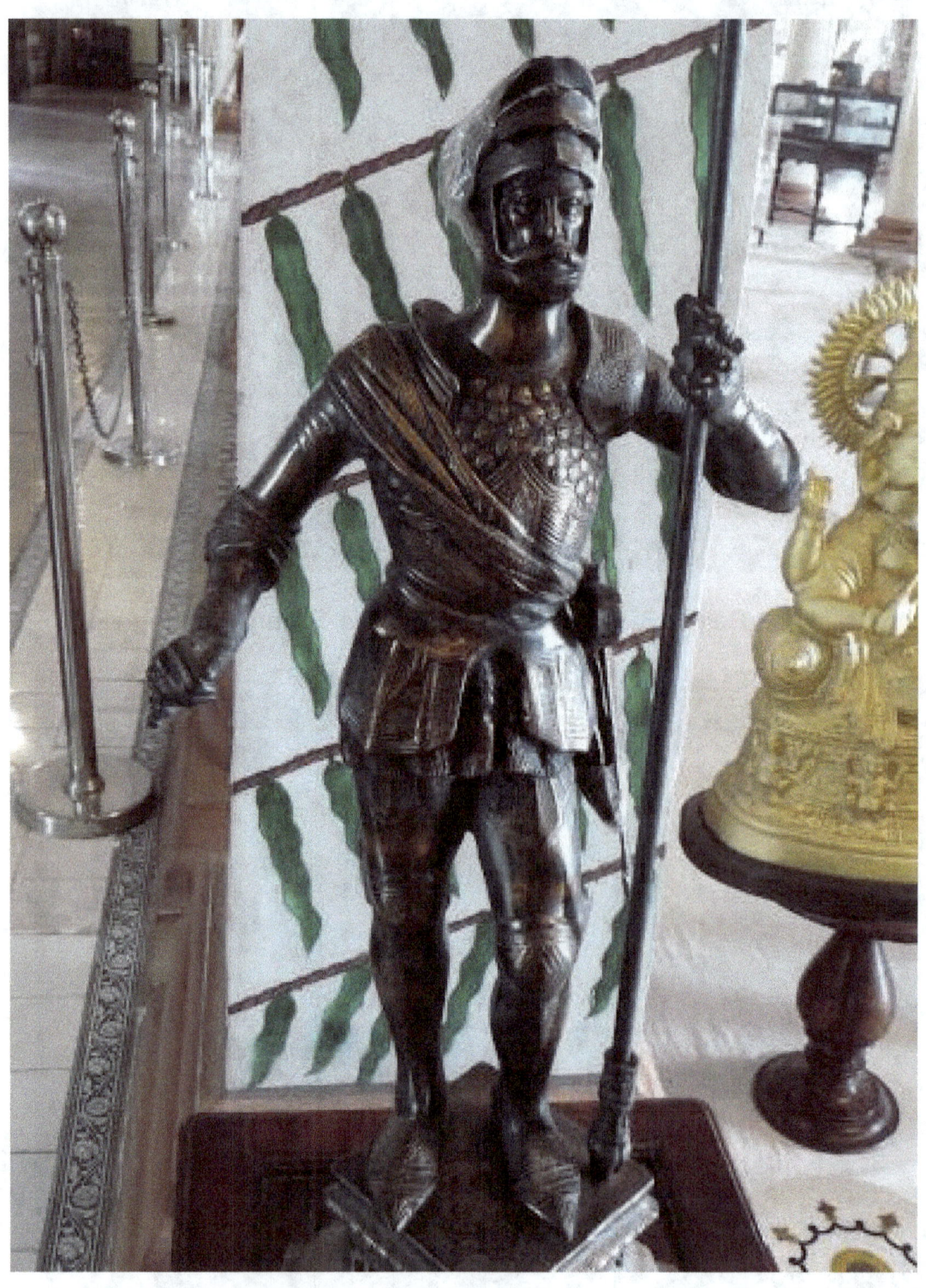

Jai Vilas Palace & Museum inside view Copper Metal Statue

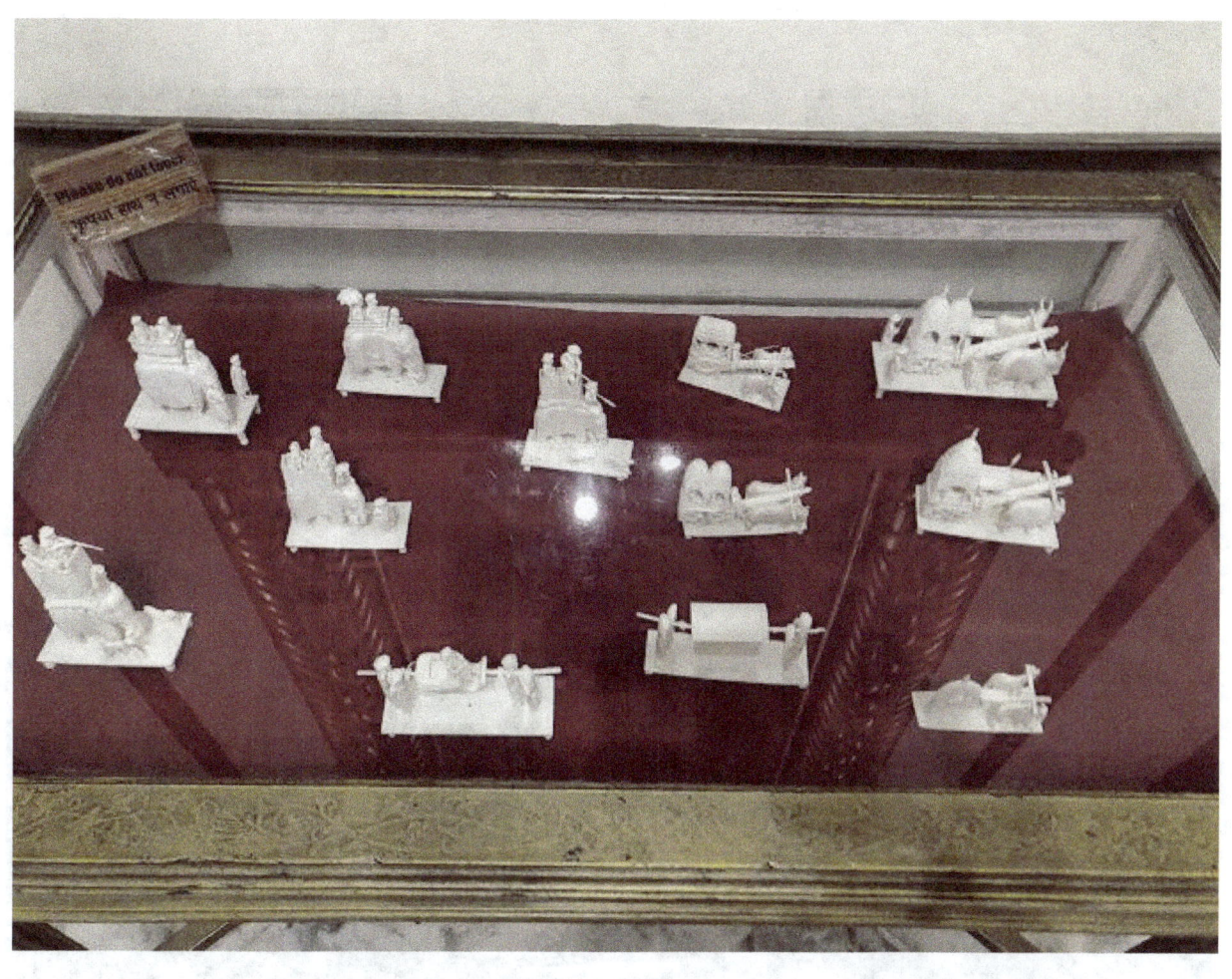

Jai Vilas Palace & Museum inside view Elephant Teeth Artifacts

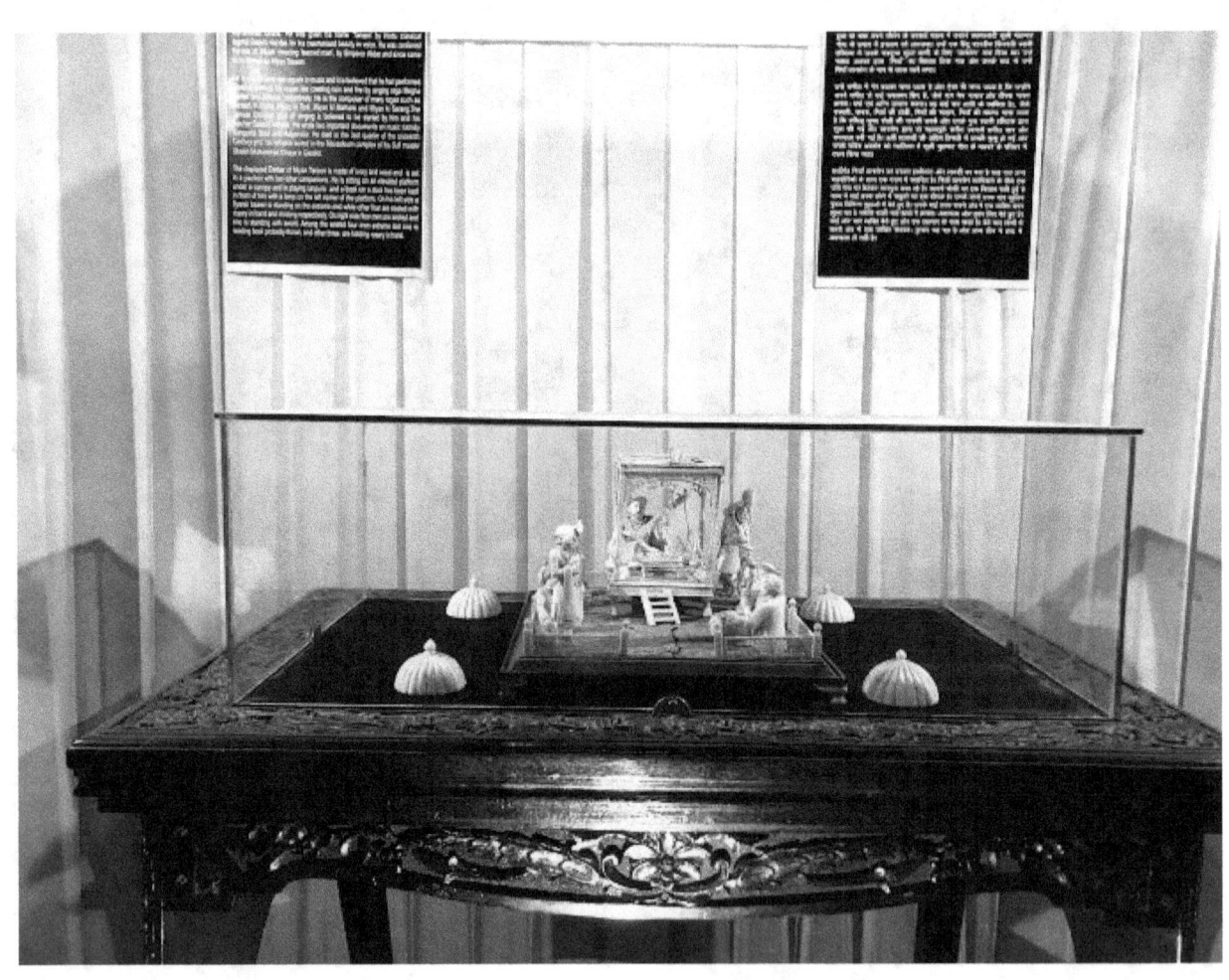

Jai Vilas Palace & Museum inside view Elephant Teeth Artifacts

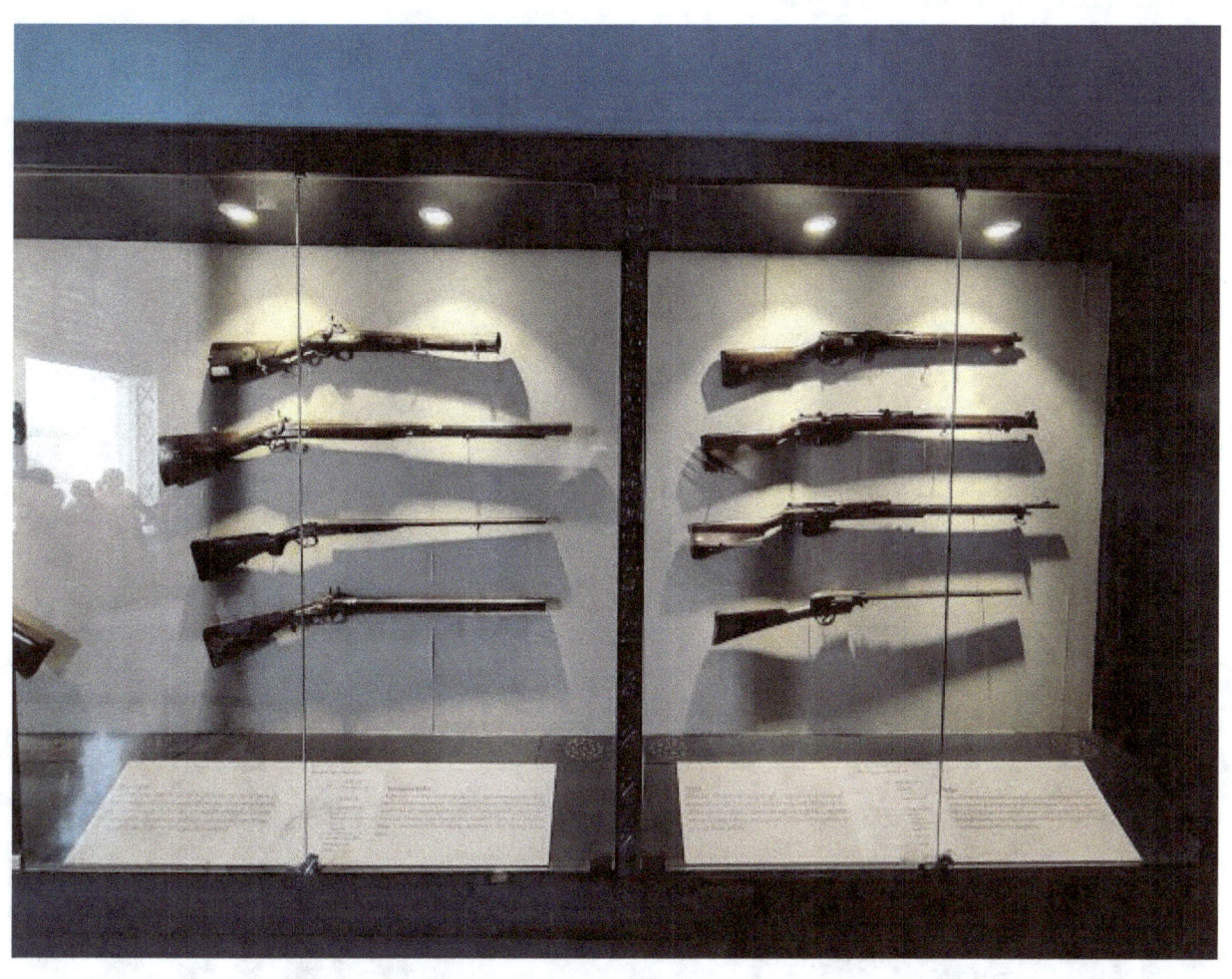
Jai Vilas Palace & Museum inside view Guns

Picture Gallery: -

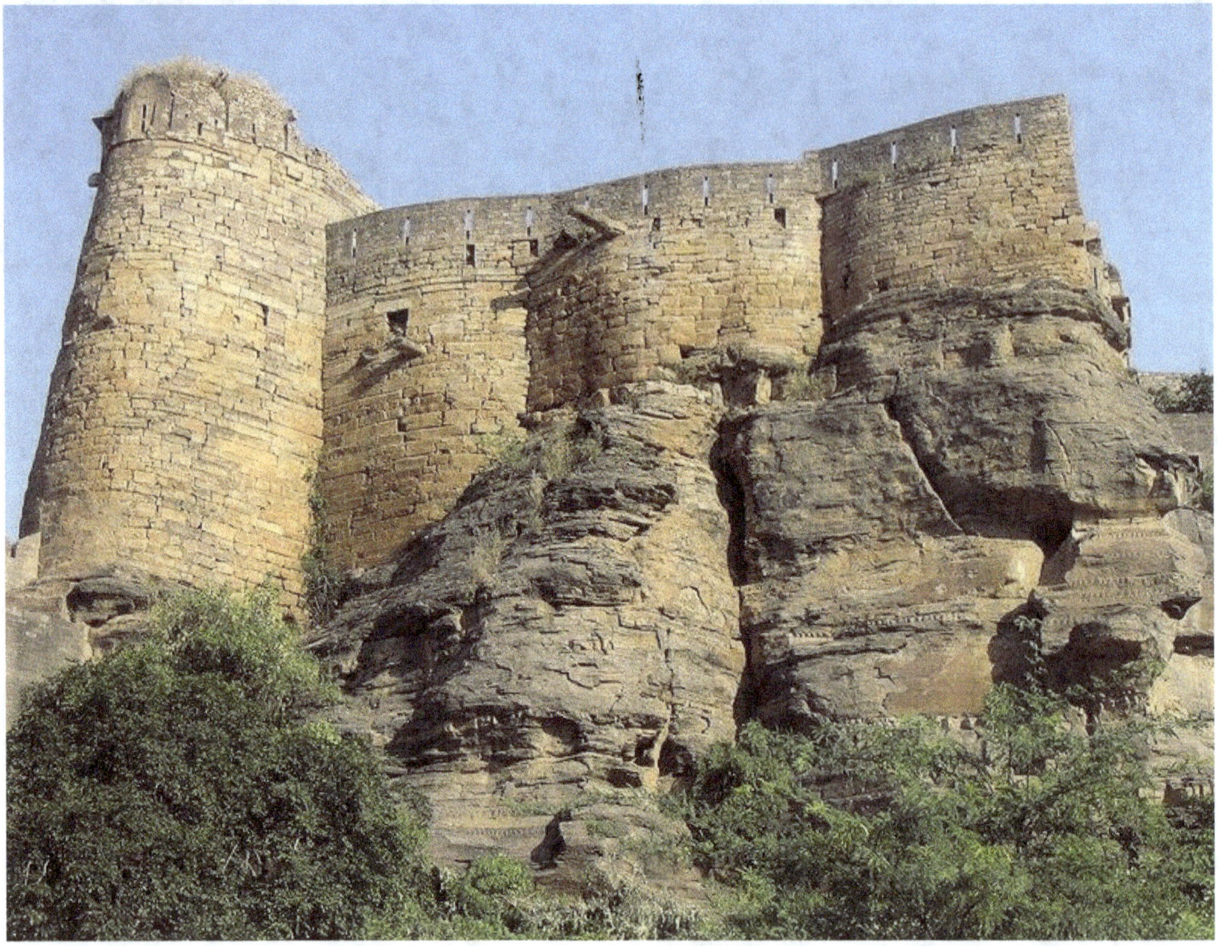

Gwalior City view from Hill top of Gwalior Fort

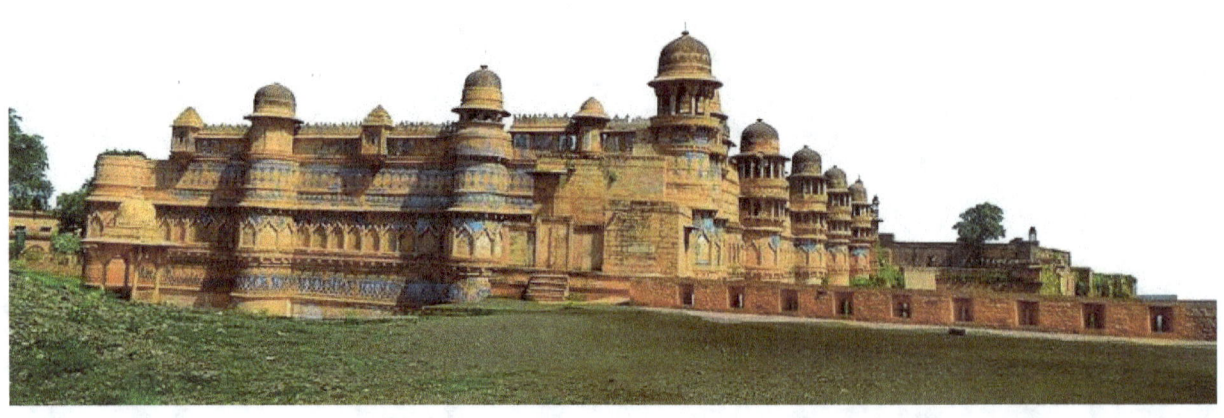

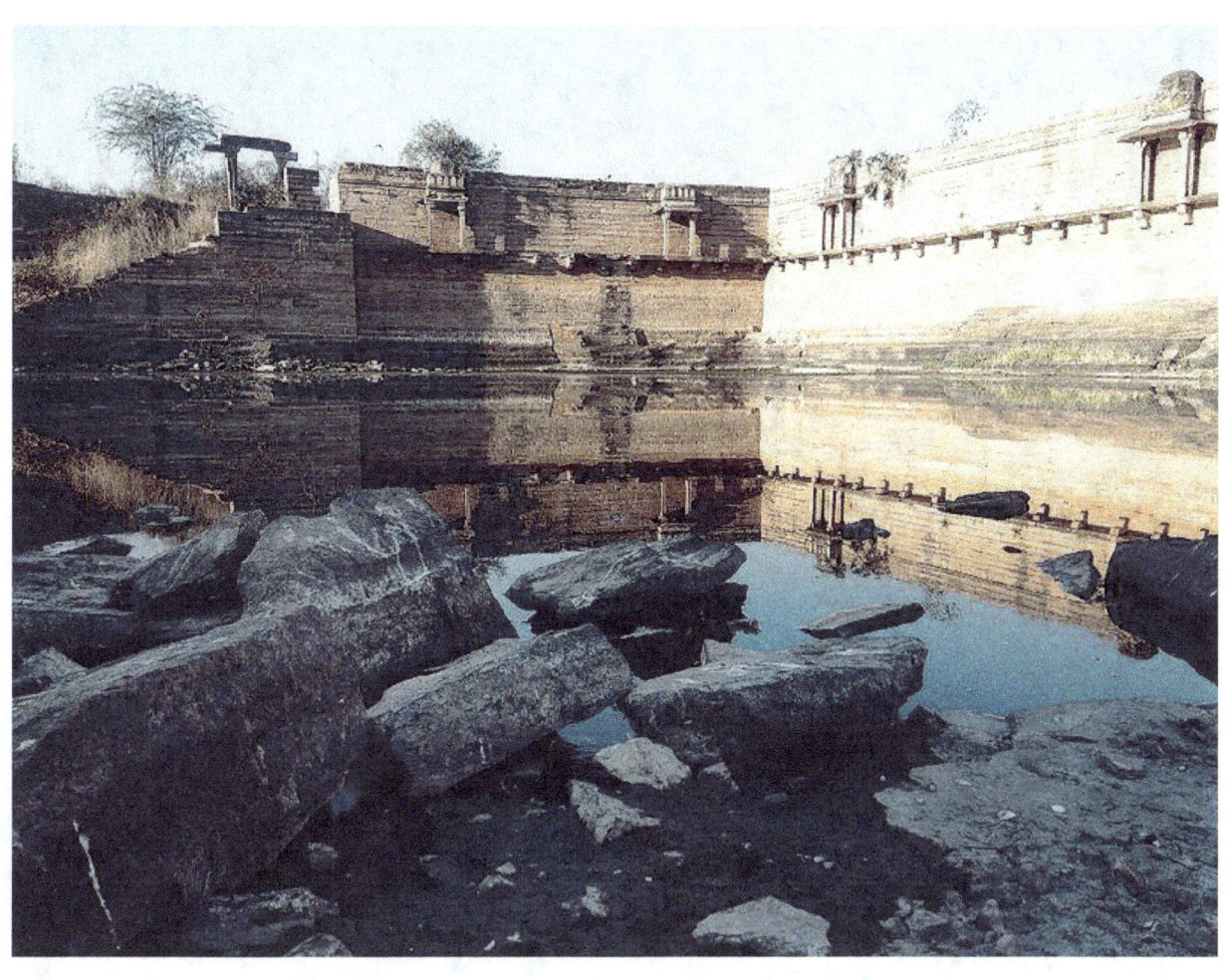

Pond inside Gwalior fort

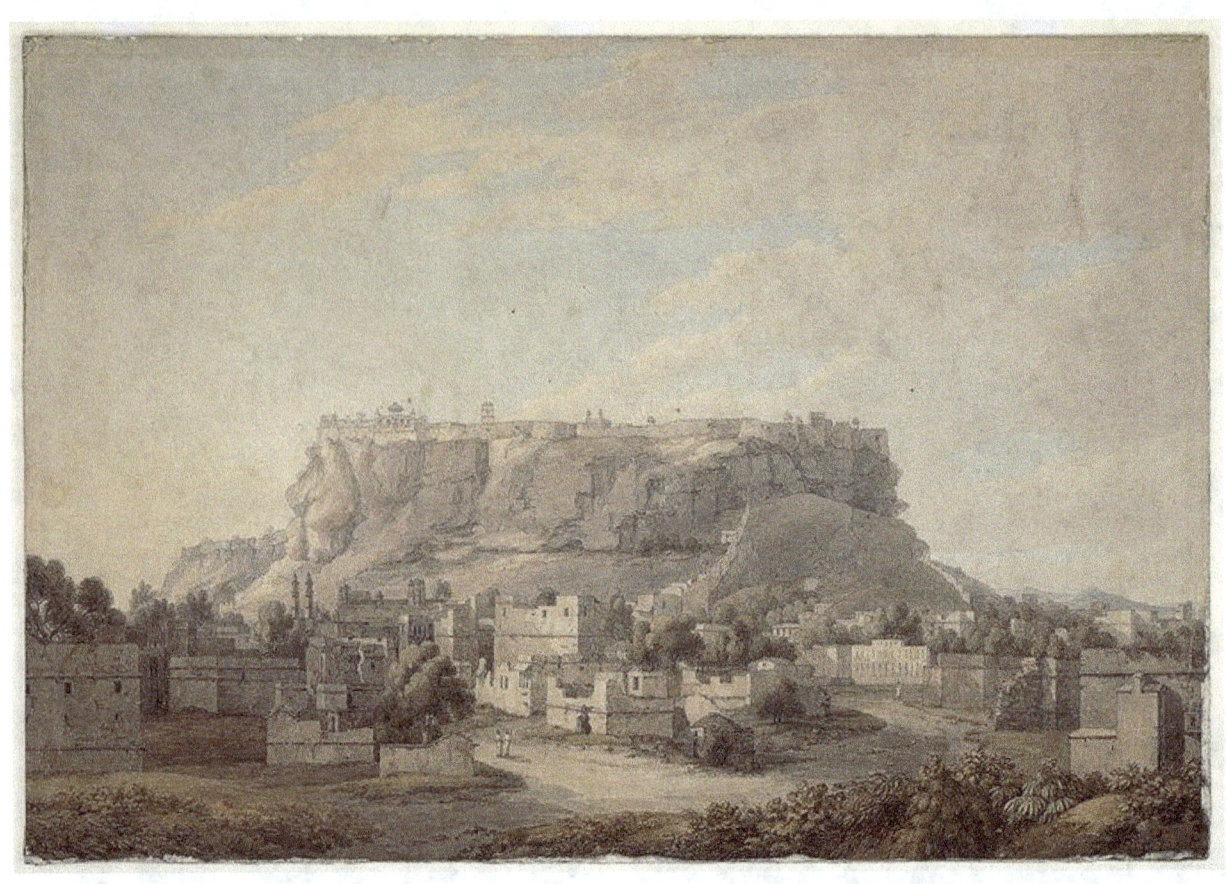
View of Gwalior Fort from the north west 1790

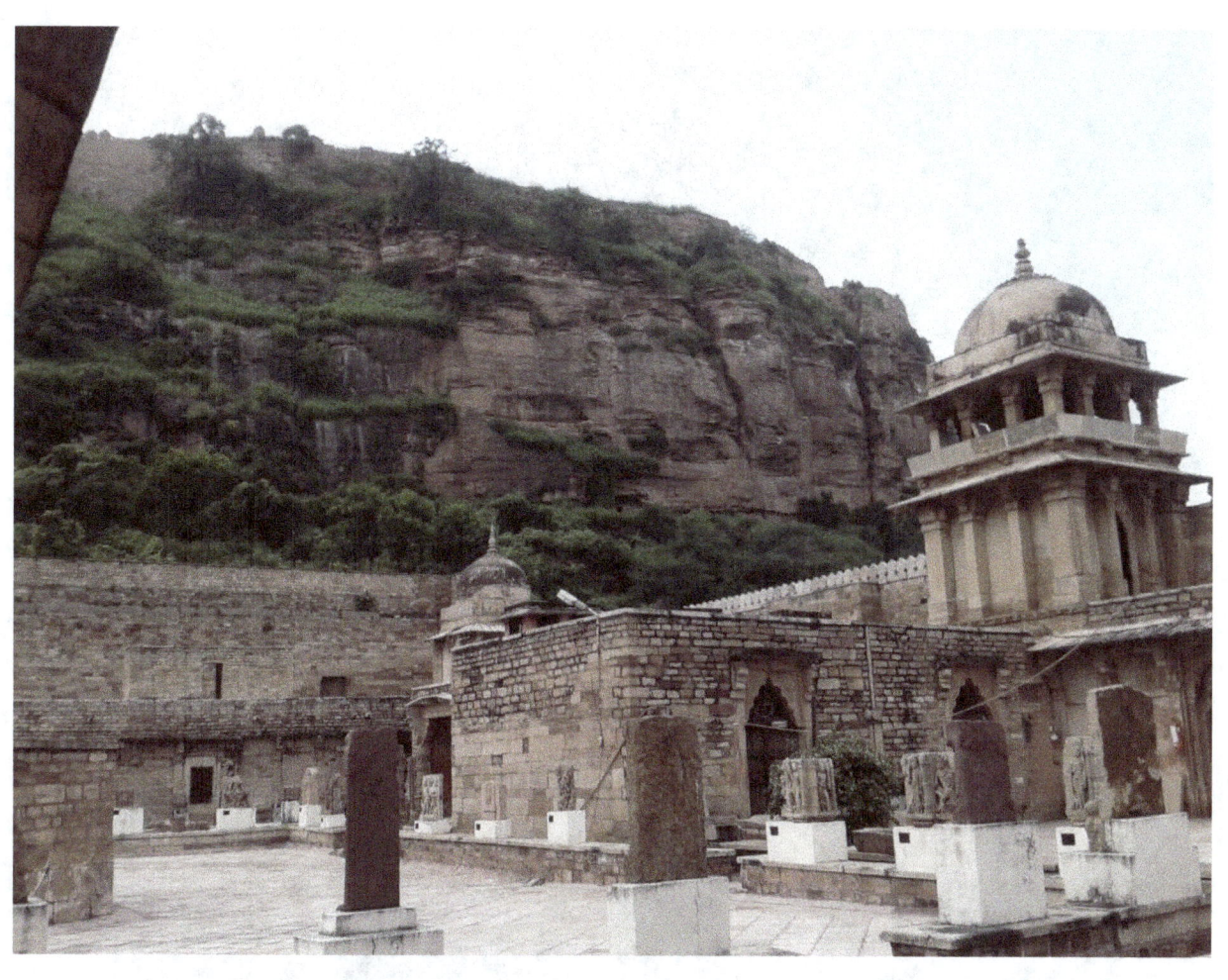
Buildings inside Gwalior fort

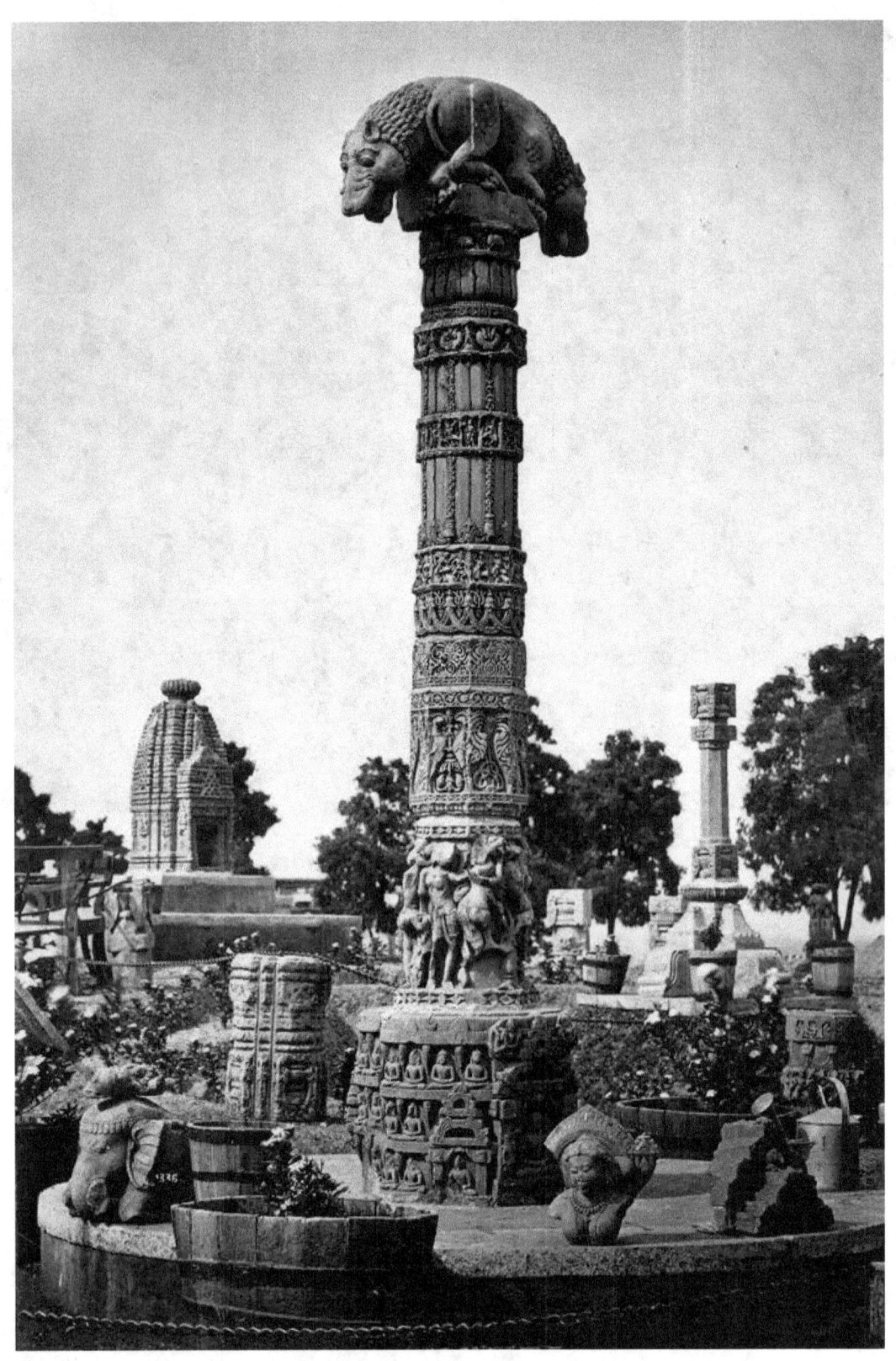

Sculptures near Teli Mandir, Gwalior Fort

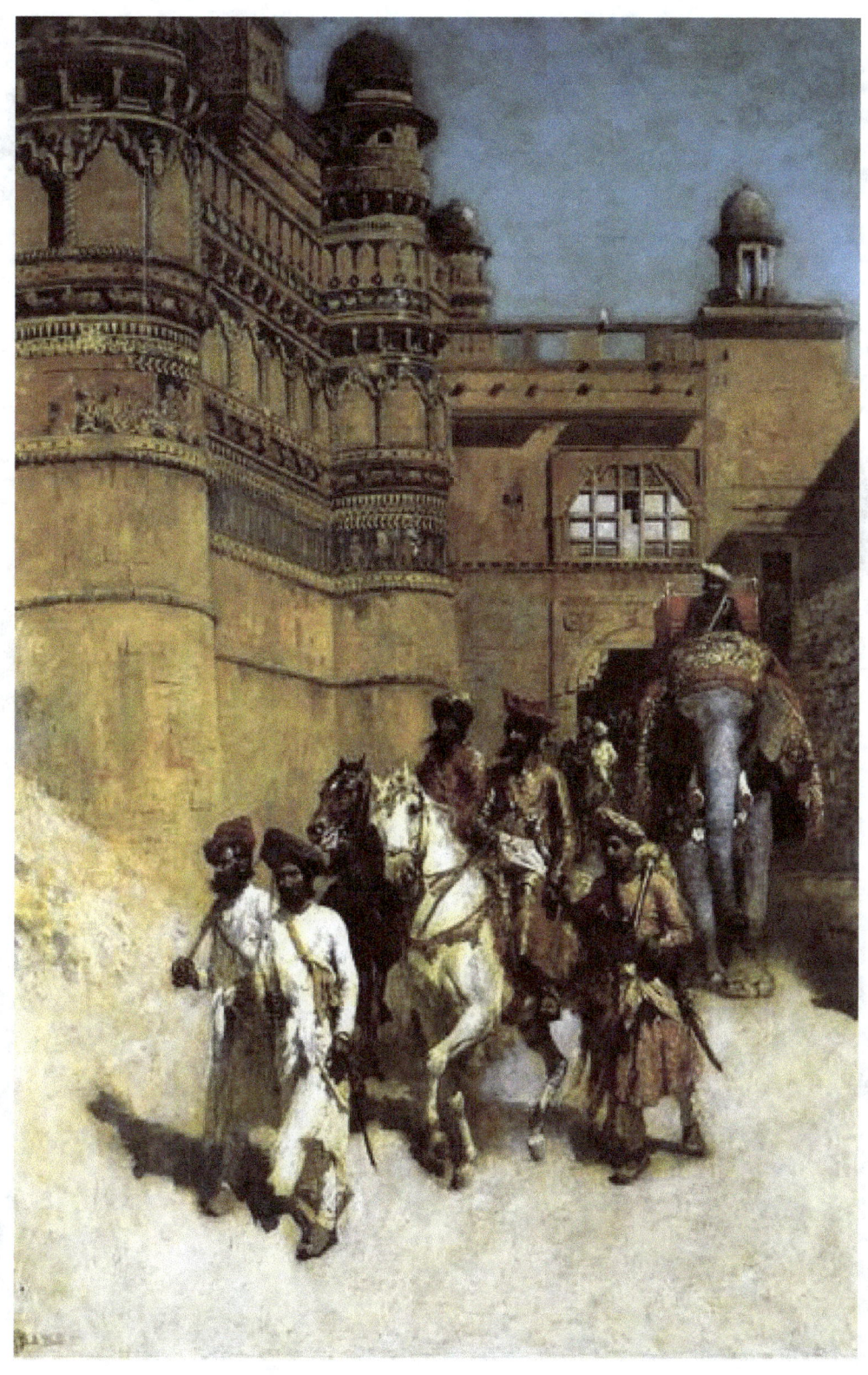

The Maharahaj-King of Gwalior before His Palace 1887

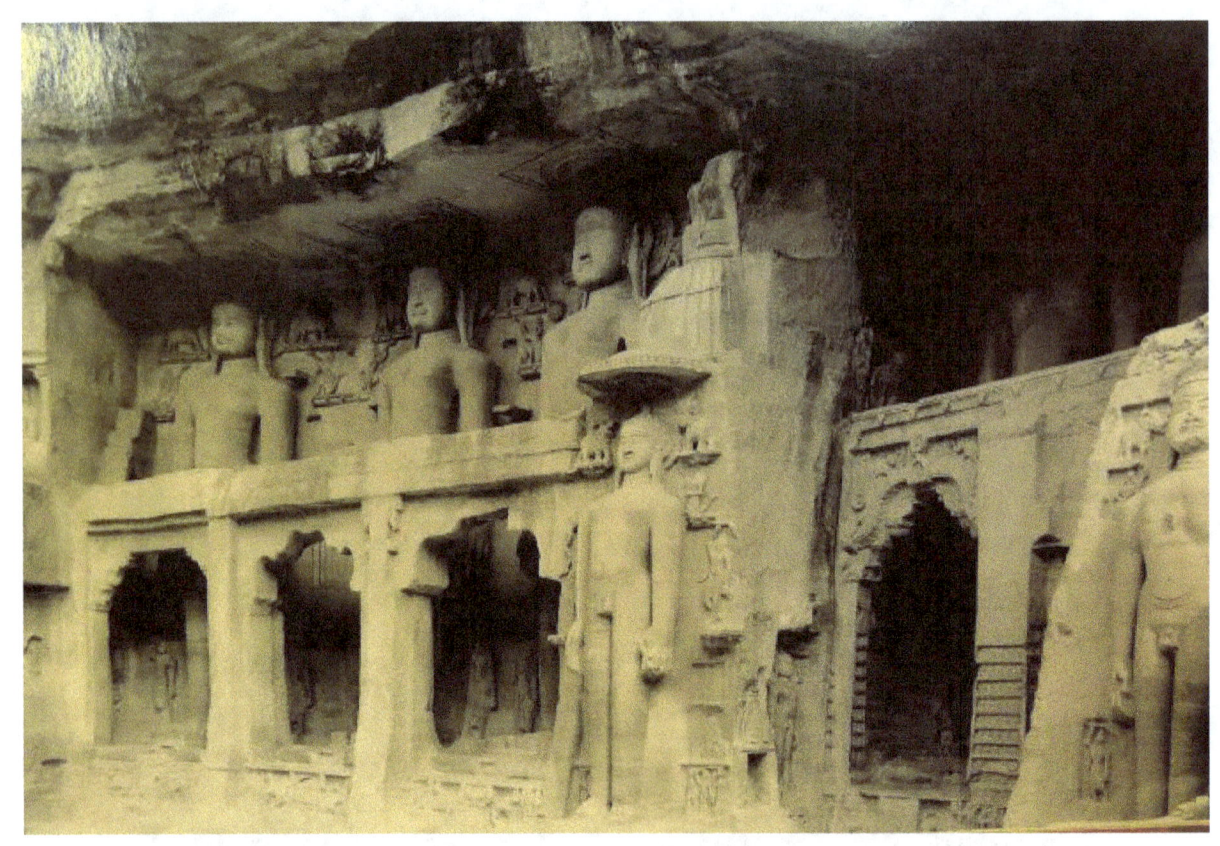

Jain Sculptures & Cave Gwalior Fort

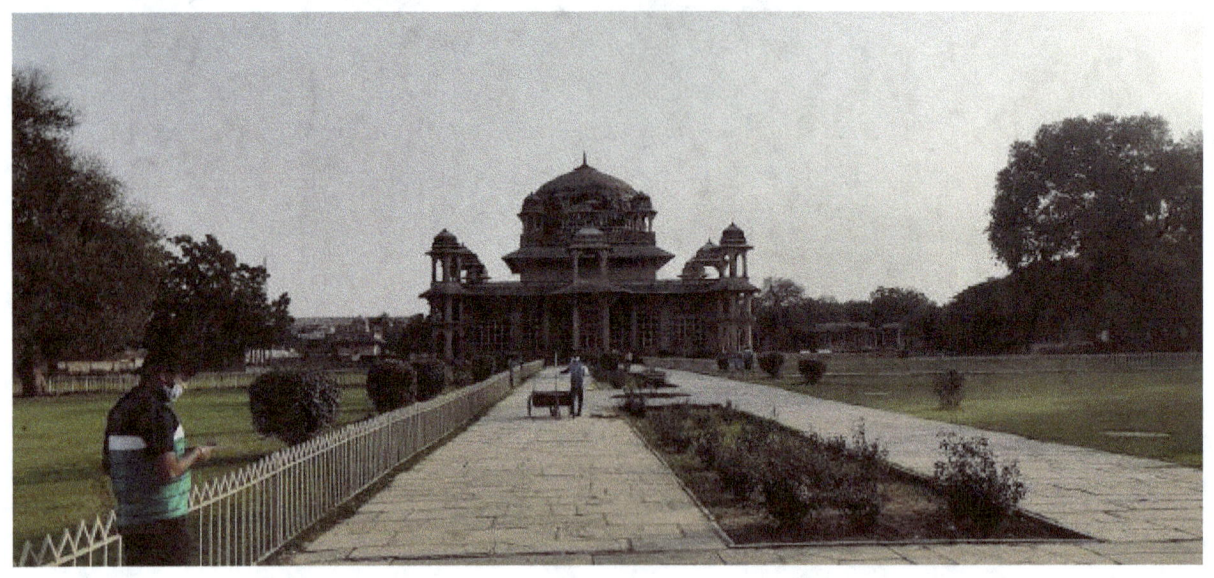

Gwalior

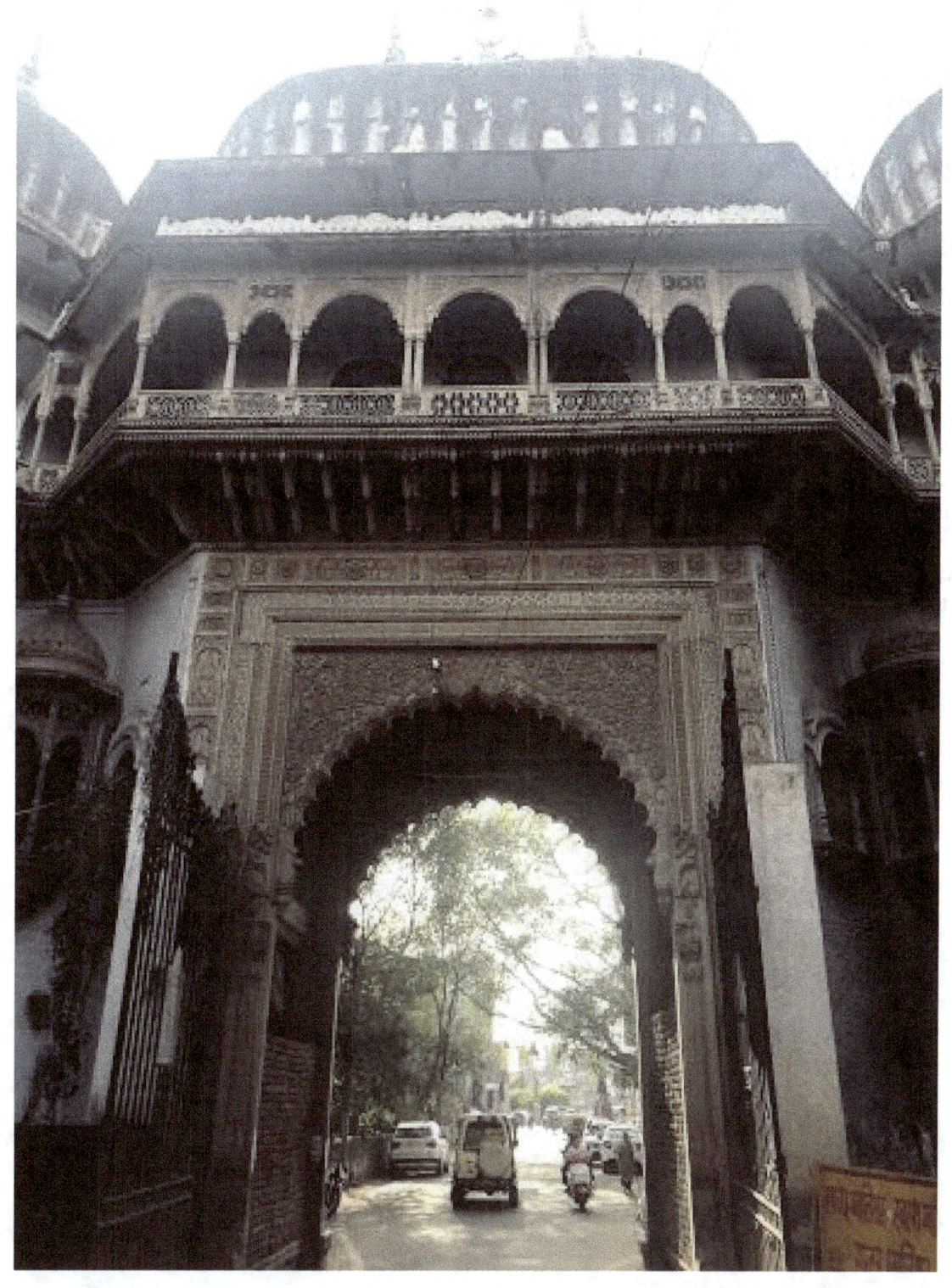

Gwalior Carved City Gate with Balcony, Road & Vehicles

References: -
Gwalior City visit Photos & Sites references

Copyright Information: -
All Rights Reserved. No Part of this Publication may be reproduced or used in any form or by any means Photographic, electronic or mechanical, including Photocopying, recording, taping or information storage and retrieval systems without the prior written permission of the Publishers & Author.
I would greatly appreciate your any contribution - even a very small one.
Please Write or Contact to Anurag Mathur:-
ANURAG MATHUR
Indian Culture & Heritage Information
Business, Research & Development
156 - CB, Bharat Nagar, Near Water Tank,
Madiyav, Sitapur Road, Lucknow U.P. PIN - 226021 INDIA
Phone Nos/Mobile Nos: +91-9415066360, +91-8319185063.
E-mails:- anuragmathu@gmail.com, anurag5551@hotmail.com
Publishing Year-2024.